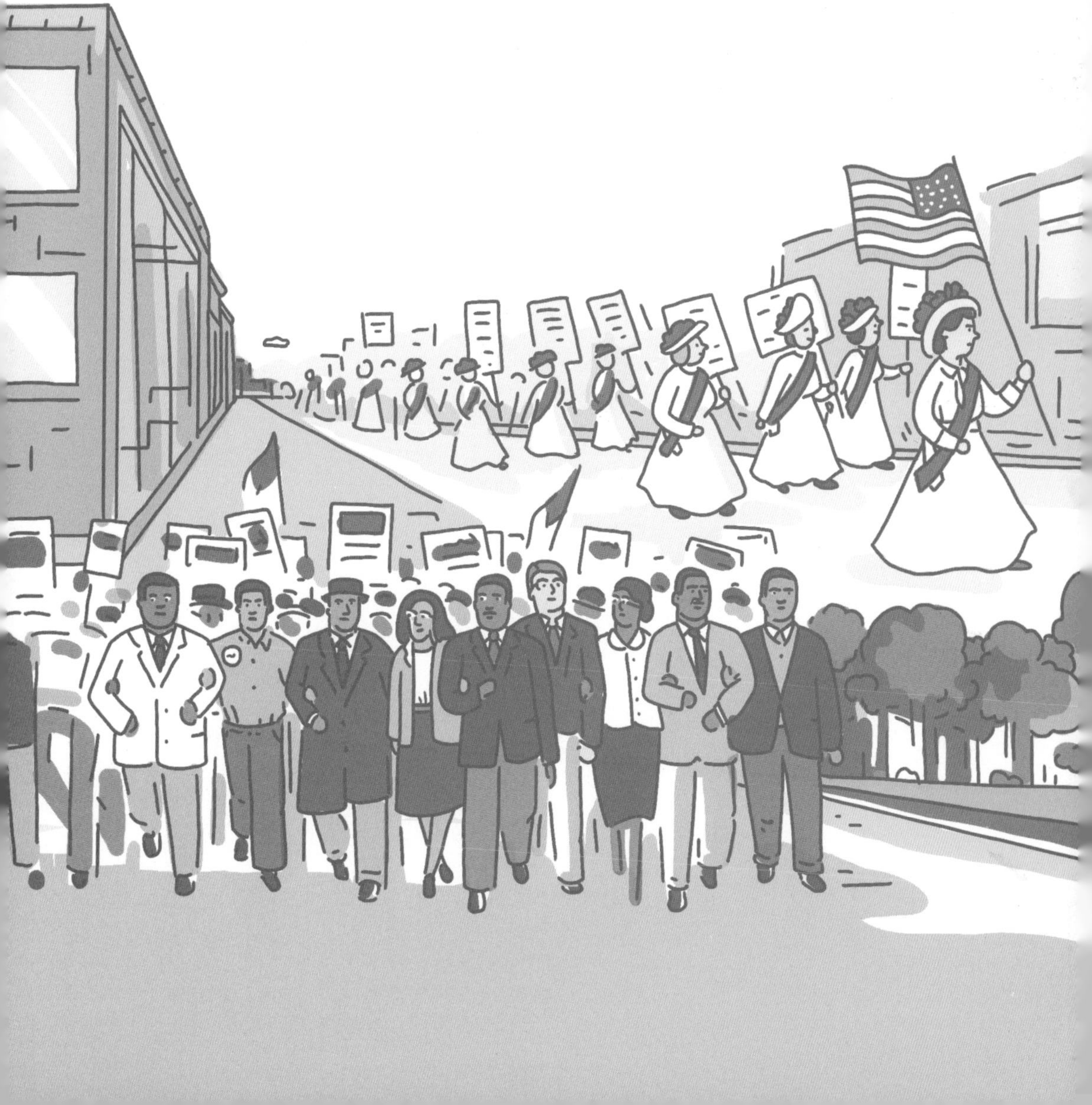

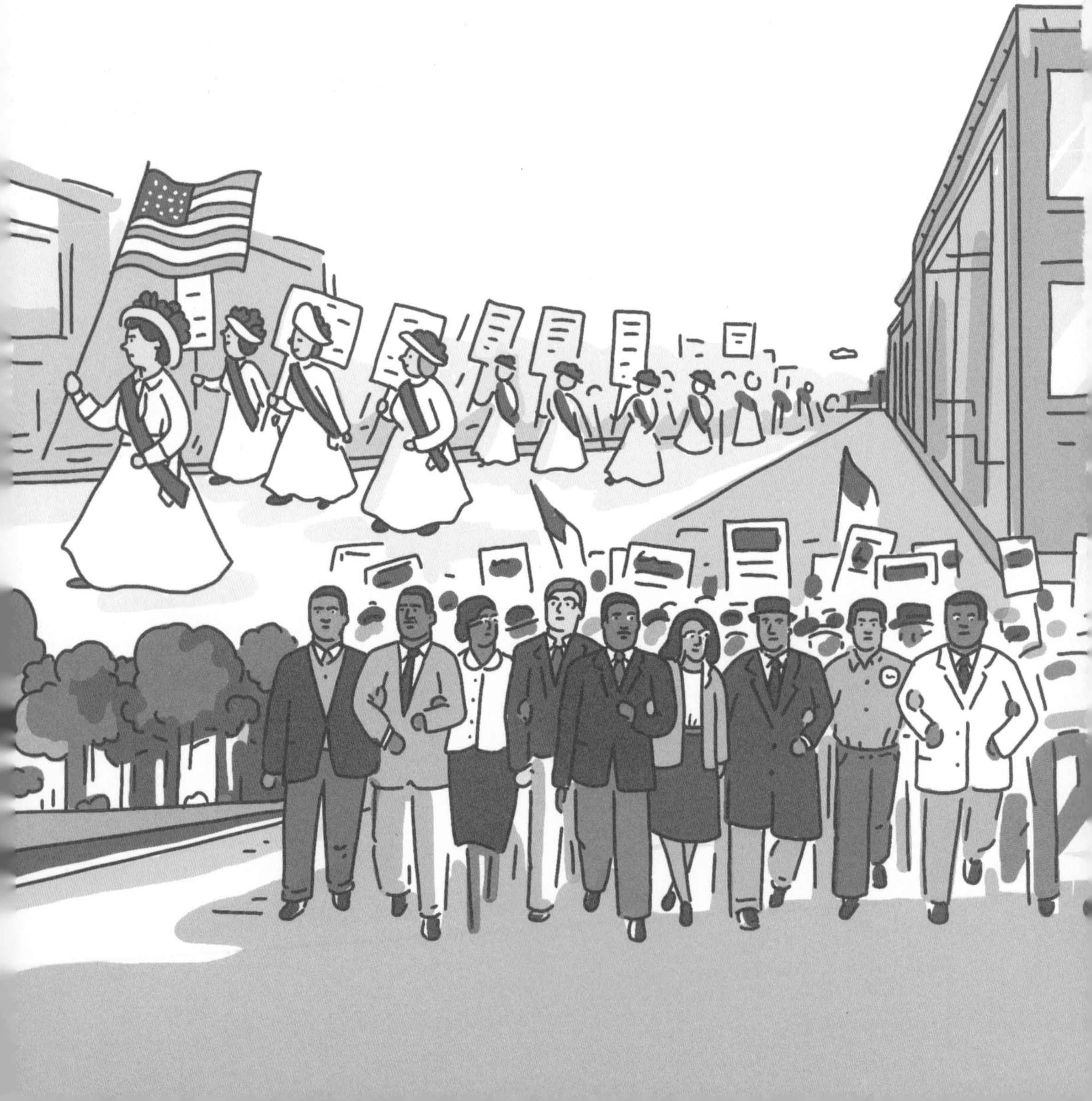

DRAWING
THE VOTE

An Illustrated Guide
to Voting in America

BY **TOMMY JENKINS**
ILLUSTRATED BY **KATI LACKER**
FOREWORD BY **MARTHA S. JONES**

ABRAMS COMICARTS, NEW YORK

Editor: Charlotte Greenbaum
Designer: Max Temescu
Managing Editor: Annalea Manalili
Production Manager: Alison Gervais

Cataloging-in-Publication Data has been applied for
and may be obtained from the Library of Congress.

ISBN 978-1-4197-3998-9
eISBN 978-1-68335-733-9

Printed and bound in China
10 9 8 7 6 5 4 3 2 1

Abrams ComicArts books are available at special discounts when
purchased in quantity for premiums and promotions as well as fundraising
or educational use. Special editions can also be created to specification.
For details, contact specialsales@abramsbooks.com or the address below.

Abrams ComicArts® is a registered trademark of Harry N. Abrams, Inc.

ABRAMS The Art of Books
195 Broadway, New York, NY 10007
abramsbooks.com

FOR MY PARENTS, WHO TAUGHT ME THE IMPORTANCE OF VOTING,
AND FOR MY WIFE, WHO SHOWS ME THE POWER OF HOPE

Contents

Foreword

The right to vote has grown out of struggle. Our national history is littered with scenes in which getting to the polls involved far more than a simple buggy or bus ride across town. Casting a ballot has rarely been as easy as showing up and dropping a paper slip in a box or pulling a lever. Each Election Day, for nearly two and a half centuries, Americans have acted as the People and chosen their elected representatives. Their votes are the products of campaigns, battles, court challenges, and the risking of lives—all so that the best promises of democracy can be tested and, as President Barack Obama often quoted from the Constitution, come closer to realizing a more perfect union.

I begin each Election Day with a personal get-out-the-vote campaign. My followers on social media know that early on the first Tuesday in November, my feed will fill with images intended to inspire us to get to the polls. They include the Constitution's 3/5ths Compromise, which reduced enslaved Americans to a figure that undercut their humanity while increasing the power of those states that allowed for human bondage. There is an engraving from 1867, *The First Vote*, that depicts a trio of black men casting their ballots in the wake of the Civil War and the constitutional revolution that abolished slavery, guaranteed citizenship, and promised black men voting rights. I always include a photograph of those who marched out of Selma, Alabama, and across the Edmund Pettus Bridge in 1965, before passage of the Voting Rights Act later that year, demanding access to the polls. Their courage was met by the raw brutality of clubs and kicks.

Drawing the Vote reminds us that every time an American citizen votes, they are taking part in the long struggle for voting rights.

If that story began as the framers of the Constitution debated how to share power in the new United States, it continues today in battles over voter identification, gerrymandering, foreign interference, and the closing of polling places. Americans still do not agree on how to ensure the right to vote, and *Drawing the Vote* explains how we got here. While, for example, access to the polls expanded for white men in the early part of the nineteenth century, it closed for black men—the descendants of enslaved people—who saw their ballots taken away in states like New York and Pennsylvania. Immigrant men were entering the body politic only by giving up their allegiances to their homelands—the price they paid for becoming part of what was still a white man's republic. At the same moment, American women—black and white—began to demand their right to vote. Still, most would wait until the twentieth century to freely cast their ballots. In our own time, after Election Days wind down, the focus is often on winners versus losers. But behind the results are the stories of how every generation of Americans has struggled to influence the outcomes.

Like the family of *Drawing the Vote* author Tommy Jenkins, my people come from North Carolina—black residents of the city of Greensboro, where their right to vote was denied for much of the state's history. My earliest forebears—like Elijah Jones, born in 1802—may have voted because only in 1835 did "free persons of color" like him lose the right to vote. That year the state limited the ballot to white men, though even they, too, struggled against a property qualification that was not lifted until 1856. Still, the color line kept African Americans from the polls. After the Civil War, men like my great-great-grandfather Sidney Dallas Jones, born in 1845, voted for the first time. He went on to become a Republican Party activist and, in 1868, helped elect the state's first African American legislators. But by 1904, the political aspirations of Sidney's sons, including those of my grandfather David Dallas Jones, had been crushed by violence, the poll tax, a grandfather clause, and literacy tests.

The women of my North Carolina family waited the longest of all for the right to cast their ballots. Racism left many of them out of the revolution that welcomed white American women to the polls. When in 1920 the Nineteenth Amendment to the Constitution was ratified, all states including North Carolina were prohibited from denying the vote based upon sex. It was, however, unclear how black women would fare. They were subject to the same race-based restrictions that kept their fathers, brothers, husbands, and sons from casting ballots on Election Day. But in Greensboro, black men and women tested these limits. Some passed literacy tests and registered. Others ran for local office. In 1951, Dr. William Hampton, a physician, was elected the first black member of Greensboro's city council. In 1960, the female students of the city's Bennett College registered black residents to vote as part of "Operation Door Knock." In 1965, the passage of the federal Voting Rights Act guaranteed all black North Carolinians the right to vote, men and women. But it took many decades of struggle to put women like my grandmother Susie Williams Jones on more equal footing—with black men *and* with all white North Carolinians.

My family stories, like those of so many American families, are what we quietly carry to the polls each Election Day. The long saga of American voting rights, as told in *Drawing the Vote,* moves me to get up earlier than usual on that first Tuesday in November to cast my ballot before heading to work. It also charges us with making certain that we all get there! Today, we are face-to-face with another era of voter suppression, and simply casting a ballot is not enough. The history of hard-won voting rights moves me to be part of the ongoing struggle to ensure that all Americans have access to the polls. It is time to think hard about the future of democracy, and to then act and ensure that its future lives up to our best ideals. Read *Drawing the Vote*, and then ask yourself what you will do next.

Martha S. Jones, an internationally recognized historian of African American history, is the Society of Black Alumni Presidential Professor and Professor of History at Johns Hopkins University. She currently serves as a president of the Berkshire Conference of Women Historians and as a member of the executive board of the Organization of American Historians. She is the author of *Birthright Citizens: A History of Race and Rights in Antebellum America* (Cambridge University Press, 2018) and *All Bound Up Together: The Women Question in African American Public Culture* (University of North Carolina Press, 2007).

Preface

When I was six or eight years old, I remember walking the two blocks to the courthouse with my dad on Election Day. After he cast his vote, my dad explained to me why voting was so important. "It is our voice," he said, "it is our connection to the rest of the state and the rest of the country." I never forgot that lesson.

Once I was old enough, I made sure I voted, but for years I took it for granted. I continued to acknowledge its importance, but I didn't understand its history. Then, suddenly, talk of illegal voting was everywhere. Next, the United States Supreme Court overturned the preclearance portion of the Voting Rights Act. In response, a number of states enacted, or attempted to enact, measures that make voting more difficult in the name of protecting the integrity of elections. My own state of North Carolina tried to impose voter IDs, and limits on early voting and polling place hours of operation. The legislature even tried to prevent college students from voting where they attend college, meaning they would have to return to their hometowns, even though elections are held on Tuesdays in November.

Rather than ensuring the right to vote, it seemed we were trying to keep people away from the polls. Once I started to research the history of voting in this country and learned about the bloody struggle to gain the right to vote, it made writing this book a necessity.

Then, in September 2019, the Democrats in the House of Representatives opened an impeachment inquiry into President Trump.

With our current twenty-four-hour news cycle, events and even scandals are broadcast immediately. While voters staying informed is easier than it has been in our nation's history, it is also more critical than it has ever been.

We all need to learn how vital voting is and that, as history shows, it can be easily taken away. We all need to learn about some of the heroes who sacrificed deeply to earn the ability to cast a ballot, people such as Fannie Lou Hamer and Thurgood Marshall.

Because I love comics and because I think the format brings a story to life, this book naturally took the form of a comic book. Comics opened up a larger world to a boy in a small southern town. Comics took me to New York, to California, and to outer space.

I hope this book takes people to the voting booth.

And I hope this book makes people realize the right to vote is fragile; we need to protect it, and the best way to protect it is to exercise it.

Get out and vote!

Tommy Jenkins
Raleigh, North Carolina
October 2019

Timeline of Key Events in US Voting History

1773 Boston Tea Party

1775 Beginning of the American Revolutionary War

1776 Declaration of Independence

1777 Articles of Confederation

1783 End of the American Revolutionary War

1787 Constitutional Convention

1787 3/5ths Compromise

1788 US Constitution ratified

1789 George Washington elected first US president

1804 12th Amendment ratified, officially creates the Electoral College

1824 John Quincy Adams elected president; first president elected who did not receive the most popular votes

1848 Seneca Falls Convention for women's rights

1850 Fugitive Slave Act passed

1860 Abraham Lincoln elected 16th president

1861 Fort Sumter fired on; Civil War begins

1865 Civil War ends

1865 Lincoln assassinated

1865 13th Amendment ratified outlawing slavery

1866 Reconstruction begins

1868 Impeachment of President Andrew Johnson initiated

1870 15th Amendment ratified giving former slaves the right to vote

1876 Rutherford B. Hayes elected president; Reconstruction ends

1890 Mississippi revises its constitution, puts limits on who can vote

1896 *Plessy v. Ferguson*

1898 *Williams v. Mississippi*; SCOTUS upholds Mississippi's constitution of 1890

1909 NAACP founded

1920 19th Amendment ratified giving women the right to vote

1954 *Brown v. Board of Education*

1955 Rosa Parks refuses to give up her seat on a public bus

1955–1956 Montgomery bus boycott

1963 US enters Vietnam War

1963 March on Washington;
Martin Luther King Jr. delivers "I Have a Dream" speech

1964 Civil Rights Act enacted

1965 March on Selma

1965 Voting Rights Act enacted

1968 Martin Luther King Jr. assassinated

1968 Richard Nixon elected president

1972 Watergate break-in

1974 Richard Nixon resigns

1975 US exits Vietnam War

1987 Fairness Doctrine abolished

1998 Impeachment of President Bill Clinton initiated

2001 NYC World Trade Center attacked

2008 Barack Obama elected; first African American president

2009 First Tea Party protests held

2010 *Citizens United v. FEC*

2013 *Shelby County v. Holder* overturns parts of the Voting Rights Act

2016 Hillary Clinton is the first woman
nominated for president by a major party

2016 Donald Trump elected president

2019 Formal impeachment inquiry of President Donald Trump initiated

VOTE

DERIVED FROM THE LATIN WORD *VOTUM*
MEANING "VOW, WISH, PROMISE"

CHAPTER 1

BY THE PEOPLE, FOR THE PEOPLE

IN 2008, **BARACK OBAMA'S** PRESIDENTIAL CAMPAIGN INSPIRED MILLIONS OF YOUNG PEOPLE.

CHANGE

IT WAS A CAMPAIGN ABOUT POSITIVE CHANGE.

YES WE CAN

A PERSON OF COLOR COULD ACTUALLY BE PRESIDENT OF THE UNITED STATES. THE AMERICAN DREAM WAS REAL.

I TEACH CREATIVE WRITING AND AMERICAN LITERATURE TO COLLEGE STUDENTS JUST NORTH OF RALEIGH, NORTH CAROLINA, AND IN 2008 MY STUDENTS WERE MOTIVATED TO VOTE.

HOW MANY OF YOU ARE GOING TO VOTE?

I'M WORKING ON A CAMPAIGN.

I VOLUNTEERED TO REGISTER PEOPLE TO VOTE.

I LIVE IN DOWNTOWN RALEIGH, AND THE NIGHT OBAMA WON THE PRESIDENCY, I TOOK OUR DOG, NOAH, FOR A WALK AND RAN INTO CROWDS OF JOYOUS PEOPLE FLOODING THE STREETS.

THE MOOD IN RALEIGH MIRRORED THE MOOD IN GRANT PARK IN CHICAGO, WHERE OBAMA SPOKE.

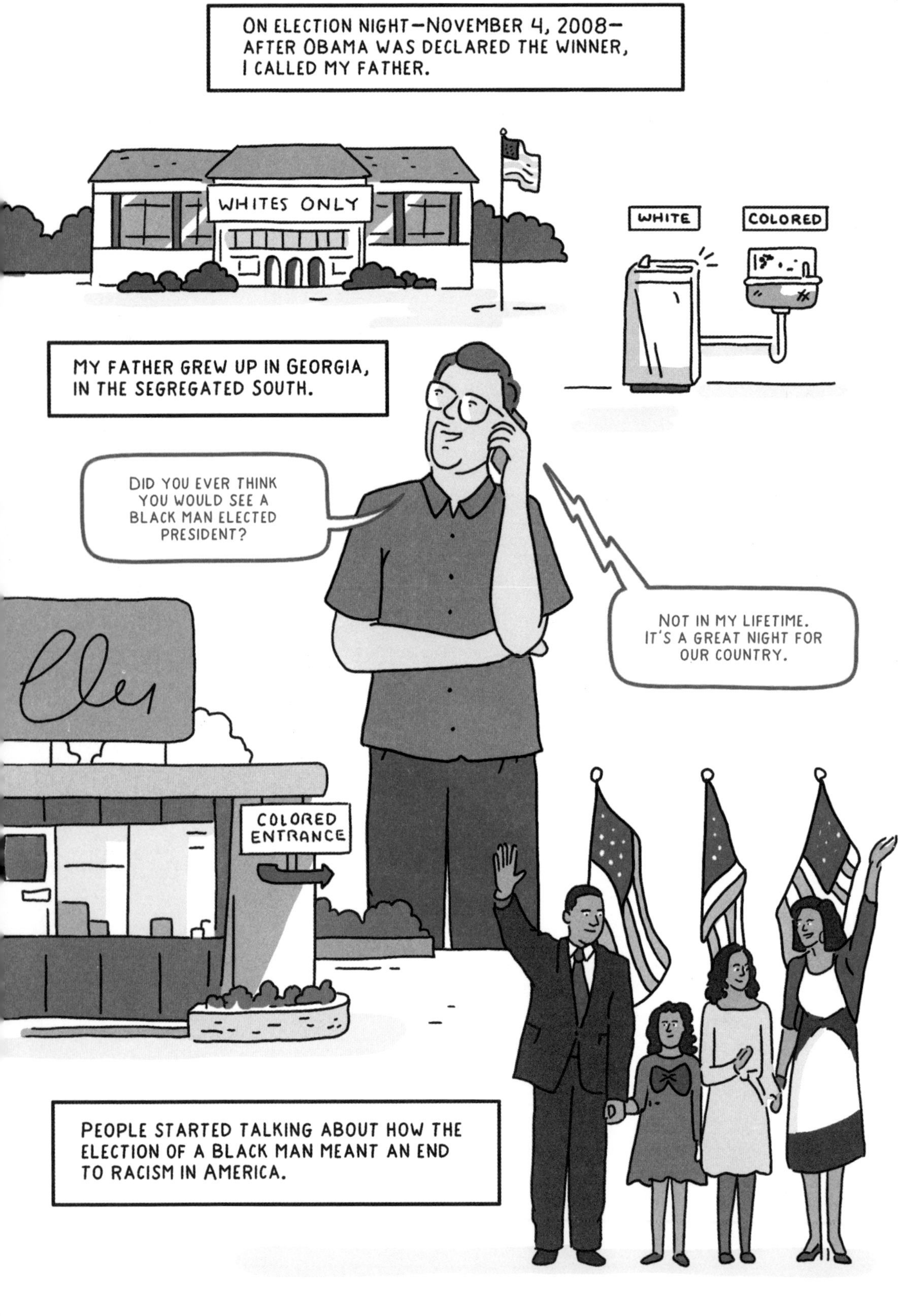

ON ELECTION NIGHT—NOVEMBER 4, 2008—AFTER OBAMA WAS DECLARED THE WINNER, I CALLED MY FATHER.
WHITES ONLY
WHITE
COLORED
MY FATHER GREW UP IN GEORGIA, IN THE SEGREGATED SOUTH.
DID YOU EVER THINK YOU WOULD SEE A BLACK MAN ELECTED PRESIDENT?
NOT IN MY LIFETIME. IT'S A GREAT NIGHT FOR OUR COUNTRY.
COLORED ENTRANCE
PEOPLE STARTED TALKING ABOUT HOW THE ELECTION OF A BLACK MAN MEANT AN END TO RACISM IN AMERICA.

BUT IT WASN'T THE END OF RACISM.

EVEN DURING OBAMA'S PRESIDENCY, RACIST POLICIES WERE BEING PUT INTO ACTION BY LAWMAKERS. MOST SIGNIFICANTLY, TWO PARTS OF THE VOTING RIGHTS ACT, WHICH PROTECTED MINORITY VOTING IN SOUTHERN STATES, WERE OVERTURNED BY THE SUPREME COURT.

INSPIRED BY THIS ACTION, REPUBLICAN-LED SOUTHERN LEGISLATURES, INCLUDING IN MY HOME STATE OF NORTH CAROLINA, BEGAN TO CHANGE VOTING REQUIREMENTS. THEY BEGAN BY REQUIRING PHOTO IDENTIFICATION . . .

FOLLOWED BY CLOSING POLLING PLACES IN MINORITY AREAS . . .

AND FINALLY, LIMITING EARLY VOTING, CAUSING LONG LINES AND LONG WAITS ON ELECTION DAYS.

WHAT HAPPENED? THIS WAS SO DISCOURAGING. THE ELECTION WOULD DETERMINE THE STUDENTS' FUTURE. YET THEY FELT POWERLESS, LIKE THERE WASN'T ANY HOPE.

MAYBE IT WAS BECAUSE PEOPLE WERE INUNDATED WITH STRANGE "NEWS" STORIES ON SOCIAL MEDIA. THESE STORIES MADE IT SEEM LIKE THERE WERE ALL KINDS OF CRAZINESS GOING ON BEHIND THE SCENES. THIS **HAD** TO CONTRIBUTE TO THE APATHY OF VOTERS.

LATER, THE CIA DISCOVERED IRREFUTABLE EVIDENCE THAT THE RUSSIANS HAD CREATED BOTS TO SPREAD THESE KINDS OF STORIES.

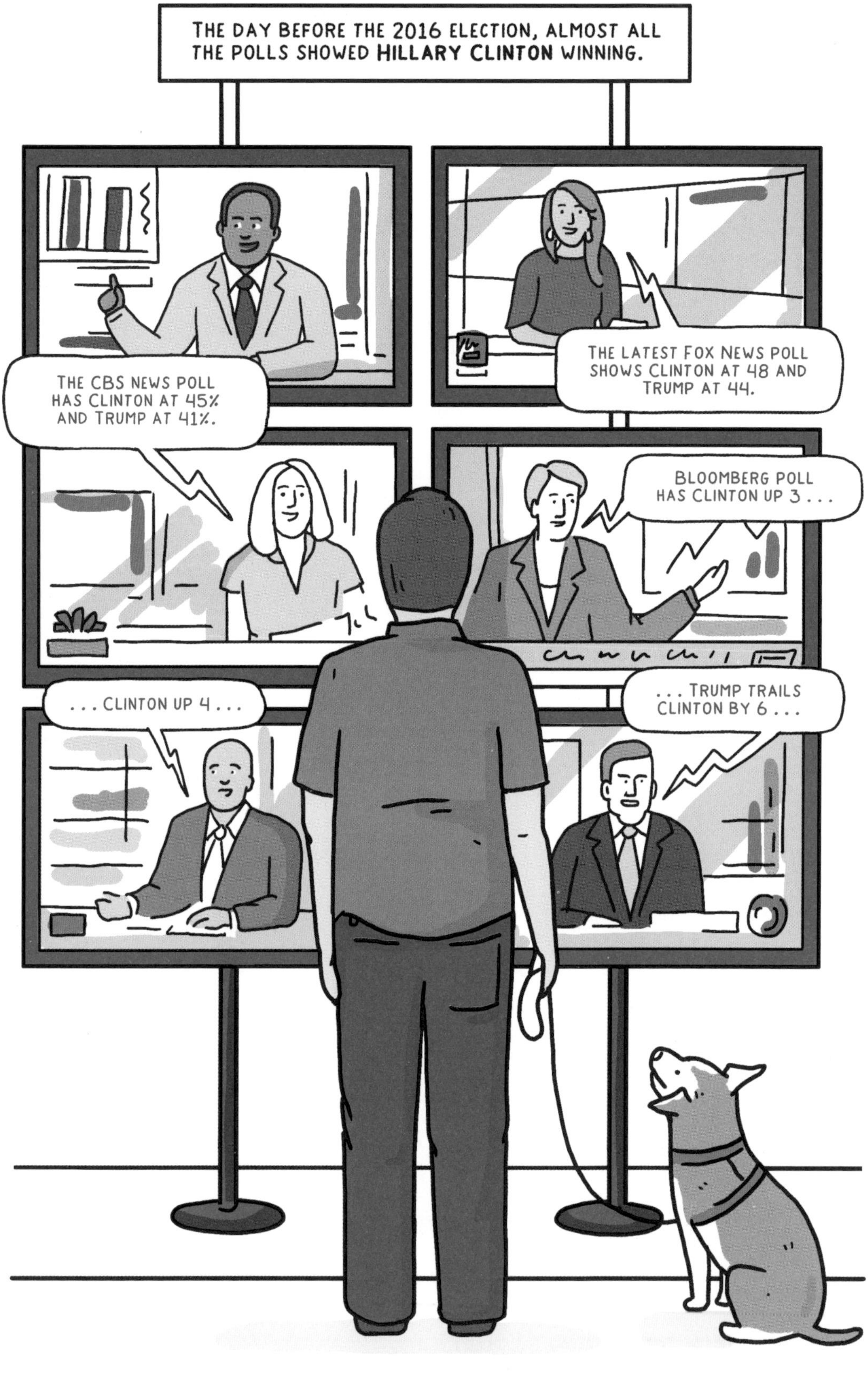
THE DAY BEFORE THE 2016 ELECTION, ALMOST ALL THE POLLS SHOWED **HILLARY CLINTON** WINNING.
THE CBS NEWS POLL HAS CLINTON AT 45% AND TRUMP AT 41%.
THE LATEST FOX NEWS POLL SHOWS CLINTON AT 48 AND TRUMP AT 44.
BLOOMBERG POLL HAS CLINTON UP 3 . . .
. . . CLINTON UP 4 . . .
. . . TRUMP TRAILS CLINTON BY 6 . . .

LATE ON ELECTION NIGHT, NOVEMBER 8, 2016, AFTER IT WAS CLEAR **DONALD TRUMP** WOULD WIN, NOAH AND I WENT FOR A WALK.

HARDLY ANYBODY WAS OUT. THERE WAS NO CELEBRATION. IT SEEMED LIKE PEOPLE DIDN'T EVEN KNOW THE ELECTION WAS HAPPENING.

IT MADE ME THINK ABOUT MY STUDENTS AND THEIR APATHY. WHAT HAPPENED? DID APATHY LEAD TO TRUMP BEING ELECTED? OR DID TRUMP'S ELECTION REVEAL HOW DEEPLY DIVIDED THE COUNTRY REALLY IS?

OBAMA'S PRESIDENCY DIDN'T UNITE THE COUNTRY. SOME PEOPLE EVEN CLAIMED OBAMA CREATED MORE DIVISIONS IN OUR POLITICS.

TRUMP'S STUNNING VICTORY SHOWED THIS. RACISM REARED ITS HEAD.

JEWS WILL NOT REPLACE US!

CHARLOTTESVILLE, VIRGINIA. AUGUST 11, 2017.

THIS WAS A "UNITE THE RIGHT" RALLY, SET UP BY WHITE SUPREMACISTS TO PROTEST THE REMOVAL OF CONFEDERATE MONUMENTS. BASICALLY, RACISTS AND FASCISTS GOT TOGETHER SO THEY COULD BE SEEN AND HEARD.

THE NEXT DAY, AUGUST 12, A WHITE SUPREMACIST RAMMED HIS CAR INTO COUNTERPROTESTERS, KILLING A WOMAN NAMED **HEATHER HEYER.**

THEN ON AUGUST 15, PRESIDENT **DONALD TRUMP** SAID:

YOU ALSO HAD SOME VERY FINE PEOPLE ON BOTH SIDES.

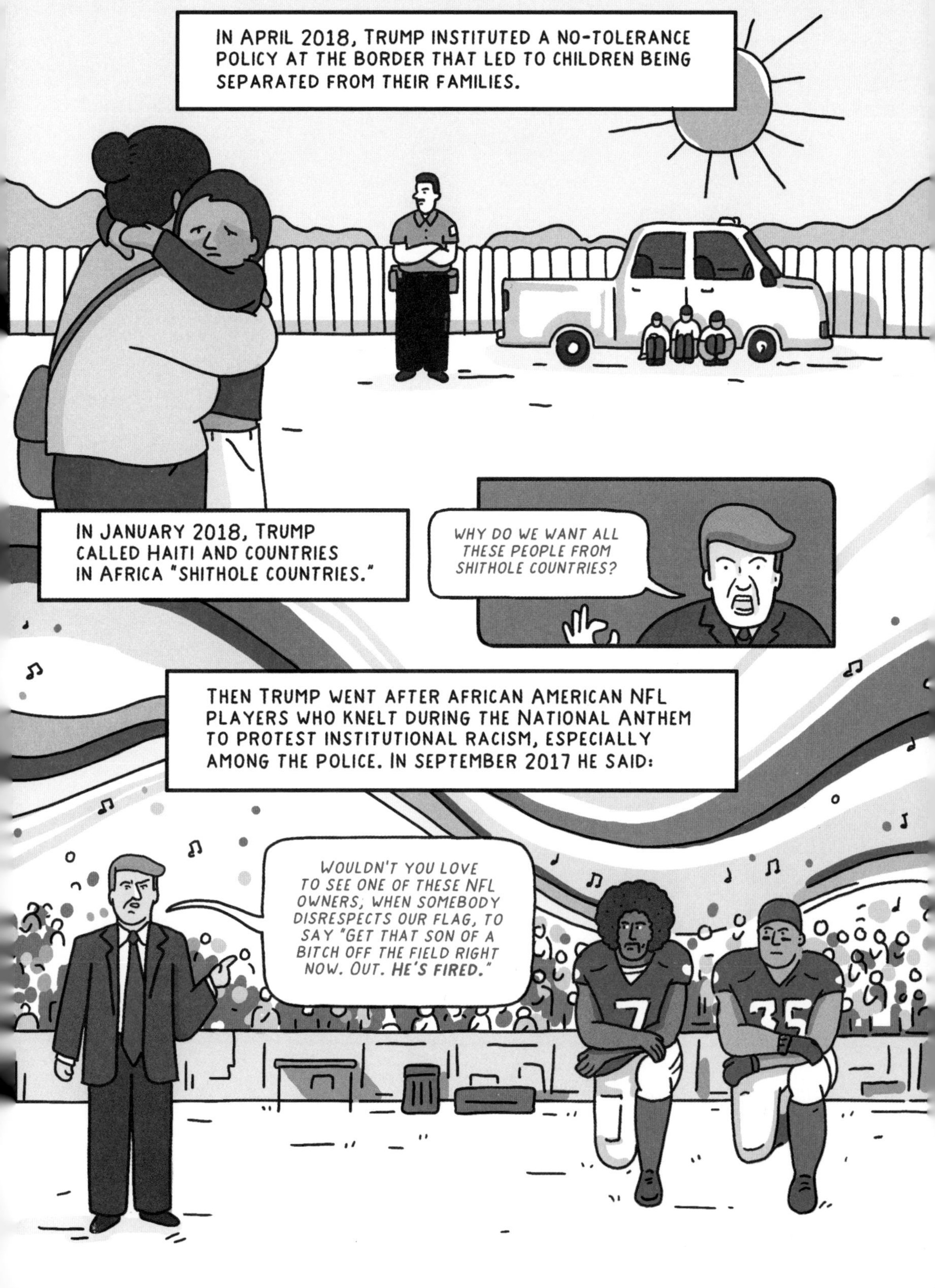
IN APRIL 2018, TRUMP INSTITUTED A NO-TOLERANCE POLICY AT THE BORDER THAT LED TO CHILDREN BEING SEPARATED FROM THEIR FAMILIES.
IN JANUARY 2018, TRUMP CALLED HAITI AND COUNTRIES IN AFRICA "SHITHOLE COUNTRIES."
WHY DO WE WANT ALL THESE PEOPLE FROM SHITHOLE COUNTRIES?
THEN TRUMP WENT AFTER AFRICAN AMERICAN NFL PLAYERS WHO KNELT DURING THE NATIONAL ANTHEM TO PROTEST INSTITUTIONAL RACISM, ESPECIALLY AMONG THE POLICE. IN SEPTEMBER 2017 HE SAID:
WOULDN'T YOU LOVE TO SEE ONE OF THESE NFL OWNERS, WHEN SOMEBODY DISRESPECTS OUR FLAG, TO SAY "GET THAT SON OF A BITCH OFF THE FIELD RIGHT NOW. OUT. HE'S FIRED."
7
35

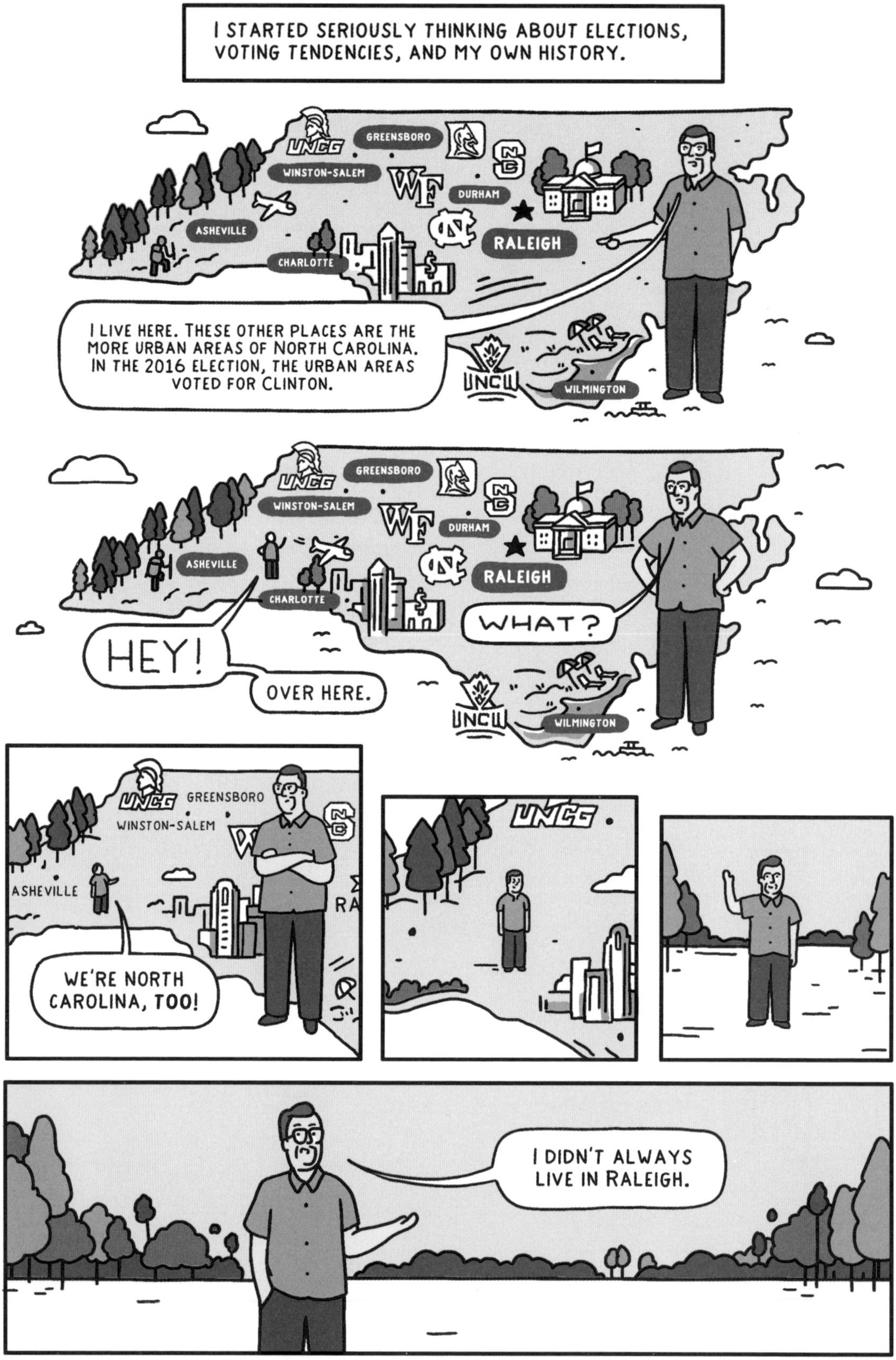
I STARTED SERIOUSLY THINKING ABOUT ELECTIONS, VOTING TENDENCIES, AND MY OWN HISTORY.
UNCG
GREENSBORO
WINSTON-SALEM
DURHAM
ASHEVILLE
RALEIGH
CHARLOTTE
I LIVE HERE. THESE OTHER PLACES ARE THE MORE URBAN AREAS OF NORTH CAROLINA. IN THE 2016 ELECTION, THE URBAN AREAS VOTED FOR CLINTON.
UNCW
WILMINGTON
HEY!
OVER HERE.
WHAT?
WE'RE NORTH CAROLINA, TOO!
I DIDN'T ALWAYS LIVE IN RALEIGH.

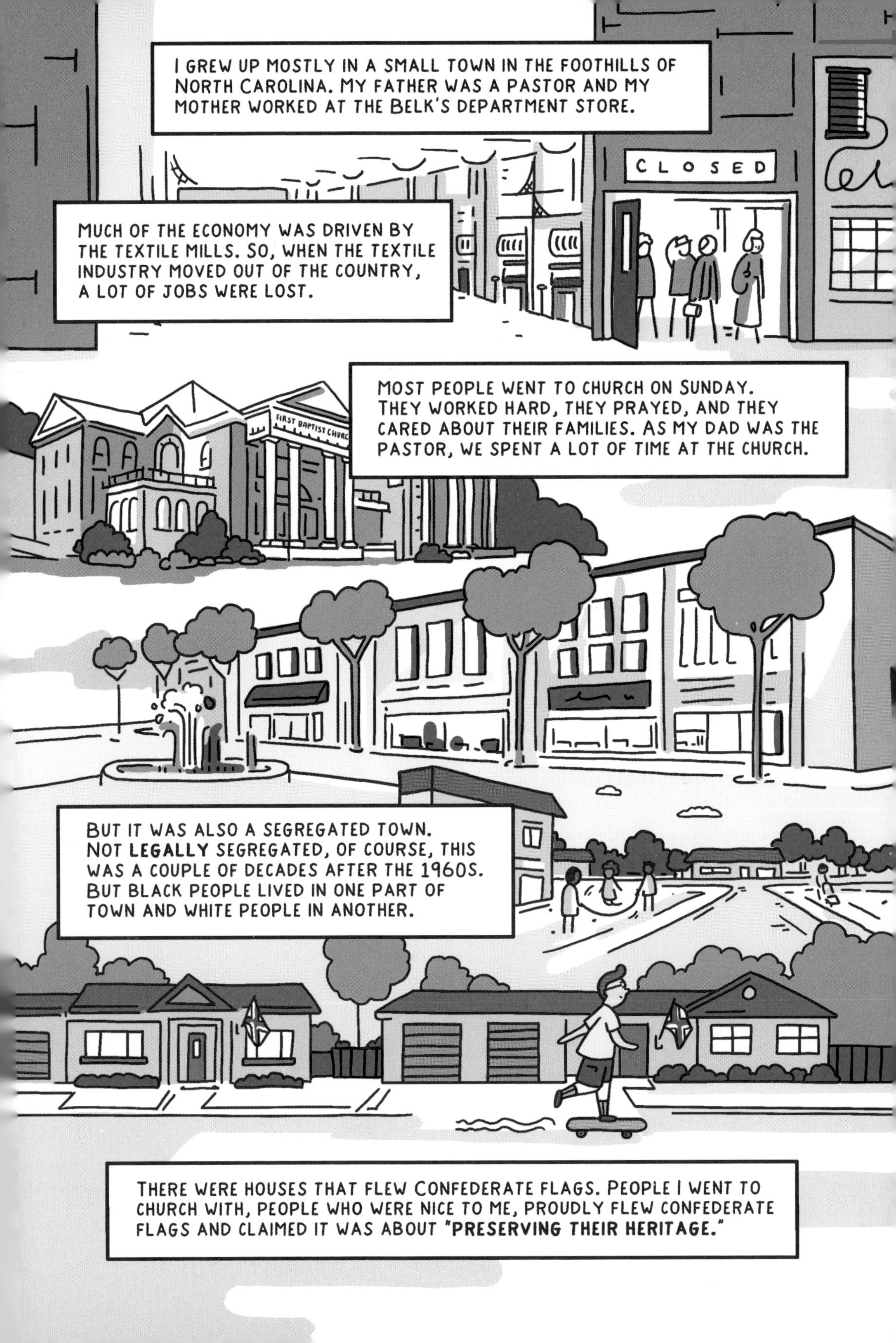
I GREW UP MOSTLY IN A SMALL TOWN IN THE FOOTHILLS OF NORTH CAROLINA. MY FATHER WAS A PASTOR AND MY MOTHER WORKED AT THE BELK'S DEPARTMENT STORE.
CLOSED
MUCH OF THE ECONOMY WAS DRIVEN BY THE TEXTILE MILLS. SO, WHEN THE TEXTILE INDUSTRY MOVED OUT OF THE COUNTRY, A LOT OF JOBS WERE LOST.
MOST PEOPLE WENT TO CHURCH ON SUNDAY. THEY WORKED HARD, THEY PRAYED, AND THEY CARED ABOUT THEIR FAMILIES. AS MY DAD WAS THE PASTOR, WE SPENT A LOT OF TIME AT THE CHURCH.
FIRST BAPTIST CHURC
BUT IT WAS ALSO A SEGREGATED TOWN. NOT **LEGALLY** SEGREGATED, OF COURSE, THIS WAS A COUPLE OF DECADES AFTER THE 1960S. BUT BLACK PEOPLE LIVED IN ONE PART OF TOWN AND WHITE PEOPLE IN ANOTHER.
THERE WERE HOUSES THAT FLEW CONFEDERATE FLAGS. PEOPLE I WENT TO CHURCH WITH, PEOPLE WHO WERE NICE TO ME, PROUDLY FLEW CONFEDERATE FLAGS AND CLAIMED IT WAS ABOUT "**PRESERVING THEIR HERITAGE.**"

HONESTLY, MEMBERS OF MY OWN FAMILY FIT THIS MOLD.

MY UNCLES

MY DAD

I GOT A JOKE. HOW MANY N[...] DOES IT TAKE—

NO.

WHAT?

I DON'T WANT TO HEAR THOSE KINDS OF JOKES. AND I DEFINITELY DON'T WANT MY SON HEARING THEM.

WE'RE JUST HAVING SOME FUN HERE. EASE UP.

NO. THAT'S NOT FUN.

COME ON, SON. RACISM ISN'T FUNNY, AND IT'S NOT RIGHT.

GOD, I LOVE MY DAD.

14

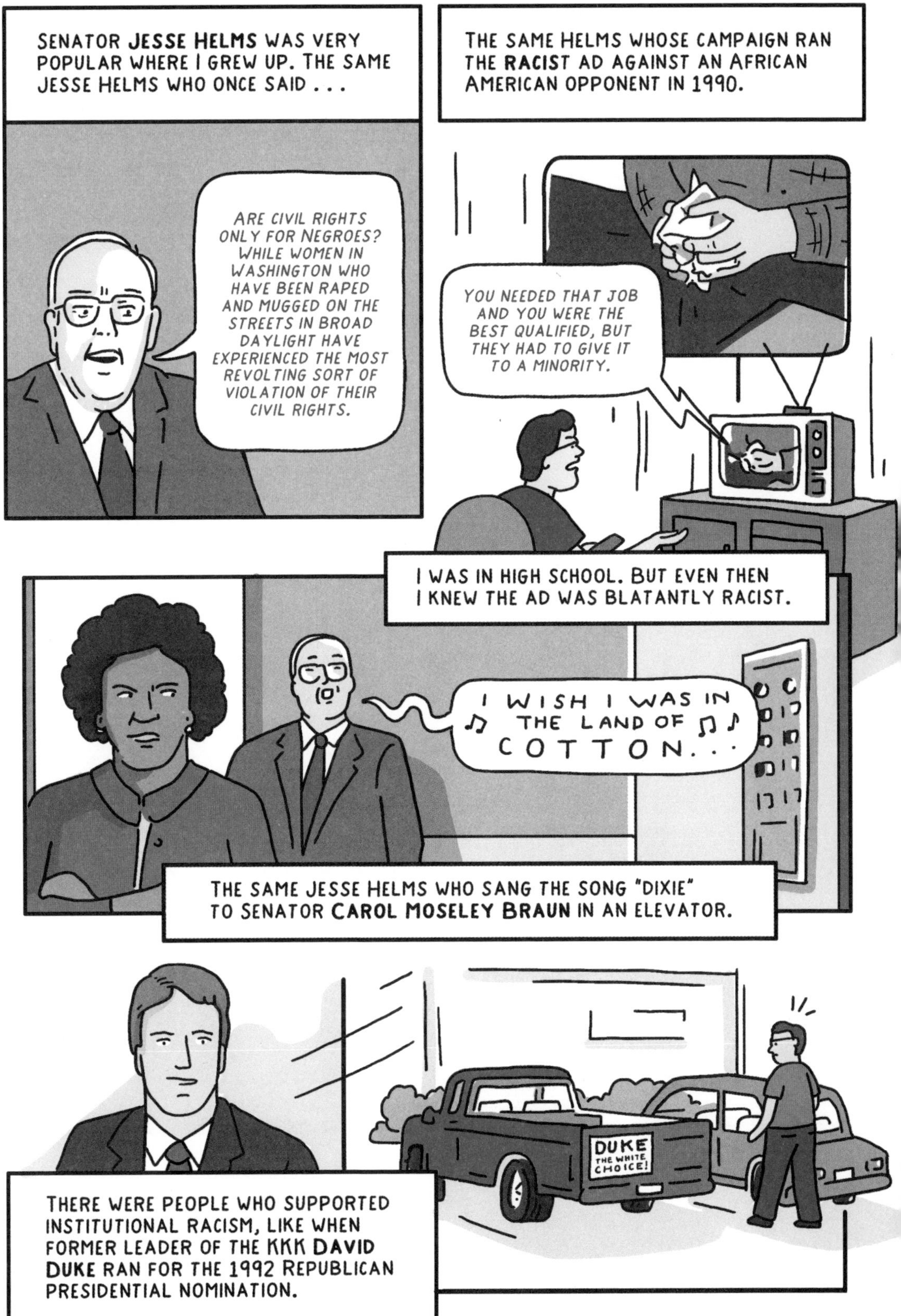
SENATOR JESSE HELMS WAS VERY POPULAR WHERE I GREW UP. THE SAME JESSE HELMS WHO ONCE SAID . . .
ARE CIVIL RIGHTS ONLY FOR NEGROES? WHILE WOMEN IN WASHINGTON WHO HAVE BEEN RAPED AND MUGGED ON THE STREETS IN BROAD DAYLIGHT HAVE EXPERIENCED THE MOST REVOLTING SORT OF VIOLATION OF THEIR CIVIL RIGHTS.
THE SAME HELMS WHOSE CAMPAIGN RAN THE RACIST AD AGAINST AN AFRICAN AMERICAN OPPONENT IN 1990.
YOU NEEDED THAT JOB AND YOU WERE THE BEST QUALIFIED, BUT THEY HAD TO GIVE IT TO A MINORITY.
I WAS IN HIGH SCHOOL. BUT EVEN THEN I KNEW THE AD WAS BLATANTLY RACIST.
I WISH I WAS IN THE LAND OF COTTON. . .
THE SAME JESSE HELMS WHO SANG THE SONG "DIXIE" TO SENATOR CAROL MOSELEY BRAUN IN AN ELEVATOR.
DUKE THE WHITE CHOICE!
THERE WERE PEOPLE WHO SUPPORTED INSTITUTIONAL RACISM, LIKE WHEN FORMER LEADER OF THE KKK DAVID DUKE RAN FOR THE 1992 REPUBLICAN PRESIDENTIAL NOMINATION.

SEE, I THOUGHT A LOT OF THOSE ATTITUDES WERE FADING AWAY. THEN, IN 2011, TRUMP EMERGED ON THE POLITICAL SCENE BY QUESTIONING IF OBAMA WAS BORN IN AMERICA. IN 2012, HE CONTINUED HIS ATTACKS.

 Donald J. Trump ✓
@realDonaldTrump

🐦 Follow

An 'extremely credible source' has called my office and told me that @BarackObama's birth certificate is a fraud.
4:23 PM- 6 Aug 2012

↩ ♺ 9,196 ♡ 6,539

AT A 2016 DEBATE, TRUMP SAID . . .

OUR INNER CITIES, AFRICAN AMERICANS, HISPANICS ARE LIVING IN HELL BECAUSE IT'S SO DANGEROUS. YOU WALK DOWN THE STREET, YOU GET SHOT.

HOW COULD WE HAVE BELIEVED RACISM WAS DEAD? IT SEEMED TO ME RACISM WAS MAKING A COMEBACK.

SO, HOW DID TRUMP GET ELECTED?

NORTH CAROLINA

| D | HILLARY CLINTON 1,976,699 | 46.5% |
| R | DONALD TRUMP 2,159,298 | 50.8% |

ALTHOUGH OBAMA WON NORTH CAROLINA, MY HOME STATE, IN 2008, TRUMP WON IT IN 2016.

VOTER TURNOUT IN NORTH CAROLINA, LIKE IN MANY STATES, WAS LOW FOR YEARS, ESPECIALLY IN MIDTERM AND STATE ELECTIONS. BUT **STATE ELECTIONS** DETERMINE WHO WHO DRAWS THE LINES OF REPRESENTATION IN THE HOUSE OF REPRESENTATIVES.

DO PEOPLE NOT VOTE BECAUSE THEY DON'T CARE? DO THEY NOT VOTE BECAUSE OF OBSTACLES LIKE PHOTO ID REQUIREMENTS?

TO CHANGE THE WORLD, YOU NEED TO CHANGE ONE PERSON AT A TIME.

WOULD YOU LIKE TO REGISTER TO VOTE?

THAT'S A WASTE OF TIME.

OVER THE YEARS I'VE VOLUNTEERED TO REGISTER PEOPLE TO VOTE.

LEADING UP TO THE 2018 MIDTERM ELECTIONS, I WAS ALMOST AFRAID TO ASK THE STUDENTS.

WONDER WOMAN + THE AMERICAN LITERARY OUTSIDER

ANY OF YOU PLAN ON VOTING?

IT WASN'T MUCH, BUT IT WASN'T COMPLETE APATHY, EITHER.

116TH CONGRESS MEMBERS ELECT—

REPUBLICANS:

DEMOCRATS:

DEMOCRATS WON THE HOUSE IN THE 2018 MIDTERMS. THIS SHOWS THE STARK DIFFERENCE BETWEEN NEW GOP HOUSE MEMBERS AND NEW DEMOCRAT HOUSE MEMBERS.

FEMALE DEMOCRATIC CANDIDATES DID ESPECIALLY WELL.

WOMEN VOTERS CLEARLY MADE A DIFFERENCE IN THE ELECTION.

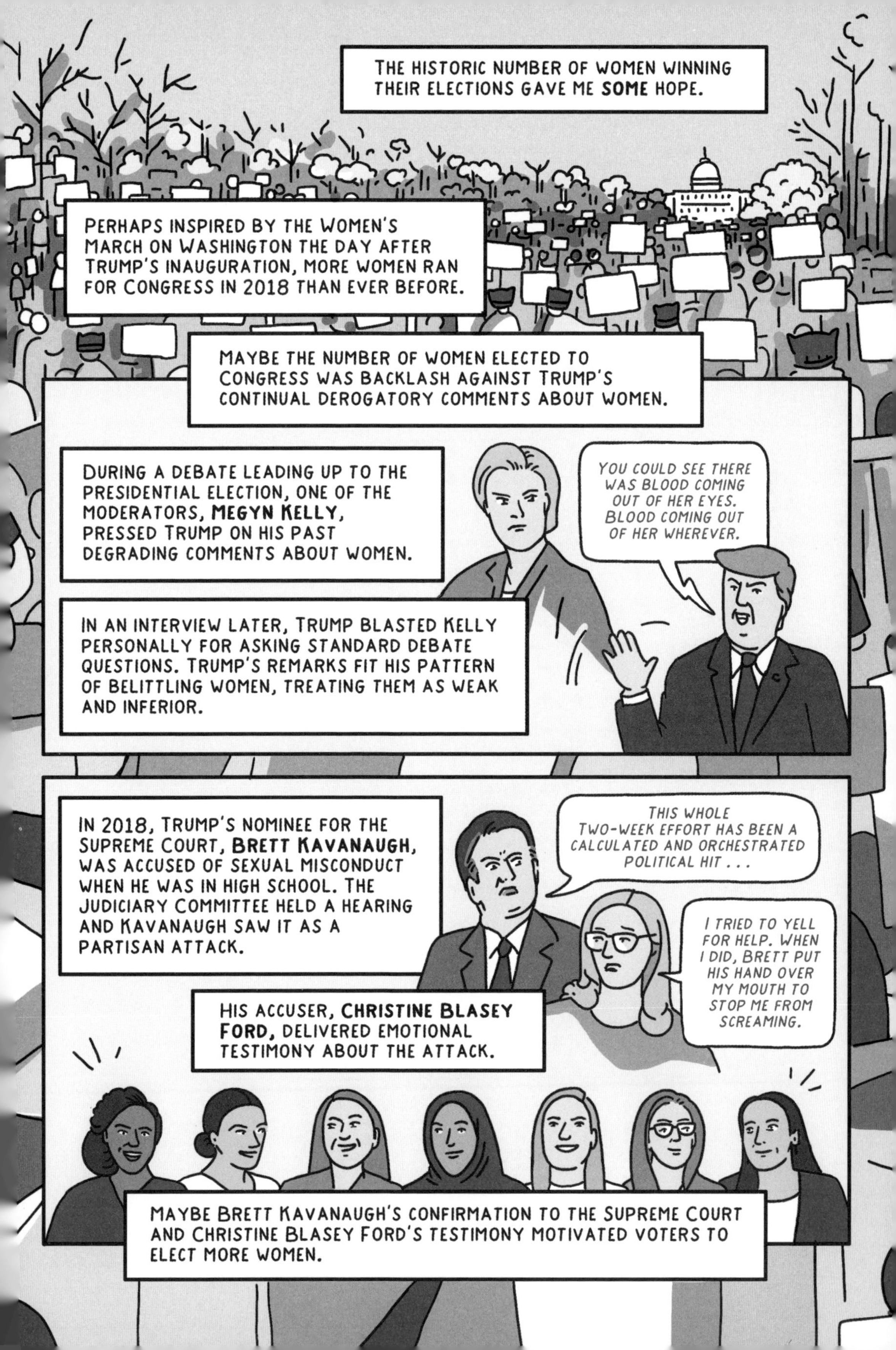
THE HISTORIC NUMBER OF WOMEN WINNING THEIR ELECTIONS GAVE ME **SOME** HOPE.
PERHAPS INSPIRED BY THE WOMEN'S MARCH ON WASHINGTON THE DAY AFTER TRUMP'S INAUGURATION, MORE WOMEN RAN FOR CONGRESS IN 2018 THAN EVER BEFORE.
MAYBE THE NUMBER OF WOMEN ELECTED TO CONGRESS WAS BACKLASH AGAINST TRUMP'S CONTINUAL DEROGATORY COMMENTS ABOUT WOMEN.
DURING A DEBATE LEADING UP TO THE PRESIDENTIAL ELECTION, ONE OF THE MODERATORS, **MEGYN KELLY**, PRESSED TRUMP ON HIS PAST DEGRADING COMMENTS ABOUT WOMEN.
YOU COULD SEE THERE WAS BLOOD COMING OUT OF HER EYES. BLOOD COMING OUT OF HER WHEREVER.
IN AN INTERVIEW LATER, TRUMP BLASTED KELLY PERSONALLY FOR ASKING STANDARD DEBATE QUESTIONS. TRUMP'S REMARKS FIT HIS PATTERN OF BELITTLING WOMEN, TREATING THEM AS WEAK AND INFERIOR.
IN 2018, TRUMP'S NOMINEE FOR THE SUPREME COURT, **BRETT KAVANAUGH**, WAS ACCUSED OF SEXUAL MISCONDUCT WHEN HE WAS IN HIGH SCHOOL. THE JUDICIARY COMMITTEE HELD A HEARING AND KAVANAUGH SAW IT AS A PARTISAN ATTACK.
THIS WHOLE TWO-WEEK EFFORT HAS BEEN A CALCULATED AND ORCHESTRATED POLITICAL HIT . . .
HIS ACCUSER, **CHRISTINE BLASEY FORD,** DELIVERED EMOTIONAL TESTIMONY ABOUT THE ATTACK.
I TRIED TO YELL FOR HELP. WHEN I DID, BRETT PUT HIS HAND OVER MY MOUTH TO STOP ME FROM SCREAMING.
MAYBE BRETT KAVANAUGH'S CONFIRMATION TO THE SUPREME COURT AND CHRISTINE BLASEY FORD'S TESTIMONY MOTIVATED VOTERS TO ELECT MORE WOMEN.

NORTH CAROLINA'S 2018 ELECTION WAS A MICROCOSM FOR THE COUNTRY AS A WHOLE. ELECTION RESULTS FAVORED BOTH REPUBLICANS AND DEMOCRATS.

TO AVOID A COURT BATTLE, ON THE NORTH CAROLINA BALLOT WAS A CONSTITUTIONAL AMENDMENT REQUIRING A PHOTO ID TO VOTE.

IT **OVERWHELMINGLY** PASSED AND WAS SEEN AS A VICTORY FOR REPUBLICANS.

THE REPUBLICAN-HELD LEGISLATURE ALSO PUT A CONSTITUTIONAL AMENDMENT ON THE BALLOT THAT WOULD GIVE THE POWER TO APPOINT JUDGES TO **THEM** RATHER THAN THE (DEMOCRAT) GOVERNOR.

THIS AMENDMENT WAS **OVERWHELMINGLY** DEFEATED AND WAS SEEN AS A VICTORY FOR DEMOCRATS.

THE LEGISLATURE WILL RECOMMEND AT LEAST TWO NOMINEES TO THE GOVERNOR VIA LEGISLATIVE ACTION NOT SUBJECT TO GUBERNATORIAL VETO...

WHILE THE REPUBLICANS KEPT A MAJORITY IN THE STATE LEGISLATURE, THEY LOST THEIR VETO-PROOF SUPERMAJORITY.

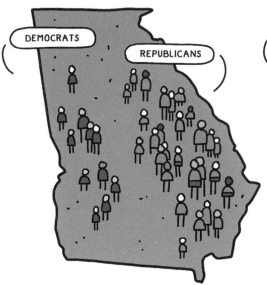

LIKE NORTH CAROLINA, GEORGIA'S REPUBLICAN SUPERMAJORITY IN THE STATE SENATE WAS BROKEN IN THE 2018 MIDTERM ELECTIONS. IT WAS A MODEST GAIN, BUT IT SHOWED HOW VOTER TURNOUT CAN MAKE A DIFFERENCE.

DEMOCRATS WON THE MOST SEATS IN THE ARIZONA HOUSE OF REPRESENTATIVES SINCE 1966.

DEMOCRATS DID WELL IN THE ARIZONA SUBURBS, PLACES THAT HAD BEEN RELIABLY REPUBLICAN FOR MANY YEARS.

ELAINE LURIA WON VIRGINIA'S 2ND CONGRESSIONAL DISTRICT AND ABIGAIL SPANBERGER WON VIRGINIA'S 7TH. TRUMP CARRIED BOTH DISTRICTS IN 2016, BUT DEMOCRATIC TURNOUT LED TO VICTORY IN THE MIDTERMS.

However, even after the people made their will known by voting in the 2018 midterm elections, some state legislatures acted out after not getting the results they wanted.

THE SYSTEM IS RIGGED ANYWAY.

THE PEOPLE VOTED, AND THE LEGISLATURE STILL JUST DOES WHAT IT WANTS.

After the 2018 election, it was discovered that Republicans committed fraud in North Carolina's 9th district by collecting absentee ballots and completing them.

In Wisconsin, the lame-duck legislature voted to limit the powers of the incoming governor. The lame-duck legislature was a majority Republican and the incoming governor was a Democrat.

JUST SIGN THE BALLOT AND WE'LL FILL IT IN.

OF COURSE, THIS IS HOW IT WORKS.

ARE YOU SURE?

ALL IN FAVOR?

AYE AYE AYE AYE

It was an obvious power grab.

The Republican House Speaker, **ROBIN VOS**, was blatant about the power grab, even though the Republican Governor was defeated by a Democrat.

[W]E ARE GOING TO HAVE A VERY LIBERAL GOVERNOR WHO IS GOING TO ENACT POLICIES THAT ARE IN DIRECT CONTRAST TO WHAT MANY OF US BELIEVE IN.

THIS LEGISLATION NEEDLESSLY DIVIDES AND WON'T DELIVER RESULTS.

In Michigan, **JOCELYN BENSON** was elected Secretary of State, **GRETCHEN WHITMER** Governor, and **DANA NESSEL** Attorney General.

The Michigan Republican-led legislature started passing bills to limit their powers.

TO BRING ABOUT CHANGE, IT TOOK PEOPLE VOTING. LARGE NUMBERS OF PEOPLE.

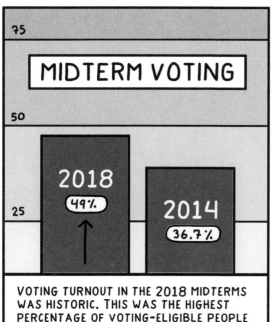

VOTING TURNOUT IN THE 2018 MIDTERMS WAS HISTORIC. THIS WAS THE HIGHEST PERCENTAGE OF VOTING-ELIGIBLE PEOPLE SINCE 1914.

A TURNOUT OF OVER 49% IS GREAT FOR A MIDTERM ELECTION. BUT THINK ABOUT IT THIS WAY: **WE ARE PRAISING A TURNOUT OF LESS THAN 50%.**

THAT MEANS THAT JUST OVER HALF OF THE VOTING-ELIGIBLE PEOPLE YOU WALK BY ON THE STREET DO **NOT** VOTE.

IT IS EVEN WORSE FOR YOUNG VOTERS. WHILE 31% VOTED IN 2018, UP FROM 20% IN 2014, THAT IS STILL **LESS THAN A THIRD.**

WHAT COULD I DO TO SHOW PEOPLE, ESPECIALLY YOUNG PEOPLE, HOW IMPORTANT VOTING IS? WHAT COULD I DO TO SHOW PEOPLE THE HARD-FOUGHT, OFTEN LIFE-AND-DEATH, HISTORY OF VOTING IN THIS COUNTRY?

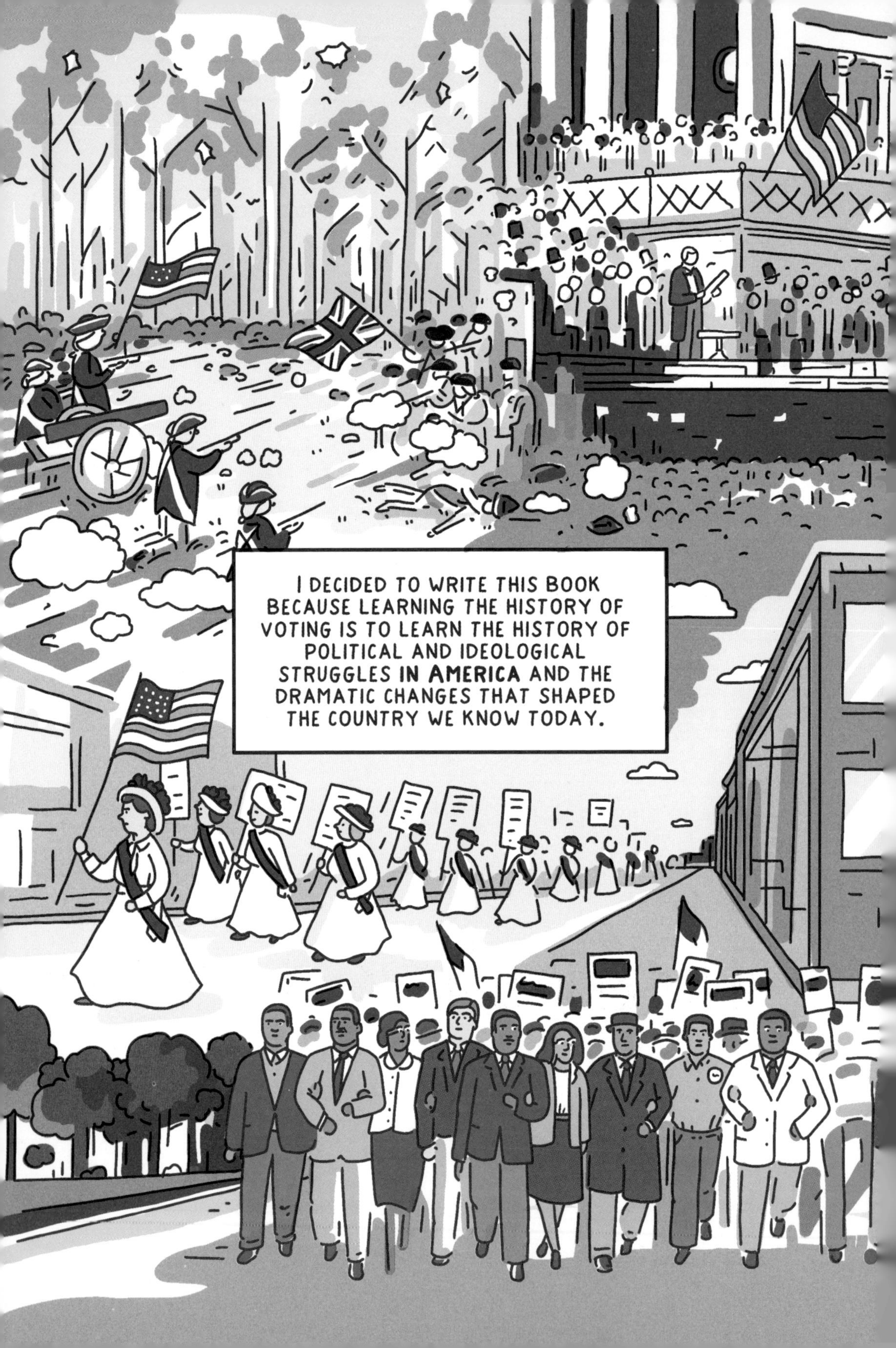
I DECIDED TO WRITE THIS BOOK BECAUSE LEARNING THE HISTORY OF VOTING IS TO LEARN THE HISTORY OF POLITICAL AND IDEOLOGICAL STRUGGLES **IN AMERICA** AND THE DRAMATIC CHANGES THAT SHAPED THE COUNTRY WE KNOW TODAY.

CHAPTER 2

THE BIRTH OF A NATION
1776–1861

WHAT EVENTUALLY BECAME THE UNITED STATES OF AMERICA WAS ORIGINALLY A GROUP OF BRITISH COLONIES. BUT THE COLONISTS GREW TIRED OF SUBMITTING TO A GOVERNMENT THOUSANDS OF MILES AWAY. A GOVERNMENT IN WHICH THEY HAD NO REPRESENTATION.

PARLIAMENT COULD ENACT WHATEVER LAWS THEY WISHED ON THE COLONIES, AND THE COLONISTS HAD NO VOTE.

WHAT ABOUT US?

THE FIGHT FOR VOTING RIGHTS BEGAN WITH THE BIRTH OF THIS NATION.

NO TAXATION WITHOUT REPRESENTATION!

THE BRITISH GOVERNMENT PUNISHED THE COLONISTS IN NUMEROUS WAYS. FOR INSTANCE, THE BRITISH PASSED THE **STAMP ACT** IN 1765, WHICH TAXED EVERY PIECE OF PRINTED PAPER USED BY THE COLONISTS.

THOSE UNGRATEFUL YANKEES WILL PAY A TAX ON **EVERY** PIECE OF PRINTED PAPER.

THE EAST INDIA COMPANY IS THE **ONLY** COMPANY TO RECEIVE A REFUND ON TAX, AND ONLY THEIR CONSIGNEES IN THE COLONIES WILL SEE THIS REDUCED PRICE.

THEY ALSO TAXED TEA, AN IMPORTANT AND POPULAR COMMODITY. THIS MEANT THAT THE EAST INDIA COMPANY HAD A MONOPOLY. TEA MERCHANTS NOT OF THE EAST INDIA COMPANY WOULD BE RUINED.

OF COURSE, MANY COLONISTS WERE UNHAPPY WITH THIS.

ON DECEMBER 16, 1773, IN BOSTON, A GUERILLA GROUP CALLED THE **SONS OF LIBERTY** BOARDED SHIPS CARRYING EAST INDIA COMPANY TEA AND TOSSED TEA INTO THE HARBOR. AS A RESULT OF THEIR ACTIONS, THE BRITISH CLOSED BOSTON HARBOR.

I'LL BE STAYING HERE AWHILE.

IN 1774, BRITAIN PASSED THE **QUARTERING ACT.**

BECAUSE OF THESE INDIGNITIES, AND THE CONTINUAL LACK OF REPRESENTATION IN PARLIAMENT, THE COLONISTS OFFICIALLY DECLARED THEIR INDEPENDENCE FROM THE BRITISH ON **JULY 4, 1776.**

HOWEVER, THE DECLARATION OF INDEPENDENCE DID NOT ESTABLISH OUR SYSTEM OF GOVERNMENT. IT WAS **NOT** THE CONSTITUTION.

ALTHOUGH IT WAS NOT CONCERNED WITH THE RIGHT TO VOTE, THE DECLARATION DID ADDRESS OTHER GRIEVANCES, INCLUDING SLAVERY.

"HE HAS WAGED CRUEL WAR AGAINST HUMAN NATURE ITSELF, BLAH, BLAH, BLAH, PERSONS OF A DISTANT PEOPLE, BLAH, BLAH, BLAH, AND CARRYING THEM INTO SLAVERY . . ."

HOLD ON, NOW! YOU CAN'T TALK ABOUT SLAVERY. WE **NEED** OUR SLAVES!

MY CONSTITUENTS IN THE NORTH DEPEND ON THE SLAVE TRADE FOR MONEY. THE MERCHANTS NEED IT.

WE SHOULD REMOVE THAT SECTION.

BUT SOME POLITICIANS, AS WE WILL SEE AGAIN AND AGAIN, REPRESENTED BY OUR GENERIC POLITICIAN, OPPOSED THIS.

THE REVOLUTIONARY WAR WAS BLOODY AND TOOK A GREAT TOLL, BUT EVENTUALLY THE COLONISTS PREVAILED.

BYE- BYE, BRITAIN!

YOU WON!

SO WHAT DO WE DO NOW?

THE SECOND CONTINENTAL CONGRESS DREW UP THE ARTICLES OF CONFEDERATION IN NOVEMBER OF 1777. BUT BECAUSE OF THE WAR, THE ARTICLES WERE NOT RATIFIED UNTIL 1781.

THESE DOCUMENTS ESTABLISHED OUR FIRST GOVERNMENT.

THE ARTICLES OF CONFEDERATION **DID NOT** GIVE THE FEDERAL GOVERNMENT MUCH POWER.

WE DON'T WANT ONE CENTRAL AUTHORITY. THE COLONIES CAN RULE THEMSELVES.

EACH NEW STATE WAS PRETTY MUCH SOVEREIGN. THE STATE LEGISLATURES SELECTED REPRESENTATIVES FOR THE CONGRESS.

HERE'S WHAT CONGRESS HAD THE AUTHORITY TO DO:

MAINTAIN AN ARMED FORCE.

I CAN'T BELIEVE I HAVE TO ACKNOWLEDGE **YOU.** I'M THE KING OF **ENGLAND!**

MAKE TREATIES AND ALLIANCES.

I HATE YOU.

THE FEELING IS MUTUAL.

NEW YORK

PENNSYLVANIA

CONGRESS WAS ALSO THE PLACE TO APPEAL DISPUTES BETWEEN STATES.

AND CONGRESS COULD MAKE MONEY. **THAT WAS ABOUT IT.**

HOW DO WE RAISE ANY MONEY?

THE FEDERAL GOVERNMENT COULD NOT COLLECT TAXES. NOR COULD IT REGULATE COMMERCE.

THE ONLY VOTING ANYONE COULD DO WAS FOR STATE AND LOCAL ELECTIONS.

THE LACK OF CENTRAL GOVERNMENT AUTHORITY LED TO PROBLEMS, SUCH AS **SHAYS'S** REBELLION.

DANIEL SHAYS WAS A FARMER, BUT HE VOLUNTEERED FOR THE CONTINENTAL ARMY. HE MADE THE RANK OF CAPTAIN, AND FOUGHT AT LEXINGTON, AMONG OTHER BATTLES.

THE SOLDIERS WERE HARDLY PAID FOR FIGHTING. THEN THEY RETURNED HOME AND FOUND OUT THEY **STILL** OWED MONEY FOR THEIR LAND AND OTHER GOODS. CREDITORS DIDN'T SUSPEND THE SOLDIERS' DEBT WHILE THEY FOUGHT.

IN 1786, SHAYS RALLIED SOME MEN, AND THEY TRIED TO TAKE THE SPRINGFIELD ARMORY.

IT WAS AN ARMED REVOLT.

SHAYS LOST AND DIDN'T OVERTHROW THE GOVERNMENT. BUT HIS REBELLION SCARED GOVERNMENT OFFICIALS.

BECAUSE OF SHAYS'S REBELLION, AND OTHER MATTERS, IT WAS CLEAR THE COUNTRY NEEDED A STRONGER CENTRAL GOVERNMENT.

SINCE THE ONLY WAY TO AMEND THE ARTICLES OF CONFEDERATION WAS BY **UNANIMOUS** VOTES OF THE STATES, THEY NEEDED A NEW ARTICLE OF GOVERNMENT.

IN MAY 1787, A CONSTITUTIONAL CONVENTION WAS HELD IN PHILADELPHIA.

REPRESENTATIVES FROM EACH STATE ATTENDED. **ALEXANDER HAMILTON** WAS SELECTED BY THE NEW YORK STATE LEGISLATURE TO REPRESENT NEW YORK.

GEORGE WASHINGTON WAS UNANIMOUSLY ELECTED AS THE CONVENTION'S PRESIDENT.

AND SO THE CONSTITUTION WAS CREATED.

WHILE WAITING FOR THE CONVENTION TO BEGIN, **JAMES MADISON** DRAFTED WHAT BECAME KNOWN AS THE **VIRGINIA PLAN.**

MADISON'S PLAN CALLED FOR A **BICAMERAL** LEGISLATURE. THAT MEANS THERE WOULD BE TWO HOUSES, OR CHAMBERS, OF THE LEGISLATURE.

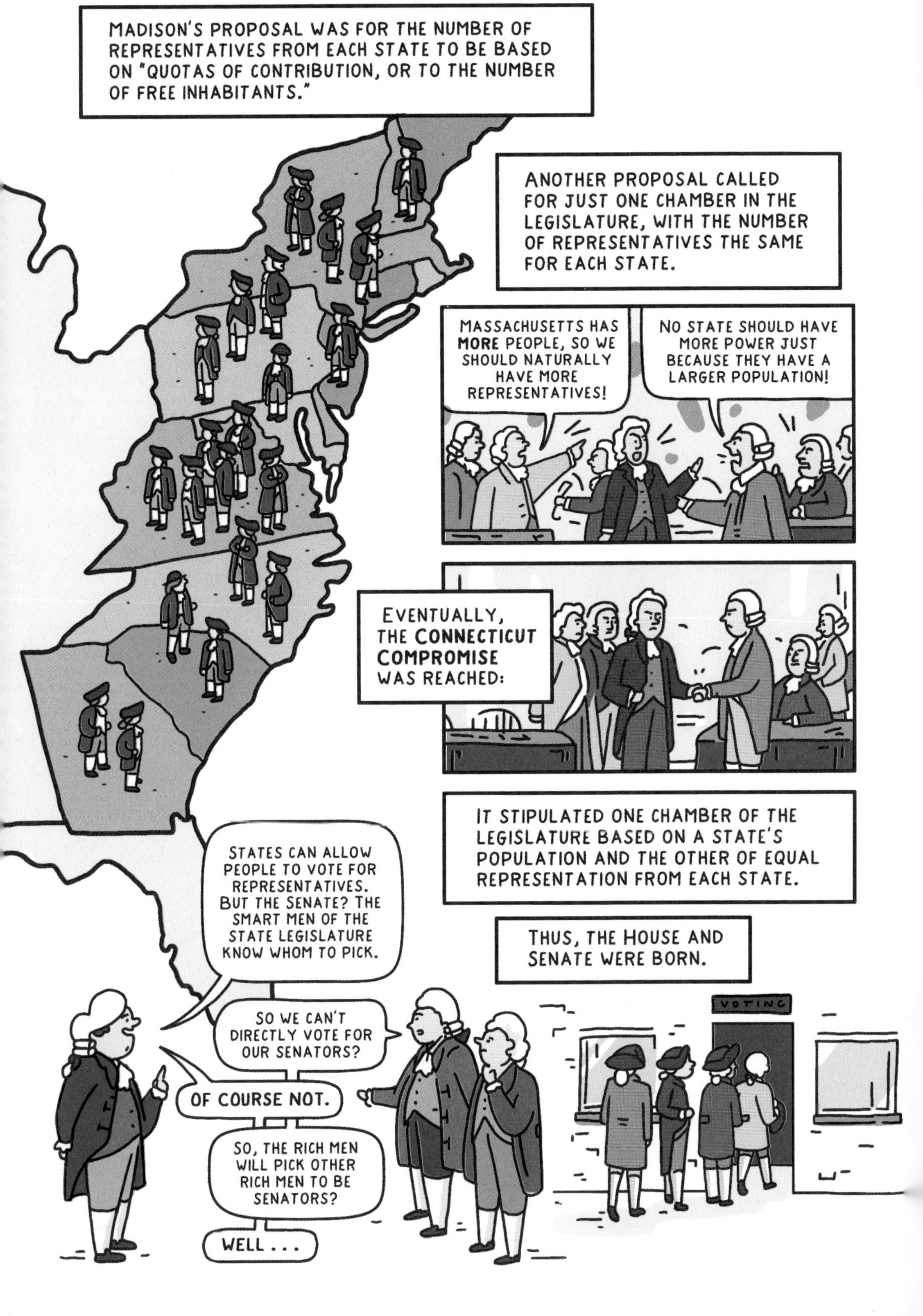
MADISON'S PROPOSAL WAS FOR THE NUMBER OF REPRESENTATIVES FROM EACH STATE TO BE BASED ON "QUOTAS OF CONTRIBUTION, OR TO THE NUMBER OF FREE INHABITANTS."
ANOTHER PROPOSAL CALLED FOR JUST ONE CHAMBER IN THE LEGISLATURE, WITH THE NUMBER OF REPRESENTATIVES THE SAME FOR EACH STATE.
MASSACHUSETTS HAS **MORE** PEOPLE, SO WE SHOULD NATURALLY HAVE MORE REPRESENTATIVES!
NO STATE SHOULD HAVE MORE POWER JUST BECAUSE THEY HAVE A LARGER POPULATION!
EVENTUALLY, THE **CONNECTICUT COMPROMISE** WAS REACHED:
IT STIPULATED ONE CHAMBER OF THE LEGISLATURE BASED ON A STATE'S POPULATION AND THE OTHER OF EQUAL REPRESENTATION FROM EACH STATE.
THUS, THE HOUSE AND SENATE WERE BORN.
STATES CAN ALLOW PEOPLE TO VOTE FOR REPRESENTATIVES. BUT THE SENATE? THE SMART MEN OF THE STATE LEGISLATURE KNOW WHOM TO PICK.
SO WE CAN'T DIRECTLY VOTE FOR OUR SENATORS?
OF COURSE NOT.
SO, THE RICH MEN WILL PICK OTHER RICH MEN TO BE SENATORS?
WELL . . .
VOTING

WHEN IT CAME TO THE EXECUTIVE BRANCH OF GOVERNMENT, SOME FAVORED HAVING A BOARD OF THREE PERSONS.

BUT THOSE WHO FAVORED A SINGLE PRESIDENT PREVAILED.

1789 PRESIDENT

CONGRATULATIONS YOU WILL BE PRESIDENT!

KNOWING THAT GENERAL WASHINGTON WOULD MOST LIKELY BE THE PRESIDENT HELPED SWAY THE DELEGATES.

THEY DID, HOWEVER, HAVE TO DECIDE HOW THE PRESIDENT WOULD BE ELECTED.

WE PROPOSE THAT THE STATE GOVERNORS SELECT THE PRESIDENT.

JAMES MADISON SAID THE FEDERAL LEGISLATURE SHOULD CHOOSE THE PRESIDENT. BUT THERE WERE SOME WHO DIDN'T CARE FOR THAT IDEA.

JAMES WILSON WAS ONE OF THE REPRESENTATIVES FROM PENNSYLVANIA.

WE PROPOSE THAT THE VOTERS DIRECTLY ELECT THE PRESIDENT.

WELL, WHO HAS THE RIGHT TO VOTE?

PERHAPS THE STATES WILL DECIDE WHO IS ELIGIBLE TO VOTE.

HOW WILL VOTERS LEARN ABOUT PRESIDENTIAL CANDIDATES?

EXACTLY. PEOPLE WILL NOT HAVE TIME TO LEARN ABOUT THESE CANDIDATES. DO WE WANT UNINFORMED PEOPLE VOTING?

TO ENSURE INFORMED VOTERS ELECTED THE PRESIDENT, THE NOTION OF THE **ELECTORAL COLLEGE** WAS BORN. EACH STATE WOULD HAVE ELECTORS WHO WOULD VOTE FOR PRESIDENT.

WE SOUTHERN STATES LAWFULLY OWN SLAVES, BUT OF COURSE, SLAVES CANNOT VOTE.

TRUE.

THIS MEANS NORTHERN STATES GET MORE VOTES. **NO WAY.** THAT'S NOT FAIR.

THE SUBSTITUTION OF ELECTORS . . . SEEMED ON THE WHOLE TO BE LIABLE TO THE FEWEST **OBJECTIONS.**

SOME, LIKE ALEXANDER HAMILTON, ARGUED THE ELECTION NEEDED MEN WHO WERE AWARE OF THE CANDIDATES AND THUS COULD MAKE INFORMED CHOICES.

WHAT MEN? **WHO?**

MEN MOST CAPABLE OF ANALYZING THE QUALITIES ADAPTED TO THE STATION AND ACTING UNDER CIRCUMSTANCES FAVORABLE TO DELIBERATION . . .

THEY SOUND LIKE **GOOD** MEN. SO WHO DECIDES HOW THESE ELECTORS ARE CHOSEN?

THE STATES, OF COURSE.

I LIKE IT!

GENTLEMEN, CAN WE DISCUSS HOW YOU DETERMINE THE POPULATION OF STATES FOR REPRESENTATION?

WE JUST, WELL, COUNT . . .

WE MADE REASONABLE COMPROMISES.

NOT ONLY DO THESE STATES ALLOW THE **ABOMINATION** OF SLAVERY TO EXIST, THEY ALSO WANT TO HAVE MORE POWER BY COUNTING THE SLAVES AS POPULATION.

THEY **DO** LIVE IN OUR STATES.

BUT WITH NO RIGHTS! THEY'RE NOT EVEN **CITIZENS!**

IF SLAVES WERE NOT COUNTED IN THE POPULATION, NORTHERN STATES WOULD CLEARLY HAVE MORE VOTES IN THE ELECTORAL COLLEGE. SOUTHERN DELEGATES DID NOT LIKE THAT IDEA.

SLAVES *DO* CONTRIBUTE TO THE ECONOMY OF THESE STATES AND TO THE NATION, SO . . .

IN ORDER TO GET THE CONSTITUTION PASSED, ALL OF THE STATES NEEDED TO SUPPORT IT. SO MADISON CAME UP WITH THE IDEA TO NOT COUNT A SLAVE AS A FULL PERSON, BUT AS **3/5THS** OF ONE.

THE **ELECTORAL COLLEGE** THUS WAS TIED, IN A WAY, TO SLAVERY.

JOHN ADAMS GLADLY SERVED AS VICE PRESIDENT TO GENERAL WASHINGTON.

CONGRATULATIONS! GEORGE WASHINGTON, YOU'VE WON THE PRESIDENCY. BY GETTING THE SECOND-MOST VOTES, JOHN ADAMS, YOU'VE WON THE CONSOLATION PRIZE OF VICE PRESIDENT!

TO ENSURE THE PRESERVATION OF DEMOCRACY, AND GUARD AGAINST A "KING"-LIKE RULER, WASHINGTON DID NOT SEEK A THIRD TERM IN OFFICE.

IN 1796, ADAMS WON THE PRESIDENCY. HOWEVER, AT THE TIME, ELECTORS FROM THE ELECTORAL COLLEGE VOTED FOR TWO PEOPLE.

CONGRATULATIONS! JOHN ADAMS, YOU'VE WON THE PRESIDENCY! THOMAS JEFFERSON, YOU'VE WON THE CONSOLATION PRIZE OF VICE PRESIDENT!

WHICH MEANT THOMAS JEFFERSON, WHO DIDN'T AGREE WITH ADAMS . . .

AND ADAMS, WHO DIDN'T AGREE WITH JEFFERSON, HAD TO WORK TOGETHER.

NEEDLESS TO SAY, THIS MEANT A DISJOINTED GOVERNMENT.

CONGRATULATIONS! YOU WON THE PRESIDENCY!

IN 1800, JEFFERSON WAS ELECTED PRESIDENT OVER JOHN ADAMS.

THOMAS JEFFERSON WORKED WITH **AARON BURR** TO SECURE THE PRESIDENCY, WHILE BURR WOULD GET THE VOTES FOR VICE PRESIDENT.

GENTLEMEN, WE MUST HAVE **SEPARATE** CANDIDATES FOR PRESIDENT AND VICE PRESIDENT SO THE MEN WILL BE ABLE TO WORK TOGETHER.

OBVIOUSLY THERE WAS A PROBLEM WITH HAVING THE SECOND-PLACE CANDIDATE BECOME THE VICE PRESIDENT.

THUS, THE 12TH AMENDMENT TO THE CONSTITUTION WAS PASSED.

THE ELECTORS SHALL MEET IN THEIR RESPECTIVE STATES, AND VOTE BY BALLOT FOR PRESIDENT AND VICE PRESIDENT . . .

Ballot

☐ President

☐ Vice President

THE 12TH AMENDMENT MEANT SEPARATE ELECTIONS FOR PRESIDENT AND VICE PRESIDENT.

THE ELECTORAL COLLEGE, OF COURSE, HAD MORE PROBLEMS. ONE OF THE BIGGEST ISSUES WAS THAT A CANDIDATE COULD WIN THE POPULAR VOTE, BUT NOT WIN THE ELECTORAL VOTE.

IN 1824, **ANDREW JACKSON** RECEIVED **10%** MORE OF THE POPULAR VOTE BUT STILL LOST TO **JOHN QUINCY ADAMS**. THERE WERE SEVERAL CANDIDATES THAT YEAR, SO THE FIELD WAS DIVERSE.

SAMUEL TILDEN, THE GOVERNOR OF NEW YORK AND THE DEMOCRATIC NOMINEE FOR PRESIDENT, LOST THE 1876 ELECTION DESPITE RECEIVING **51%** OF THE POPULAR VOTE. **RUTHERFORD B. HAYES** RECEIVED **48%**.

GROVER CLEVELAND WAS THE INCUMBENT IN 1888. HE WON THE POPULAR VOTE **48.6%** TO **47.8%**, BUT THE ELECTORS GAVE THE PRESIDENCY TO **BENJAMIN HARRISON**.

AL GORE, IN 2000, RECEIVED **48.4%** OF THE POPULAR VOTE, WHILE **GEORGE W. BUSH** RECEIVED **47.9%**. THE SUPREME COURT EVEN STOPPED A RECOUNT IN FLORIDA.

HILLARY CLINTON, IN 2016, RECEIVED OVER 3 MILLION MORE VOTES THAN DONALD TRUMP BUT STILL LOST THE ELECTORAL COLLEGE.

WE DON'T REALLY HAVE VOTING STATISTICS FOR THE EARLIEST ELECTIONS.

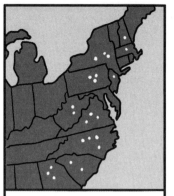

THE FIRST REAL STATISTICS ON VOTING PARTICIPATION COME FROM 1828, WHEN 57.6% OF THE VOTING POPULATION VOTED FOR PRESIDENT.

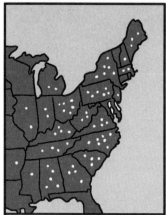

IN 1840, THAT NUMBER ROSE TO 80.2%. IT STAYED MOSTLY IN THE 70S UNTIL 1904, WHEN 65.2% VOTED.

WOW, THAT'S A LOW NUMBER.

IN 1924, 48.9% VOTED.

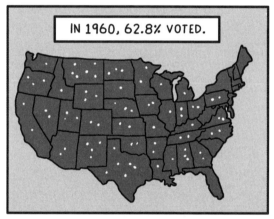

IN 1960, 62.8% VOTED.

IN 2016, 55.5% VOTED.

IN THE AVERAGE MIDTERM ELECTIONS, ONLY ABOUT 40% OF THE VOTING POPULATION ACTUALLY VOTES.

THIS IS TERRIBLE.

WE HAVE A LOT MORE DATA CONCERNING VOTING NOW, BUT WE CAN EXAMINE FACTORS THAT HAD SIGNIFICANT IMPACTS ON VOTING IN THE 1800S. FOR EXAMPLE, SLAVERY WAS NOT JUST A MAJOR POLITICAL ISSUE IN THE 1800S, IT WAS A MAJOR VOTING ISSUE, TOO.

THE SOUTHERN STATES ALWAYS VOTED TO KEEP SLAVERY. BUT THEY OF COURSE WOULD NOT ALLOW SLAVES TO VOTE.

IN 1850, THE FUGITIVE SLAVE ACT ENRAGED THOSE OPPOSED TO SLAVERY.

THE FUGITIVE SLAVE ACT ALLOWED SLAVE OWNERS TO GO INTO FREE STATES AND CAPTURE THEIR RUNAWAY SLAVES. IT ALSO SAID ANY PEOPLE HELPING A RUNAWAY SLAVE COULD BE FINED AND GO TO PRISON.

ABRAHAM **LINCOLN** WAS ELECTED IN 1860, AND SHORTLY THEREAFTER . . .

SOUTH CAROLINA OPENED FIRE ON FORT SUMTER . . .

AND THE SOUTHERN STATES SECEDED.

THUS, THE CIVIL WAR BEGAN.

CHAPTER 3

UNITED WE STAND, DIVIDED WE FALL

1865–1900

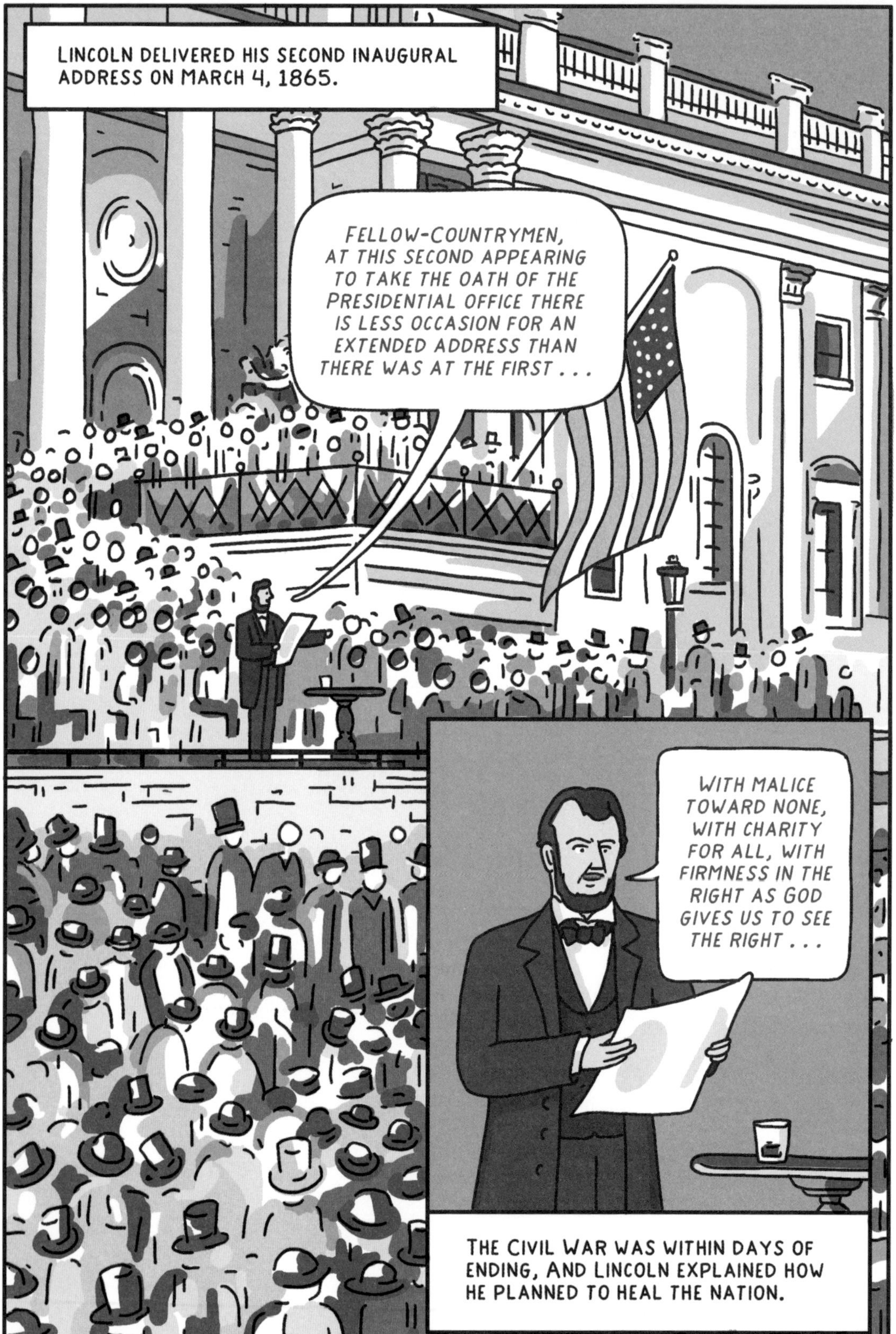
LINCOLN DELIVERED HIS SECOND INAUGURAL ADDRESS ON MARCH 4, 1865.
FELLOW-COUNTRYMEN, AT THIS SECOND APPEARING TO TAKE THE OATH OF THE PRESIDENTIAL OFFICE THERE IS LESS OCCASION FOR AN EXTENDED ADDRESS THAN THERE WAS AT THE FIRST . . .
WITH MALICE TOWARD NONE, WITH CHARITY FOR ALL, WITH FIRMNESS IN THE RIGHT AS GOD GIVES US TO SEE THE RIGHT . . .
THE CIVIL WAR WAS WITHIN DAYS OF ENDING, AND LINCOLN EXPLAINED HOW HE PLANNED TO HEAL THE NATION.

THE CIVIL WAR DIVIDED THE NATION AND RAGED FROM 1861 TO 1865. THE FIGHTING WAS BLOODY, WITH THOUSANDS DEAD OR WOUNDED IN BATTLES LIKE BULL RUN, VICKSBURG, AND GETTYSBURG.

BULL RUN

VICKSBURG

GETTYSBURG

EVENTUALLY, THE UNION FORCES TOOK CONTROL OF THE WAR, AND ON APRIL 9, 1865, GENERAL **ROBERT E. LEE** SURRENDERED TO GENERAL **ULYSSES S. GRANT** AT THE APPOMATTOX COURT HOUSE IN VIRGINIA.

AS PART OF THE SURRENDER, LEE AND HIS MEN WOULD **NOT** BE IMPRISONED **NOR** FACE CHARGES FOR TREASON.

I'M READY TO GO HOME.

DOES THIS MEAN WE HAVE TO PUT UP WITH ALL THE **NEGROES**?

THE WAR WAS OVER, AND SOLDIERS WHO HAD BEEN AWAY FOR YEARS RETURNED HOME.

THEN, ON APRIL 14 . . .

SIC SEMPER TYRANNIS!

"THUS ALWAYS TO TYRANTS."

MR. PRESIDENT? **MR. PRESIDENT?**

THE ASSASSINATION OF THE PRESIDENT BY **JOHN WILKES BOOTH** MEANT THAT THE POST–CIVIL WAR RECONSTRUCTION WOULD BE VERY DIFFERENT FROM WHAT LINCOLN HAD IN MIND.

ANDREW JOHNSON WAS SWORN IN AS THE 17TH PRESIDENT ON APRIL 15, 1865.

I DO.

YOU ARE A WISE MAN, SIR.

JOHNSON WAS FROM TENNESSEE. HE HAD HIS OWN PLANS FOR RECONSTRUCTION. HE ORDERED THAT THE LAND BE GIVEN **BACK** TO THE MEN WHO OWNED IT BEFORE THE WAR. HE ALSO LET THE SOUTHERN STATES DECIDE THEIR GOVERNMENTS.

AFTER THE CIVIL WAR, THERE WERE MILLIONS OF FREED SLAVES WHO HAD NO PLACE TO GO.

WHAT ARE WE GOING TO DO WITH ALL THESE SO-CALLED "FREE" SLAVES?

MAKE SURE THEY KNOW THEIR **PLACE.**

IN 1866, REPUBLICANS TOOK OVER CONGRESS IN A LANDSLIDE. **SCHUYLER COLFAX** BECAME SPEAKER OF THE HOUSE.

COLFAX BELIEVED THEY COULD OVERRIDE THE PRESIDENT'S VETOES. SO, THEY STARTED BY REMOVING CIVILIAN GOVERNMENTS IN THE SOUTH.

PEOPLE WHO HAD HELD POSITIONS OF AUTHORITY UNDER THE CONFEDERACY WERE PROHIBITED FROM VOTING AND HOLDING ELECTED OFFICE.

THADDEUS STEVENS, FROM PENNSYLVANIA, WAS ANOTHER LEADER OF THE RADICAL REPUBLICAN TAKEOVER OF 1866.

WE HOLD IT TO BE THE DUTY OF THE GOVERNMENT TO INFLICT PUNISHMENT ON THE REBEL BELLIGERENTS, AND SO WEAKEN THEIR HANDS THAT THEY CAN NEVER AGAIN ENDANGER THE UNION.

THE RADICAL REPUBLICANS FAVORED HARSH MEASURES FOR THE SOUTH DURING RECONSTRUCTION.

THE REPUBLICANS ENACTED RADICAL RECONSTRUCTION WHERE THE MILITARY COULD OVERSEE ELECTIONS AND MAKE SURE THAT FORMER SLAVES WERE REPRESENTED.

EVERY MAN, NO MATTER WHAT HIS RACE OR COLOR; EVERY EARTHLY BEING WHO HAS AN IMMORTAL SOUL, HAS AN EQUAL RIGHT TO JUSTICE, HONESTY, AND FAIR PLAY WITH EVERY OTHER MAN . . .

FORMER SLAVES EQUAL? YOU HAVE LOST YOUR MIND, SIR.

CONGRESS APPROVED THE 15TH AMENDMENT IN FEBRUARY OF 1869.

THE RIGHT OF THE CITIZENS OF THE UNITED STATES TO VOTE SHALL NOT BE DENIED OR ABRIDGED BY THE UNITED STATES OR BY ANY STATE ON ACCOUNT OF RACE, COLOR, OR PREVIOUS CONDITION OF SERVITUDE.

FOR THE FIRST TIME, FORMER SLAVES WERE ABLE TO VOTE IN THE SOUTH.

VOTE

WE REALLY GET TO VOTE?

WE ARE HERE TO PROTECT YOU SO YOU CAN.

AND BECAUSE OF THE GREAT NUMBER OF FORMER SLAVES VOTING, THERE WERE SIGNIFICANT CHANGES IN CONGRESS.

VOTE

IN 1870 AND 1871, SIX AFRICAN AMERICAN MEN FROM FORMER CONFEDERATE STATES TOOK OFFICE IN THE US HOUSE OF REPRESENTATIVES. THEY WERE ALL REPUBLICANS.

THROUGHOUT THE 1870S, DURING RECONSTRUCTION, AN ADDITIONAL EIGHT AFRICAN AMERICANS TOOK OFFICE FROM FORMER CONFEDERATE STATES. AGAIN, ALL WERE REPUBLICANS.

HIRAM REVELS WAS APPOINTED TO SERVE OUT A TERM IN THE US SENATE BY THE MISSISSIPPI LEGISLATURE IN 1870. HE BECAME THE FIRST BLACK US SENATOR.

IN 1874, BLANCHE BRUCE WAS ELECTED THE FIRST AFRICAN AMERICAN US SENATOR. HE WAS FROM MISSISSIPPI AND, AS STIPULATED AT THE TIME, ELECTED BY THE STATE LEGISLATURE.

ULYSSES S. GRANT WAS ELECTED PRESIDENT IN 1868. HE CONTINUED MOST OF THE POLICIES OF THE RADICAL REPUBLICANS.

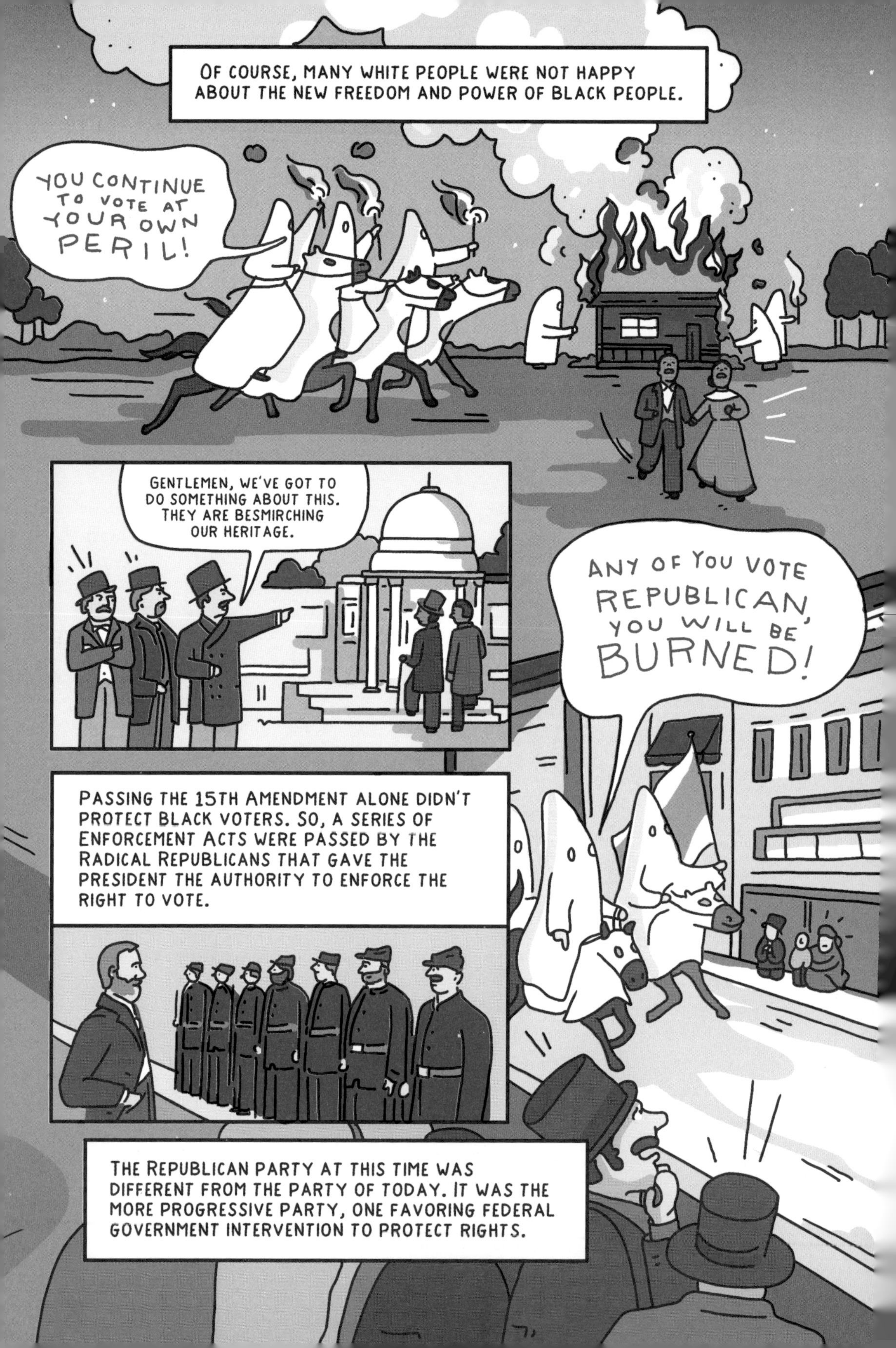

OF COURSE, MANY WHITE PEOPLE WERE NOT HAPPY ABOUT THE NEW FREEDOM AND POWER OF BLACK PEOPLE.
YOU CONTINUE TO VOTE AT YOUR OWN PERIL!
GENTLEMEN, WE'VE GOT TO DO SOMETHING ABOUT THIS. THEY ARE BESMIRCHING OUR HERITAGE.
ANY OF YOU VOTE REPUBLICAN, YOU WILL BE BURNED!
PASSING THE 15TH AMENDMENT ALONE DIDN'T PROTECT BLACK VOTERS. SO, A SERIES OF ENFORCEMENT ACTS WERE PASSED BY THE RADICAL REPUBLICANS THAT GAVE THE PRESIDENT THE AUTHORITY TO ENFORCE THE RIGHT TO VOTE.
THE REPUBLICAN PARTY AT THIS TIME WAS DIFFERENT FROM THE PARTY OF TODAY. IT WAS THE MORE PROGRESSIVE PARTY, ONE FAVORING FEDERAL GOVERNMENT INTERVENTION TO PROTECT RIGHTS.

THE WHITE LEAGUE IN LOUISIANA AND MISSISSIPPI STEPPED IN TO INTIMIDATE BLACK AND REPUBLICAN VOTERS. PART OF THEIR OFFICIAL PLATFORM READ . . .

UNITE WITH US IN AN EARNEST EFFORT TO REESTABLISH A WHITE MAN'S GOVERNMENT IN THE CITY AND THE STATE.

THE IGNORANT RACES SHOULDN'T VOTE!

OF COURSE, THIS MEANT BEATING UP BLACK PEOPLE TRYING TO VOTE, AND ANY REPUBLICAN VOTERS.

THE RED SHIRTS, WHO, YES, WORE RED SHIRTS, FORMED IN MISSISSIPPI AND THE CAROLINAS. THESE GROUPS WERE ALIGNED WITH THE DEMOCRATIC PARTY. THEY ALSO KEPT FORMER SLAVES FROM VOTING.

SHOW HIM, BOYS! SHOW HIM WHAT HE GETS FOR VOTING.

RED SHIRTS

WE WILL BE REDEEMED!

ALL OF THESE GROUPS WANTED TO PROHIBIT VOTING.

THE PRESIDENTIAL ELECTION OF 1876 WAS VERY TIGHT.

TILDEN! TILDEN!

WE WANT HAYES!

WE HAY

TILDEN

TILDEN

HAYES

HAYES

TILDEN for PRESIDENT!

SAMUEL J. TILDEN WAS GOVERNOR OF NEW YORK.

HAYES for PRESIDENT!

RUTHERFORD B. HAYES WAS A REPUBLICAN: THE PARTY OF LINCOLN.

HERE'S YOUR BALLOT. YOU WILL VOTE DEMOCRAT.

OR ELSE. REMEMBER, WE DON'T WANT THEM NEGRO-LOVERS IN OFFICE.

VOTE TODAY!

Ballot

TILDEN ☒

HAYES ☐

AT THIS TIME, THE PARTY HANDED OUT THE BALLOTS TO PEOPLE WHO COULDN'T READ SO THEY WOULD VOTE "CORRECTLY."

DON'T EVEN THINK ABOUT VOTING.

IF YOU KNOW WHAT'S GOOD FOR YOU, YOU'LL GET OUT OF HERE.

CLICK

THE NIGHT OF THE ELECTION, IT APPEARED TILDEN HAD IT.

THE DEMOCRATS ARE BACK!

CONGRATULATIONS, MR. PRESIDENT.

NOT SO FAST...

IT'S NOT OVER!

WHAT DO YOU MEAN, "NOT SO FAST"?

WHAT?

YEAH, WHAT ARE YOU TALKING ABOUT?

THE ELECTORAL VOTES IN FLORIDA, LOUISIANA, AND SOUTH CAROLINA HAVE NOT BEEN CERTIFIED. THERE IS REPORTED FRAUD AND INTIMIDATION TO KEEP PEOPLE FROM VOTING REPUBLICAN.

ARE YOU KIDDING?!

ON JANUARY 29, 1877, CONGRESS PASSED A LAW TO SET UP AN **ELECTORAL COMMISSION** TO INVESTIGATE THE PRESIDENTIAL ELECTION. THE COMMISSION CONSISTED OF FIVE MEMBERS FROM THE HOUSE, FIVE MEMBERS FROM THE SENATE, AND FIVE SUPREME COURT JUSTICES. SO IT WAS, IN THEORY, BIPARTISAN.

THE COMMISSION DECIDED HAYES RECEIVED 185 ELECTORAL VOTES AND TILDEN 184.

CONGRATULATIONS! **FINALLY.**

ONCE AGAIN, THE WINNER OF THE POPULAR VOTE DID NOT WIN THE PRESIDENTIAL ELECTION.

SO, IF WE END RECONSTRUCTION, YOU'LL GO ALONG WITH THE **ELECTORAL COMMISSION**?

THAT'S RIGHT. YOU WILL BE PRESIDENT, MR. HAYES, BUT THE FEDERAL GOVERNMENT WILL CEASE INTERFERING IN THE SOUTH.

IT WAS SPECULATED THAT A COMPROMISE WAS REACHED: IN EXCHANGE FOR THE DEMOCRATS AGREEING TO NOT BLOCK HIS WIN, HAYES WOULD END RECONSTRUCTION AND THE SOUTH WOULD BE LEFT TO HANDLE ITS OWN BUSINESS.

THE COMPROMISE MEANT THE US TROOPS REMAINING IN THE SOUTH WOULD LEAVE.

Y'ALL LEAVE AND DON'T COME BACK!

WELL, LOOKS LIKE WE'RE BACK IN CHARGE.

THE COMPROMISE ALSO MEANT SOUTHERN STATES COULD DEAL WITH FORMER SLAVES WITHOUT NORTHERN INTERFERENCE.

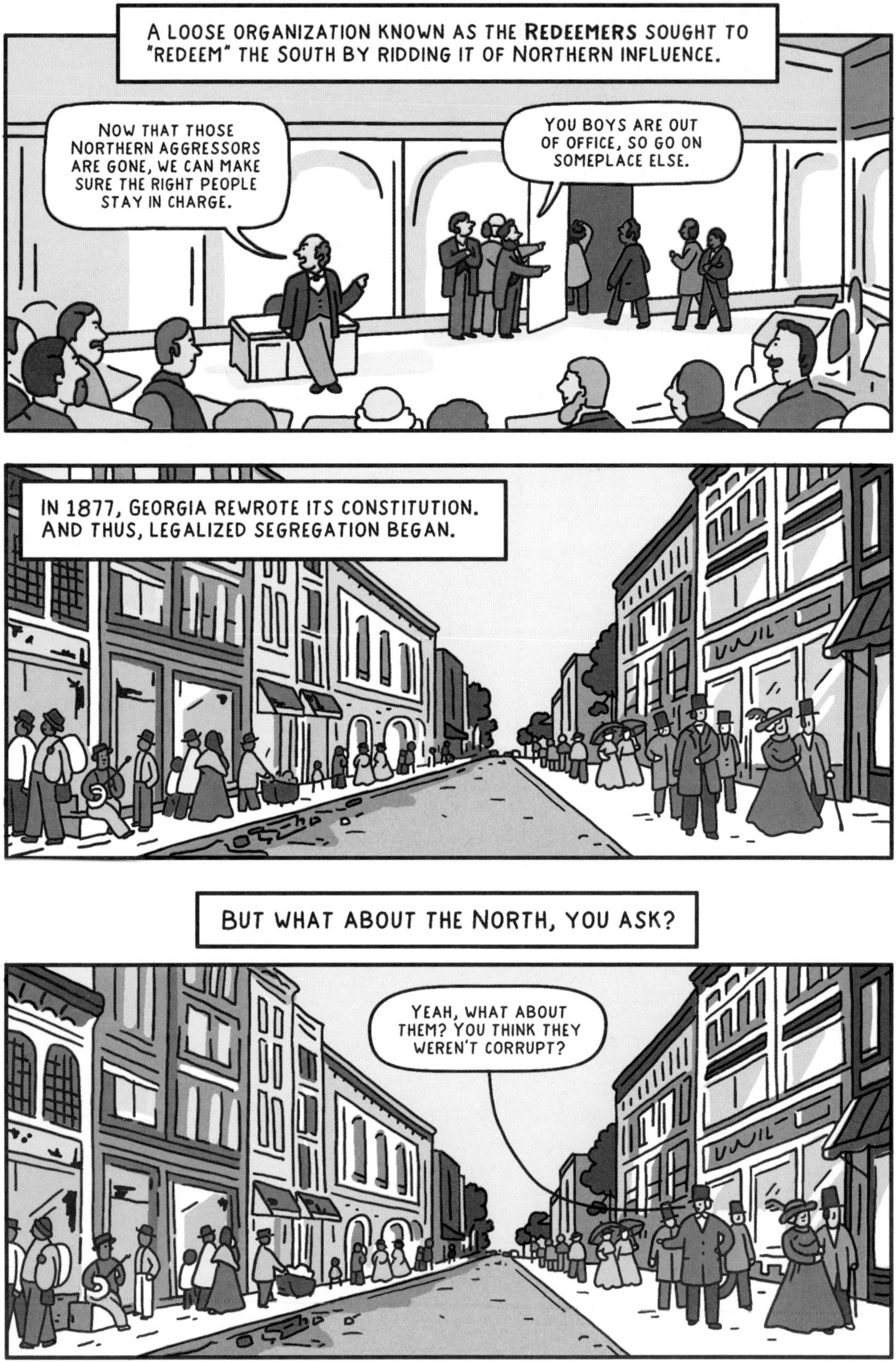
A LOOSE ORGANIZATION KNOWN AS THE **REDEEMERS** SOUGHT TO "REDEEM" THE SOUTH BY RIDDING IT OF NORTHERN INFLUENCE.
NOW THAT THOSE NORTHERN AGGRESSORS ARE GONE, WE CAN MAKE SURE THE RIGHT PEOPLE STAY IN CHARGE.
YOU BOYS ARE OUT OF OFFICE, SO GO ON SOMEPLACE ELSE.
IN 1877, GEORGIA REWROTE ITS CONSTITUTION. AND THUS, LEGALIZED SEGREGATION BEGAN.
BUT WHAT ABOUT THE NORTH, YOU ASK?
YEAH, WHAT ABOUT THEM? YOU THINK THEY WEREN'T CORRUPT?

OF COURSE, THE SOUTH WAS NOT THE ONLY REGION WITH PROBLEMS.

WE'RE GOING TO AMERICA!

IMMIGRATION TO THE UNITED STATES BOOMED IN THE 19TH CENTURY, ESPECIALLY IN THE LARGER NORTHERN CITIES.

WHERE ARE YOU GUYS FROM?

WE'RE FROM IRELAND! WE'VE REACHED THE LAND OF OPPORTUNITY.

BY 1850, ALMOST 130,000 IRISH IMMIGRANTS ALONE LIVED IN NEW YORK CITY. BUT NOT EVERYONE WAS WELCOMING TO IMMIGRANTS.

NO IRISH!

WHAT DO YOU MEAN, "NO IRISH"?

YOU'LL HAVE TO TAKE YOUR BUSINESS ELSEWHERE.

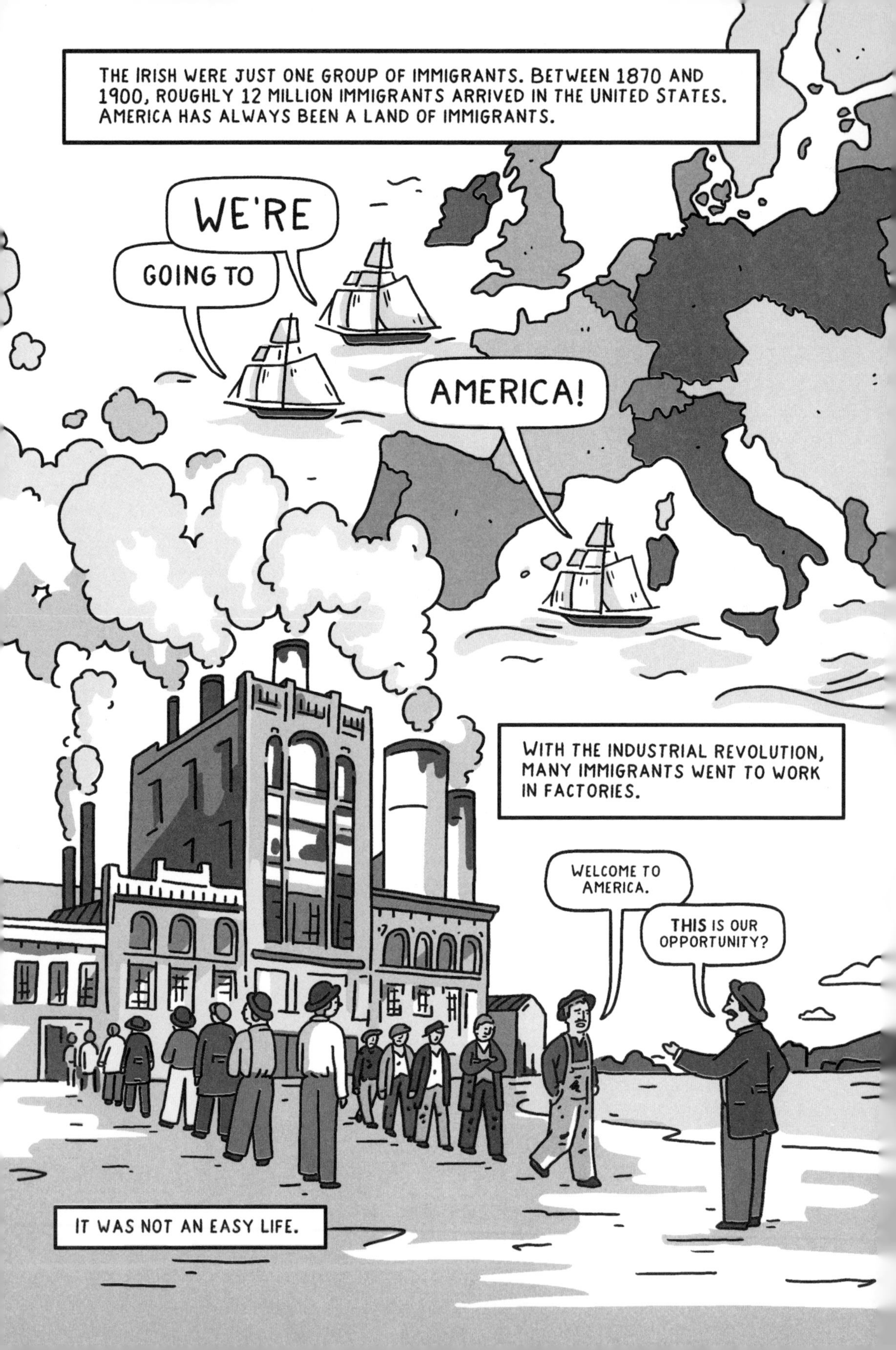
THE IRISH WERE JUST ONE GROUP OF IMMIGRANTS. BETWEEN 1870 AND 1900, ROUGHLY 12 MILLION IMMIGRANTS ARRIVED IN THE UNITED STATES. AMERICA HAS ALWAYS BEEN A LAND OF IMMIGRANTS.
WE'RE
GOING TO
AMERICA!
WITH THE INDUSTRIAL REVOLUTION, MANY IMMIGRANTS WENT TO WORK IN FACTORIES.
WELCOME TO AMERICA.
THIS IS OUR OPPORTUNITY?
IT WAS NOT AN EASY LIFE.

COME ON IN TO TAMMANY HALL. **IRISH** ARE WELCOME.

TAMMANY HALL WAS ONE OF THE MOST POWERFUL POLITICAL MACHINES IN NEW YORK.

THAT'S RIGHT. COME IN. WE CAN HELP.

THE MACHINE WAS PART OF A POLITICAL PARTY. BASICALLY, THEY RECRUITED MEN TO JOIN WITH THE PROMISE OF INCENTIVES.

YOU VOTE WITH US, AND GET YOUR FRIENDS TO VOTE FOR US, AND WE'LL HAVE A GOOD JOB FOR YOU. **IF** WE ARE ELECTED.

DON'T GO OVER THERE! YOU NEED TO JOIN US.

FORGET THOSE GUYS!

BOTH DEMOCRATS AND REPUBLICANS HAD POLITICAL MACHINES.

WE'VE GOT TO FIND A GOOD JOB FOR HIM BECAUSE HE GOT US 2,000 VOTES.

THE MACHINES BECAME VERY POWERFUL. THROUGH LOCAL BOSSES THEY CONTROLLED NEIGHBORHOODS AND OTHER SOCIAL GROUPS. THEY COULD COUNT ON THE VOTES OF THESE GROUPS BECAUSE THEY GAVE FAVORS IN RETURN.

TAMMANY HALL SAW ALL OF THESE IRISH IMMIGRANTS MOVING TO NEW YORK, AND THEY BECAME PART OF THE TAMMANY HALL DEMOCRATIC MACHINE.

I DON'T REALLY **LIKE** THE IRISH, BUT THEY SURE ARE USEFUL.

THIS MADE FOR AN ODD MIX OF DEMOCRATIC VOTERS. THEY HAD THE FORMER CONFEDERATE STATES BUT ALSO LARGE SWATHS OF IMMIGRANTS.

WE'RE VOTING WITH **THOSE** GUYS?

JOBS

WILLIAM "BOSS" TWEED RAN TAMMANY HALL UNTIL HIS DEATH IN 1878.

TWEED WAS VERY POWERFUL. HE COULD GET PEOPLE CITY JOBS FOR SUPPORTING DEMOCRATIC CANDIDATES.

WHILE IN THE SOUTH, THE DEMOCRATIC PARTY WAS ONE OF KEEPING OUT BLACKS, IN THE NORTH, THE DEMOCRATIC PARTY BEGAN TO EMERGE AS ONE IN FAVOR OF LABOR, IMMIGRANTS, AND CATHOLICS.

THIS PARTY IS A MESS.

HERE'S YOUR BALLOT **ALREADY** MARKED.

VOTE TODAY

AND REMEMBER THAT AT THIS TIME, THERE WAS NO SECRET BALLOT. THE PARTY GAVE THE BALLOT TO PEOPLE TO JUST HAND IN.

THE 1870S AND 1880S BECAME KNOWN AS THE GILDED AGE AS EXECUTIVES GOT RICHER AND RICHER.

BETTER AND BETTER EACH DAY, MR. ROCKEFELLER. HOW GOES IT FOR YOU, MR. MORGAN?

BUSINESS IS **BOOMING** FOR ME. HOW ABOUT YOU, MR. CARNEGIE?

MY BANK IS DOING WELL.

THE REPUBLICAN PARTY WAS EMERGING AS THE PARTY OF BIG BUSINESS, BUT IT ALSO INCLUDED NEWLY FREED SLAVES, FORMER ABOLITIONISTS, AND PROTESTANT PIETISTS.

THIS PARTY IS A MESS!

ALCOHOL IS A SIN. WE SHOULD OUTLAW IT. CATHOLICS ARE NOT TRUE CHRISTIANS.

TARIFFS AND INDUSTRY ARE THE MOST IMPORTANT ISSUES.

AND FARMERS, ESPECIALLY THOSE OUT WEST, WERE FEELING LEFT OUT.

DOES ANYBODY CARE ABOUT **US**?

61

IN KANSAS, **MARY LEASE** BEGAN ORGANIZING FOR FARMERS' RIGHTS, AND THE PEOPLE'S PARTY, OR **POPULISTS**, WERE FORMED.

THIS IS NO LONGER A GOVERNMENT OF THE PEOPLE, BY THE PEOPLE, AND FOR THE PEOPLE, BUT A GOVERNMENT OF WALL STREET, BY WALL STREET, AND FOR WALL STREET.

THE POPULISTS DID VERY WELL IN THE KANSAS STATE ELECTIONS OF 1890.

YOU SEE WHAT'S GOING ON IN KANSAS? WE NEED TO GET IN ON THAT.

THE POPULIST PARTY GAINED TRACTION NATIONWIDE, AND **WILLIAM JENNINGS BRYAN** BECAME ITS FACE.

BRYAN for PRESIDENT 1896!

YOU LOST, BUT YOU CAN RUN AGAIN.

LOSER

THE DEMOCRATS CO-OPTED, OR WELCOMED IN, THE POPULISTS. SO BRYAN BECAME THEIR NOMINEE FOR PRESIDENT IN 1896.

IN THE FIRST PRESIDENTIAL ELECTION OF THE 20TH CENTURY, BRYAN LOST AGAIN.

LINCOLN ONCE SAID, "A HOUSE DIVIDED AGAINST ITSELF CANNOT STAND." ALTHOUGH THE UNION WAS PRESERVED AFTER THE CIVIL WAR, DIVISIONS CONTINUED TO PLAGUE THE COUNTRY, AND EQUALITY REMAINED A DISTANT DREAM.

CHAPTER 4

RECLAIMING HER TIME!

1807–2016

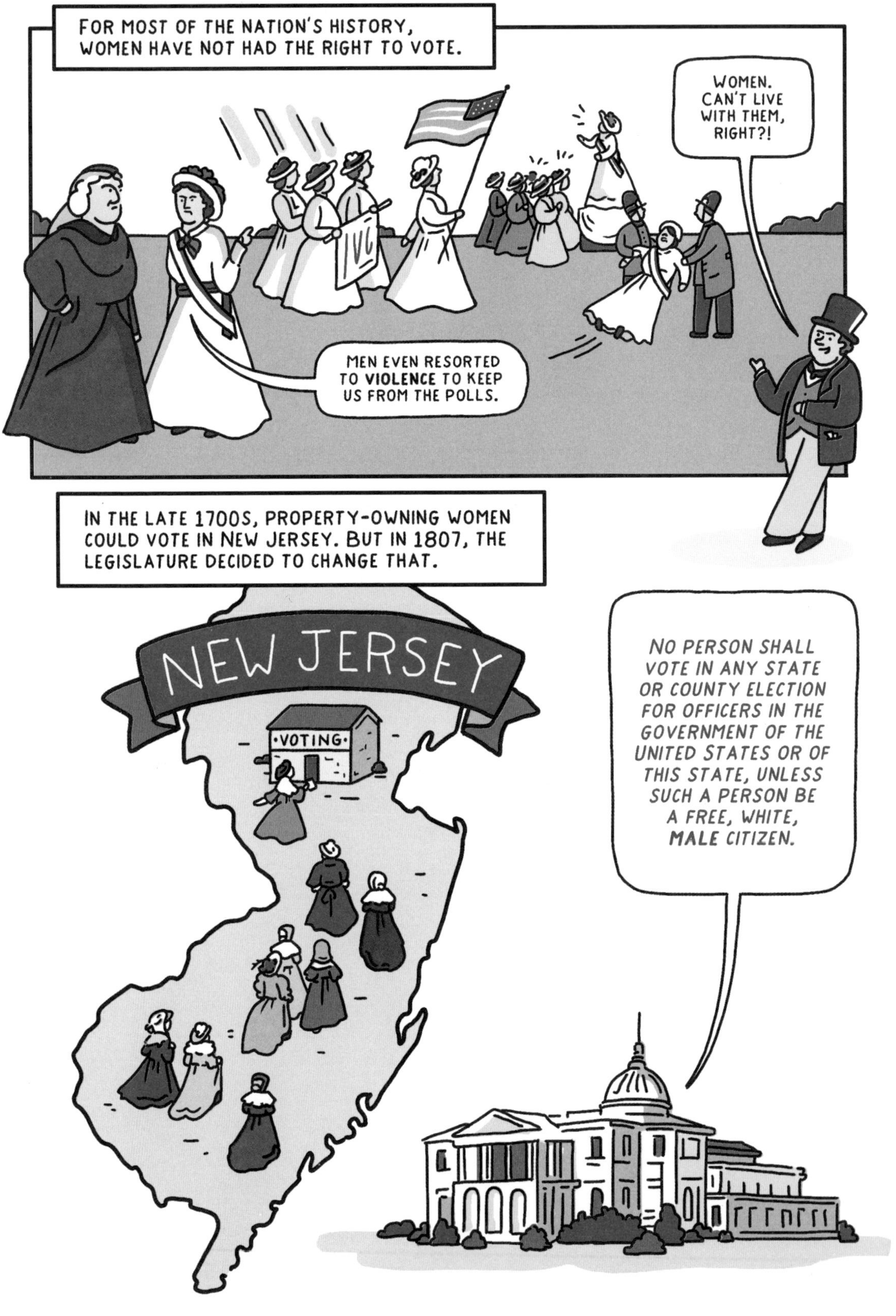
FOR MOST OF THE NATION'S HISTORY, WOMEN HAVE NOT HAD THE RIGHT TO VOTE.
IVC
MEN EVEN RESORTED TO **VIOLENCE** TO KEEP US FROM THE POLLS.
WOMEN. CAN'T LIVE WITH THEM, RIGHT?!
IN THE LATE 1700S, PROPERTY-OWNING WOMEN COULD VOTE IN NEW JERSEY. BUT IN 1807, THE LEGISLATURE DECIDED TO CHANGE THAT.
NEW JERSEY
VOTING
*NO PERSON SHALL VOTE IN ANY STATE OR COUNTY ELECTION FOR OFFICERS IN THE GOVERNMENT OF THE UNITED STATES OR OF THIS STATE, UNLESS SUCH A PERSON BE A FREE, WHITE, **MALE** CITIZEN.*

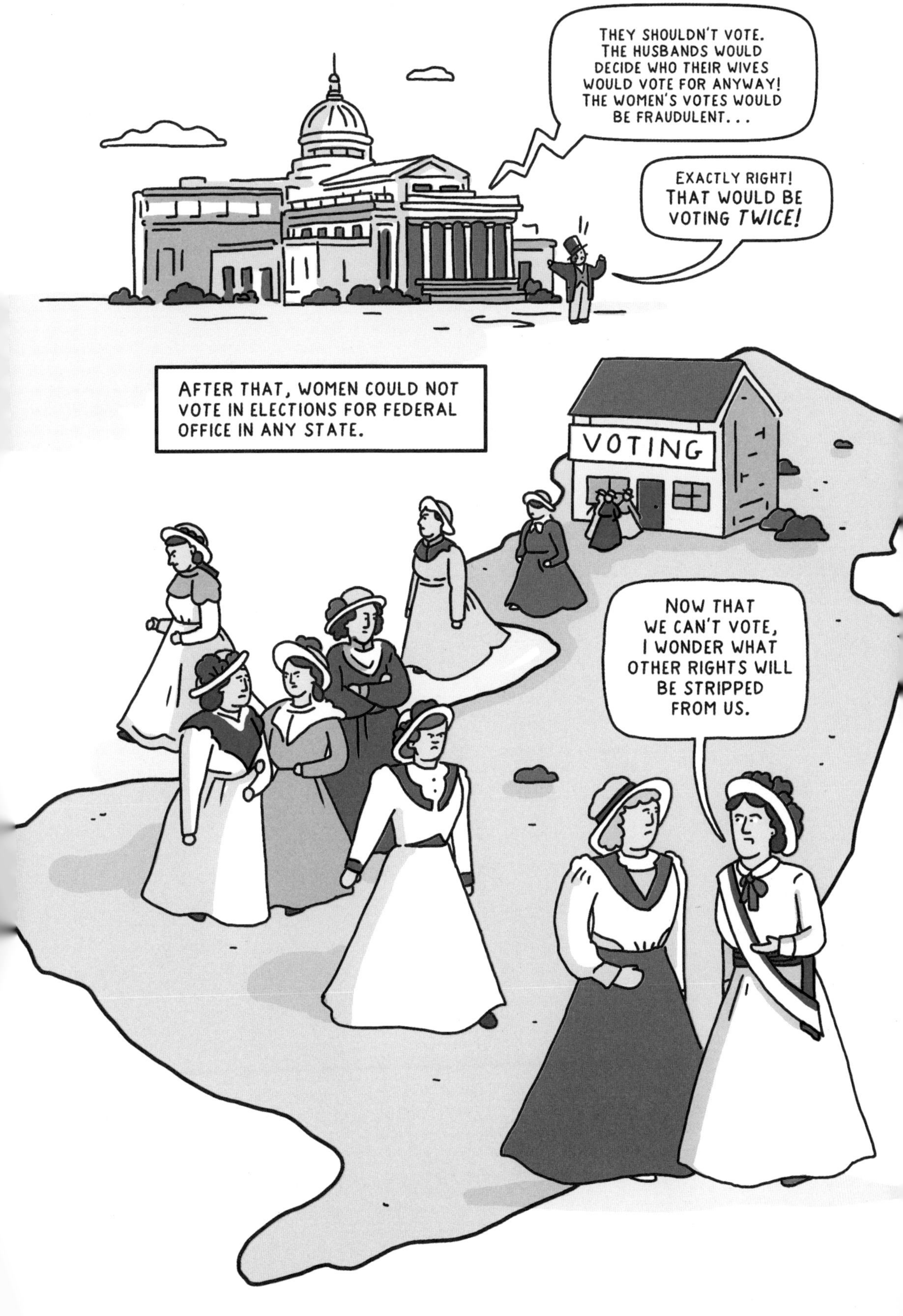
THEY SHOULDN'T VOTE. THE HUSBANDS WOULD DECIDE WHO THEIR WIVES WOULD VOTE FOR ANYWAY! THE WOMEN'S VOTES WOULD BE FRAUDULENT...
EXACTLY RIGHT! THAT WOULD BE VOTING *TWICE!*
AFTER THAT, WOMEN COULD NOT VOTE IN ELECTIONS FOR FEDERAL OFFICE IN ANY STATE.
VOTING
NOW THAT WE CAN'T VOTE, I WONDER WHAT OTHER RIGHTS WILL BE STRIPPED FROM US.

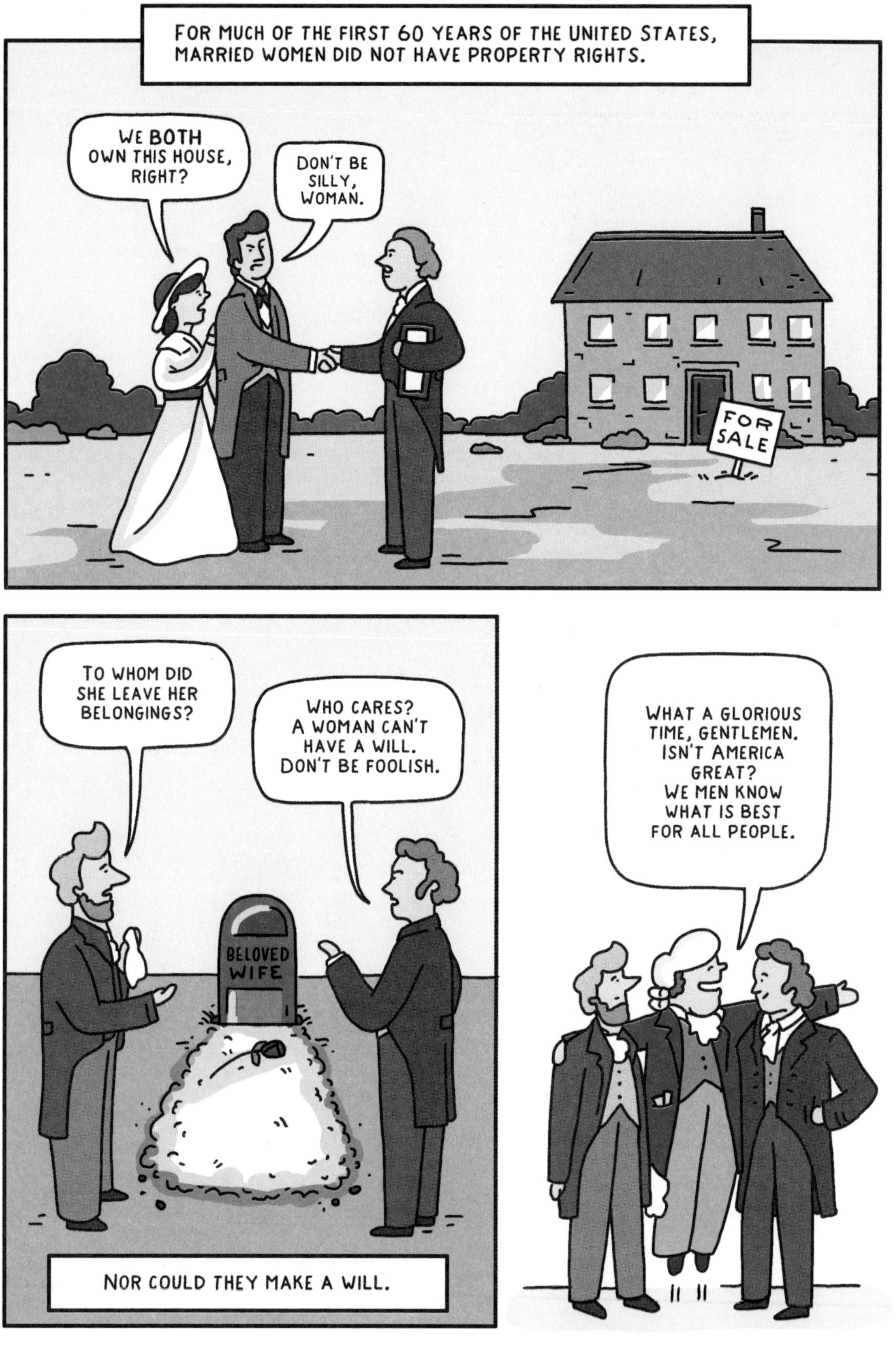
FOR MUCH OF THE FIRST 60 YEARS OF THE UNITED STATES, MARRIED WOMEN DID NOT HAVE PROPERTY RIGHTS.
WE BOTH OWN THIS HOUSE, RIGHT?
DON'T BE SILLY, WOMAN.
FOR SALE
TO WHOM DID SHE LEAVE HER BELONGINGS?
WHO CARES? A WOMAN CAN'T HAVE A WILL. DON'T BE FOOLISH.
BELOVED WIFE
NOR COULD THEY MAKE A WILL.
WHAT A GLORIOUS TIME, GENTLEMEN. ISN'T AMERICA GREAT? WE MEN KNOW WHAT IS BEST FOR ALL PEOPLE.

IN 1862, **EDITH JOYNER** SOUGHT A DIVORCE FROM HER HUSBAND. HE HAD HORSEWHIPPED HER. THE CASE WENT TO THE NORTH CAROLINA SUPREME COURT, AND CHIEF JUSTICE **RICHMOND MUMFORD PEARSON** RULED THE FOLLOWING:

IT FOLLOWS THAT THE LAW GIVES THE HUSBAND POWER TO USE SUCH A DEGREE OF FORCE AS IS NECESSARY TO MAKE THE WIFE BEHAVE HERSELF AND KNOW HER PLACE.

DIVORCE DENIED!

BECAUSE WOMEN DIDN'T HAVE THE RIGHT TO VOTE, THEY COULD NOT ELECT SYMPATHETIC LEGISLATORS TO CHANGE THE LAWS.

WOMEN HAD NO ONE TO SPEAK FOR THEM. AT LEAST, NO ONE WHO COULD ACTUALLY PASS FEDERAL LAWS.

REGARDLESS, WOMEN **STILL** SOUGHT THE VOTE.

NOW LISTEN HERE. WOMEN DO NOT HAVE THE CAPACITY TO **UNDERSTAND** THE ISSUES NOR SHOULD THEY TRY. THEY SHOULD LEAVE THESE MATTERS TO THEIR HUSBANDS.

MANY WOMEN REFUSED TO BACK DOWN, INCLUDING **ELIZABETH CADY STANTON** AND **LUCRETIA MOTT.**

WOMEN DO NOT JUST DO WHAT MEN SAY! WE ARE INDIVIDUALS WITH OUR OWN MINDS, SIR.

YOU THINK WOMEN DON'T HAVE THEIR OWN OPINIONS?

STANTON

MOTT

ELIZABETH CADY STANTON RAN FOR CONGRESS IN 1866, EVEN THOUGH SHE COULDN'T VOTE FOR HERSELF.

VOTE FOR ELIZABETH STANTON FOR THE HOUSE OF REPRESENTATIVES!

YOU FORGET YOUR PLACE! **WOMEN** ARE NOT FIT TO BE LEADERS.

VICTORIA WOODHULL WAS THE FIRST WOMAN TO RUN FOR PRESIDENT. SHE RAN ON THE EQUAL RIGHTS PARTY IN 1872.

WOODHULL *for* PRESIDENT

A VOTE FOR VICTORIA WOODHULL IS A VOTE FOR EQUAL RIGHTS FOR ALL.

I'M SORRY. YOU'VE BOTH LOST IN **CRUSHING DEFEATS.**

YOU LOSE!

LOSERS!

SOME MUNICIPALITIES AND COUNTIES DID ALLOW WOMEN TO VOTE IN LOCAL ELECTIONS.

LOCAL ELECTION

OVER THERE, LADY.

FEDERAL ELECTION

IN FACT, IN ARGONIA, KANSAS, **SUSANNA SALTER** WAS ELECTED THE FIRST FEMALE MAYOR IN THE US IN 1887.

YOU WON! YOU ARE MAYOR OF A SMALL TOWN!

BIG DEAL. POPULATION OF 376.

THAT IS **SOMETHING,** I GUESS.

BUT NOT **NEARLY** ENOUGH.

LADIES, STOP COMPLAINING. WHY DON'T YOU GO MAKE US SOME SANDWICHES?

STOP IT WITH YOUR FAKE COMPLAINTS. MEN KNOW WHAT IS BEST.

WE WILL NOT **BACK DOWN!**

MEANWHILE, ON JULY 19 AND 20, 1848, A "CONVENTION TO DISCUSS THE SOCIAL, CIVIL AND RELIGIOUS CONDITION AND RIGHTS OF WOMAN" WAS HELD IN SENECA FALLS, NEW YORK.

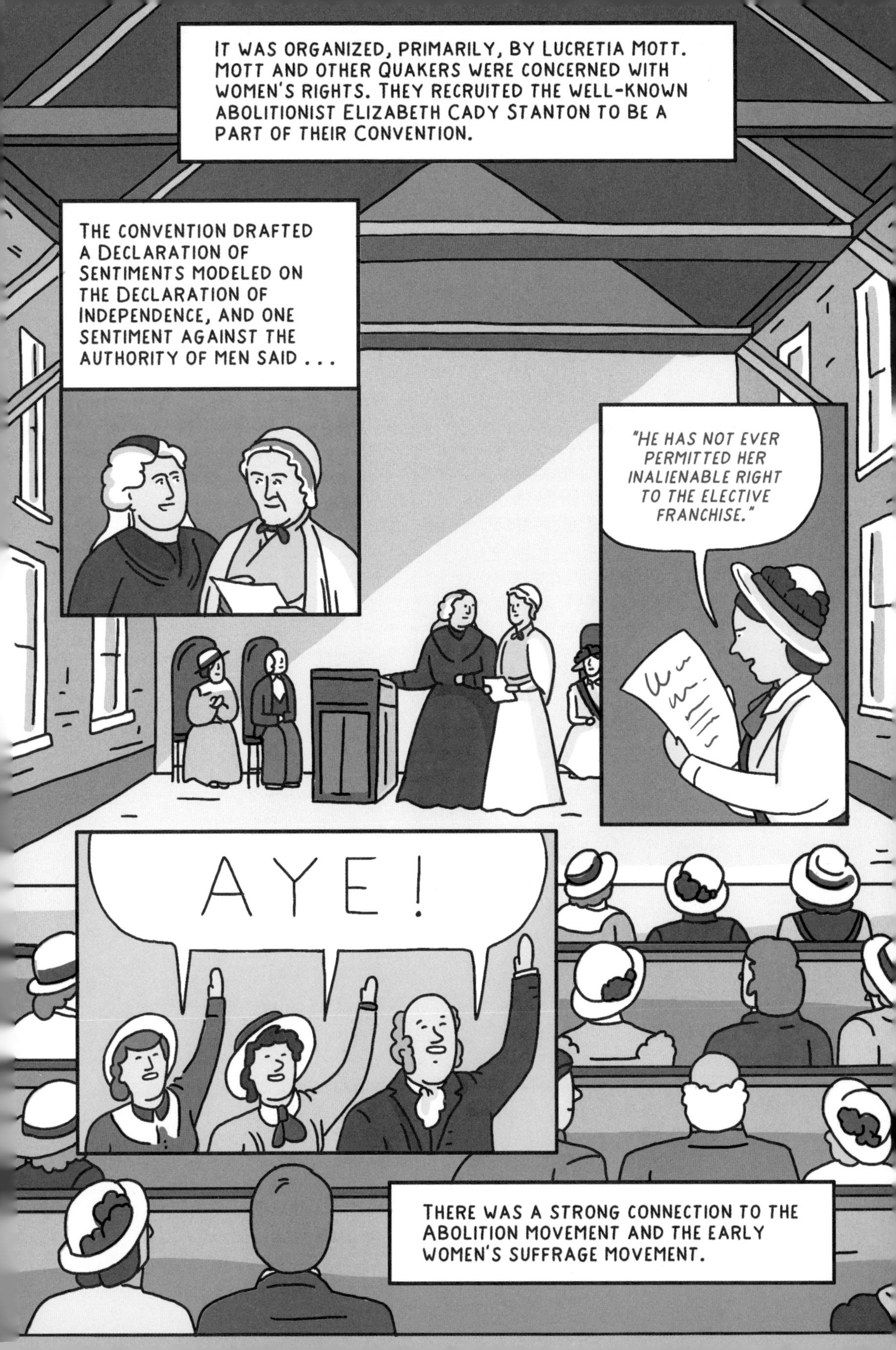
IT WAS ORGANIZED, PRIMARILY, BY LUCRETIA MOTT. MOTT AND OTHER QUAKERS WERE CONCERNED WITH WOMEN'S RIGHTS. THEY RECRUITED THE WELL-KNOWN ABOLITIONIST ELIZABETH CADY STANTON TO BE A PART OF THEIR CONVENTION.
THE CONVENTION DRAFTED A DECLARATION OF SENTIMENTS MODELED ON THE DECLARATION OF INDEPENDENCE, AND ONE SENTIMENT AGAINST THE AUTHORITY OF MEN SAID . . .
"HE HAS NOT EVER PERMITTED HER INALIENABLE RIGHT TO THE ELECTIVE FRANCHISE."
AYE!
THERE WAS A STRONG CONNECTION TO THE ABOLITION MOVEMENT AND THE EARLY WOMEN'S SUFFRAGE MOVEMENT.

ONE PROMINENT ABOLITIONIST IN ATTENDANCE WHO SUPPORTED THE DECLARATION WAS **FREDERICK DOUGLASS.**

WE HOLD WOMAN TO BE JUSTLY ENTITLED TO ALL WE CLAIM FOR MAN. WE GO FARTHER, AND EXPRESS OUR CONVICTION THAT ALL POLITICAL RIGHTS WHICH IT IS EXPEDIENT FOR MAN TO EXERCISE, IT IS EQUALLY SO FOR WOMEN.

THIS WAS A FIRST STEP IN BRINGING THE ISSUE OF WOMEN'S SUFFRAGE TO THE FOREFRONT.

WOMEN AND NEGROES AREN'T **SMART** ENOUGH TO VOTE.

NOW THE WORK OF TRYING TO CHANGE THE LAW BEGAN, BUT THERE WERE MANY OBSTACLES, BOTH EXPECTED AND UNEXPECTED.

THE PREJUDICE AGAINST COLOR, OF WHICH WE HEAR SO MUCH, IS STRONGER THAN THAT AGAINST SEX.

WE CAN WIN THE RIGHT FOR **BOTH** WOMEN AND BLACKS TO VOTE AT THE SAME TIME!

WHILE MANY TURNED THEIR ATTENTION TO THE ISSUE OF FORMER SLAVES AND VOTING, STANTON AND OTHERS SAW AN OPPORTUNITY TO RIGHT MORE THAN ONE WRONG.

MEN, HOWEVER, HAD OTHER IDEAS. TAKE RESPECTED ABOLITIONIST **WENDELL PHILLIPS.**

MY FRIENDS, WE MUST TAKE UP BUT ONE QUESTION AT A TIME, AND THIS HOUR BELONGS EXCLUSIVELY TO THE NEGRO.

THE BEST WOMEN I KNOW DO NOT WANT TO VOTE.

OR POPULAR JOURNALIST AND ABOLITIONIST **HORACE GREELEY.**

WE CAN DO BOTH!

BUT WILL THEY DO BOTH?

VOTE

THE 15TH AMMENDMENT PASSES!

OF COURSE, CONGRESS WOULD NOT DO BOTH.

THIS DOESN'T MENTION WOMEN.

IT PROHIBITS DENYING VOTING BASED ON "RACE, COLOR, OR PREVIOUS CONDITION OF SERVITUDE."

VOT

THAT'S RIGHT. THE 15TH AMENDMENT DIDN'T ADDRESS GENDER.

THE 1869 CONVENTION OF THE AMERICAN EQUAL RIGHTS ASSOCIATION (AERA) WAS VERY CONTENTIOUS BECAUSE OF THE 15TH AMENDMENT, WITH SOME SUPPORTING IT AND OTHERS NOT SUPPORTING IT BECAUSE IT ONLY ADDRESSED BLACK MEN.

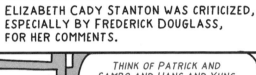

ELIZABETH CADY STANTON WAS CRITICIZED, ESPECIALLY BY FREDERICK DOUGLASS, FOR HER COMMENTS.

THINK OF PATRICK AND SAMBO AND HANS AND YUNG TUNG . . . WHO CANNOT READ THE DECLARATION OF INDEPENDENCE . . . MAKING LAWS FOR . . . SUSAN B. ANTHONY.

[THIS] CREATES AN ANTAGONISM EVERYWHERE BETWEEN EDUCATED, REFINED WOMEN AND THE LOWER ORDERS OF MEN, ESPECIALLY IN THE SOUTH.

STANTON'S COMMENTS CAUSED DOUGLASS TO SPLIT WITH THE AERA. HER OFFENSIVE ATTITUDE ALSO OVERLOOKED THE CONTRIBUTIONS OF AFRICAN AMERICAN SUFFRAGETTES. WOMEN LIKE . . .

SOJOURNER TRUTH — FRANCES HARPER — IDA B. WELLS — FANNIE BARRIER WILLIAMS

THESE BRAVE WOMEN HAD TO STRUGGLE WITH THE PREJUDICE OF **MEN** AND **WOMEN**.

SUSAN B. ANTHONY AND STANTON LED THE NATIONAL WOMAN SUFFRAGE ASSOCIATION. LUCY STONE, AN ABOLITIONIST, HEADED UP THE AMERICAN WOMAN SUFFRAGE ASSOCIATION.

THE NWSA FAVORED A CONSTITUTIONAL AMENDMENT.

THE AWSA SOUGHT CHANGE THROUGH THE STATES AS EACH STATE COULD DECIDE WHO VOTES.

NO MAN IS GOOD ENOUGH TO GOVERN ANY WOMAN WITHOUT HER CONSENT.

SUSAN B. ANTHONY WAS A FOUNDER OF THE NWSA. SHE WAS A PASSIONATE ADVOCATE FOR CHANGE. SHE DIDN'T SUPPORT THE 15TH AMENDMENT SINCE IT DID NOT INCLUDE WOMEN.

ANTHONY BEGAN WORKING WITH STANTON IN 1851.

ARE YOU TRYING TO VOTE?!

I AM.

LOCK HER UP!

ANTHONY ALSO THOUGHT THE COURTS COULD BRING ABOUT WOMEN'S SUFFRAGE.

THE CONSTITUTION "NOWHERE GIVES THE POWER TO *PREVENT* VOTING."

OTHERS AGREED WITH ANTHONY. **VIRGINIA MINOR**, THE OTHER WOMAN BEING ARRESTED, TRIED TO REGISTER TO VOTE IN MISSOURI.

THE CONSTITUTION OF THE UNITED STATES DOES NOT CONFER THE RIGHT OF SUFFRAGE ON **ANYONE.**

THE SUPREME COURT DIDN'T AGREE WITH HER. CHIEF JUSTICE **MORRISON WAITE** SAID:

UNDAUNTED, SUSAN B. ANTHONY DRAFTED AN AMENDMENT HERSELF.

THE *RIGHTS* OF CITIZENS OF *THE UNITED STATES* SHALL *NOT* BE *DENIED* OR *ABRIDGED* BY THE *UNITED* STATES OR BY ANY STATES ON ACCOUNT OF SEX.

MEMBERS OF CONGRESS SYMPATHETIC TO WOMEN'S SUFFRAGE PRESENTED ANTHONY'S AMENDMENT.

THIS WILL ENSURE WOMEN THE RIGHT TO VOTE.

IT DIDN'T WORK.

WHAT AN **OUTRAGE!** THIS AMENDMENT WILL DESTROY THE FABRIC OF AMERICAN LIFE.

NO NO! NO NO! NO!

IN 1890, THE NATIONAL WOMAN SUFFRAGE ASSOCIATION AND THE AMERICAN WOMAN SUFFRAGE ASSOCIATION MERGED TOGETHER.

THE 15TH AMENDMENT DIDN'T HELP, AND THE COURTS DIDN'T HELP YOU. JUST GIVE UP, YOU LOSERS.

THIS IS TAKING A **LONG** TIME.

NAWSA

VOTES for WOMEN

CARRIE CHAPMAN CATT WAS A TEACHER AND JOURNALIST FROM IOWA. SHE WAS INSTRUMENTAL IN TURNING THE NEW ORGANIZATION INTO AN EFFICIENT MACHINE.

ROLL UP YOUR SLEEVES, SET YOUR MIND TO MAKING HISTORY, AND WAGE SUCH A FIGHT FOR LIBERTY THAT THE WHOLE WORLD WILL RESPECT OUR SEX.

CARRIE CHAPMAN CATT HELPED GET HEADQUARTERS ESTABLISHED IN EACH STATE.

FOR GOD'S SAKE, WOMEN. GET BACK IN THE KITCHEN!

THIS HELPED MOBILIZE WOMEN, AND MEN, ACROSS THE COUNTRY.

THERE NEVER WILL BE COMPLETE EQUALITY UNTIL WOMEN THEMSELVES HELP TO MAKE LAWS AND ELECT LAWMAKERS.

WELL, IT TOOK A FEW MORE YEARS . . .

AND A LOT MORE DEMONSTRATIONS THAT LED UP TO ONE BIG MARCH.

ONE OF THE FIRST-EVER PROTESTS IN FRONT OF THE WHITE HOUSE WAS MADE BY WOMEN IN 1917.

THIS IS A LOT OF POTENTIAL VOTERS. IF THE PARTY SUPPORTS THIS, THAT MEANS MORE **VOTES** FOR US.

IT HAD AN EFFECT ON PROMINENT POLITICIANS.

INCLUDING PRESIDENT **WOODROW WILSON.** PREVIOUSLY, HE HAD BEEN LUKEWARM IN HIS COMMITMENT TO WOMEN'S SUFFRAGE.

I REGARD THE CONCURRENCE OF THE SENATE IN THE CONSTITUTIONAL AMENDMENT PROPOSING THE EXTENSION OF SUFFRAGE TO WOMEN AS VITALLY ESSENTIAL . . .

THE SENATE APPROVED THE 19TH AMENDMENT ON JUNE 4, 1919. IT WAS THE SAME WORDING AS SUSAN B. ANTHONY WROTE ALMOST 50 YEARS BEFORE.

OF COURSE, IT REQUIRES TWO-THIRDS OF STATES TO RATIFY AN AMENDMENT, AND MOST OF THE SOUTHERN STATES VOTED "NO."

NO!

YES!

HOWEVER, TENNESSEE VOTED "YES" AND THE AMENDMENT PASSED.

WE WON!

WE DID IT! I WAS RIGHT ALL ALONG. I CALLED IT.

THE 19TH AMENDMENT WAS ADOPTED IN 1920, 72 YEARS AFTER SENECA FALLS.

ALTHOUGH IT TOOK A LONG TIME, ITS PASSAGE DID SHOW THE SLOW-CHANGING DYNAMICS OF WOMEN IN POLITICS. JUST OVER 60 YEARS LATER . . .

SOME LEADERS ARE BORN WOMEN.

GERALDINE FERRARO WAS THE FIRST WOMAN SELECTED AS THE VICE PRESIDENTIAL NOMINEE OF A MAJOR PARTY IN 1984. DEMOCRATIC PRESIDENTIAL CANDIDATE **WALTER MONDALE** HOPED IT WOULD HELP WIN OVER WOMEN VOTERS IN HIS BID TO DEFEAT INCUMBENT REPUBLICAN **RONALD REAGAN.**

WE SAY KEEP YOUR CHANGE, WE'LL KEEP OUR GOD, OUR GUNS, AND OUR CONSTITUTION.

SARAH PALIN BECAME THE REPUBLICAN CANDIDATE FOR VICE PRESIDENT IN 2008. SHE ENERGIZED REPUBLICAN **JOHN MCCAIN'S** CAMPAIGN BY APPEALING TO TRADITIONAL CONSERVATIVES AND SUBURBAN MOTHERS.

I BELIEVE THAT THE RIGHTS OF WOMEN AND GIRLS IS THE UNFINISHED BUSINESS OF THE 21ST CENTURY.

HILLARY CLINTON BECAME THE FIRST MAJOR PARTY NOMINEE FOR PRESIDENT IN 2016. SHE EVEN WON THE POPULAR VOTE.

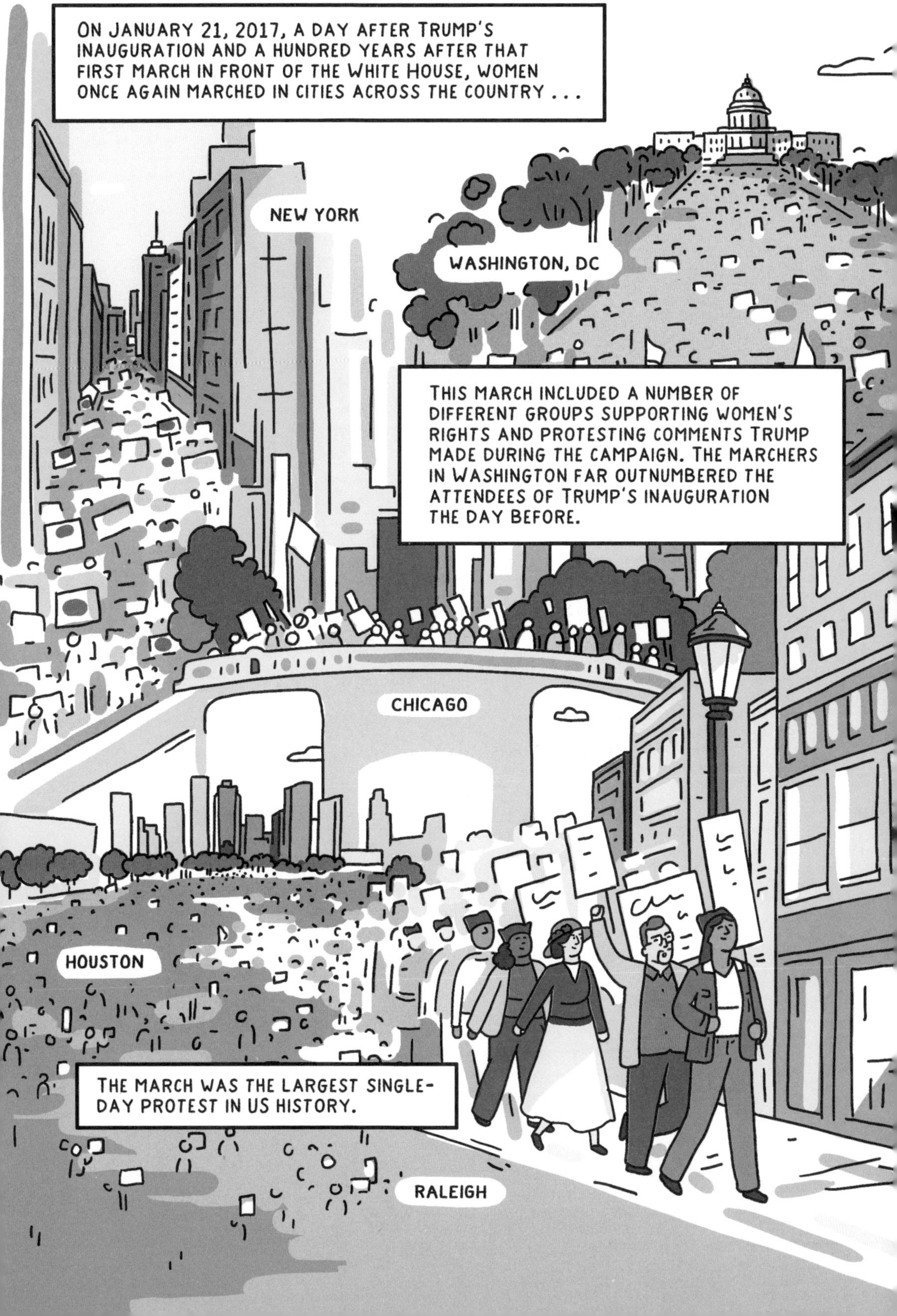
ON JANUARY 21, 2017, A DAY AFTER TRUMP'S INAUGURATION AND A HUNDRED YEARS AFTER THAT FIRST MARCH IN FRONT OF THE WHITE HOUSE, WOMEN ONCE AGAIN MARCHED IN CITIES ACROSS THE COUNTRY . . .
NEW YORK
WASHINGTON, DC
THIS MARCH INCLUDED A NUMBER OF DIFFERENT GROUPS SUPPORTING WOMEN'S RIGHTS AND PROTESTING COMMENTS TRUMP MADE DURING THE CAMPAIGN. THE MARCHERS IN WASHINGTON FAR OUTNUMBERED THE ATTENDEES OF TRUMP'S INAUGURATION THE DAY BEFORE.
CHICAGO
HOUSTON
THE MARCH WAS THE LARGEST SINGLE-DAY PROTEST IN US HISTORY.
RALEIGH

CHAPTER 5

JIM CROW STRIKES BACK!
1890–1965

AT THE START OF THE 20TH CENTURY, AFRICAN AMERICANS RECEIVED THE "PRIZE" OF JIM CROW! IT RULED THE LAW AND SOCIAL ETIQUETTE OF THE SOUTHERN STATES. OF COURSE, THIS DIDN'T HAPPEN OVERNIGHT.

PRETTY BIG STRETCH OF LAND, HUH? CONGRATULATIONS!

THIS PERIOD ALSO SAW THE PROLIFERATION OF A PHRASE THAT BECAME NEAR AND DEAR TO THE HEARTS, AND MINDS, OF WHITE, SOUTHERN POLITICIANS.

SEPARATE BUT EQUAL!

THERE WAS MORE GOING ON THAN JUST SEGREGATION. LET'S GO BACK TO 1890. THAT'S WHEN MISSISSIPPI REVISED ITS CONSTITUTION.

JUDGE **S. S. CALHOON** PRESIDED OVER THE MISSISSIPPI CONSTITUTIONAL CONVENTION OF 1890. THE GOAL WAS TO DRAFT A CONSTITUTION TO ENSURE THE RULE OF WHITE PEOPLE.

MISSISSIPPI

THE NEW CONSTITUTION PASSED.

ANOTHER "WIN" FOR AFRICAN AMERICANS!

ALL IN FAVOR?

AYE!

THE NEW CONSTITUTION PUT INTO LAW PROVISIONS FOR REGISTERING TO VOTE. THE NEW PROVISIONS PLACED RESTRICTIONS ON WHO COULD VOTE.

REGISTER TO VOTE

YOU HAVE TO PAY THE TAX.

YOU HAVE TO PASS THE LITERACY AND UNDERSTANDING TEST.

THERE WAS MORE GOING ON WITH JIM CROW AT THIS TIME AS WELL. **HOMER PLESSY** CHALLENGED THE LAW THAT PEOPLE OF COLOR HAD TO SIT IN SEPARATE TRAIN CARS.

PLESSY'S FIGHT WENT ALL THE WAY TO THE SUPREME COURT. IN 1896, THE COURT DECIDED AGAINST PLESSY IN *PLESSY V. FERGUSON*.

WE CONSIDER THE UNDERLYING FALLACY OF THE PLAINTIFF'S ARGUMENT TO CONSIST IN THE ASSUMPTION THAT THE ENFORCED SEPARATION OF THE TWO RACES STAMPS THE COLORED RACE WITH A BADGE OF INFERIORITY.

WHITES ONLY

LIKE THE SUPREME COURT SAID: "SEGREGATION DOESN'T SHOW **BIAS**."

SEE? SEPARATE BUT EQUAL IS RIGHT!

YOU GUYS GO OVER THERE AND DON'T COME ANY CLOSER. WE **TOLD** YOU THAT YOU HAD IT AS GOOD AS US. THIS IS **EQUALITY**.

IN 1898, THE SUPREME COURT, IN THE CASE *WILLIAMS V. MISSISSIPPI,* RULED THAT THE MISSISSIPPI CONSTITUTION OF 1890 DID NOT VIOLATE THE 14TH AMENDMENT IN DENYING VOTING RIGHTS.

WE FIND FOR THE STATE OF MISSISSIPPI.

HOORAY!

SEPARATE BUT EQUAL WAS THE LAW IN ALL OF THE FORMER CONFEDERATE STATES. AND 10 OF THESE FORMER STATES ADOPTED CONSTITUTIONS SIMILAR TO MISSISSIPPI'S BETWEEN 1890 AND 1908.

YOU NEGROES **STAY** OVER THERE.

BY THE EARLY 20TH CENTURY, MOST SOUTHERN STATES HAD STRICT POLL TAXES AND LITERACY TESTS FOR PEOPLE TO BE ELIGIBLE TO VOTE. THE LITERACY TESTS WERE ARBITRARY, AND MOST WERE GIVEN ORALLY.

POLL TAXES MEANT YOU HAD TO PAY A TAX TO VOTE.

I DON'T HAVE A DOLLAR.

THEN YOU CAN'T VOTE. NEXT!

I DON'T HAVE A DOLLAR. WHAT ABOUT ME?

DON'T WORRY. YOU CAN BE GRANDFATHERED IN.

MY GRANDFATHER WHAT?

JUST TAKE A LOOK BACK AND SEE THAT YOUR GRANDFATHER VOTED.

IF SOMEONE'S GRANDFATHER VOTED BEFORE A CERTAIN DATE, THEN THEY DIDN'T HAVE TO PAY THE TAX.

·VOTING·

VOTE HERE

HEY! I THINK THAT'S GRANDDADDY RIGHT THERE!

THEN YOU CAN VOTE.

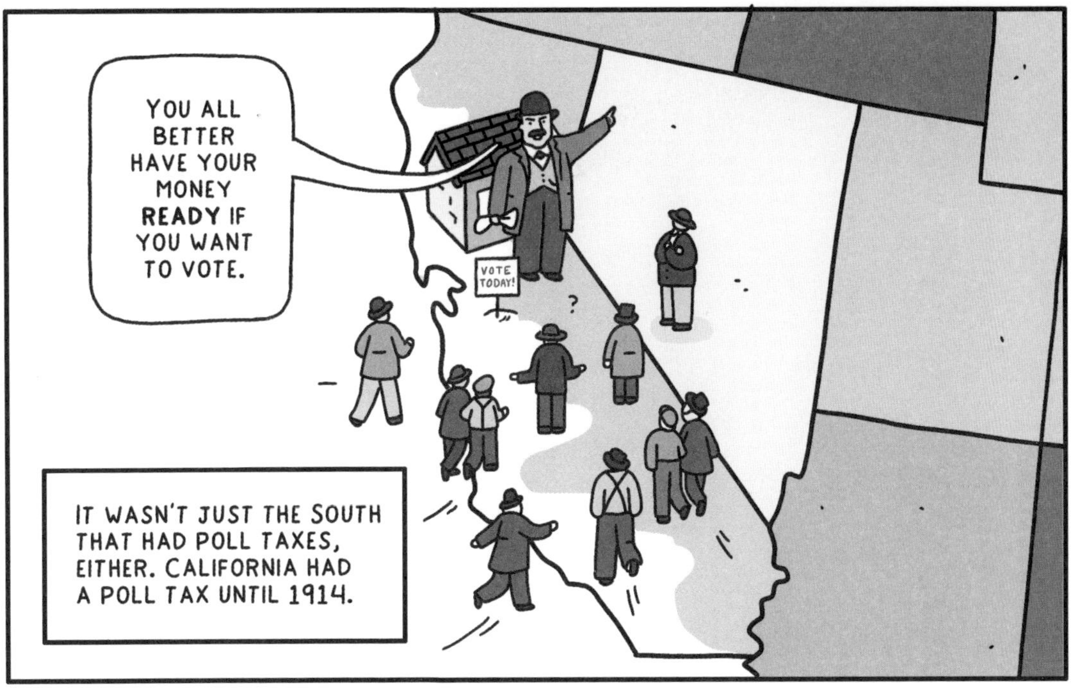
YOU ALL BETTER HAVE YOUR MONEY **READY** IF YOU WANT TO VOTE.
VOTE TODAY!
IT WASN'T JUST THE SOUTH THAT HAD POLL TAXES, EITHER. CALIFORNIA HAD A POLL TAX UNTIL 1914.

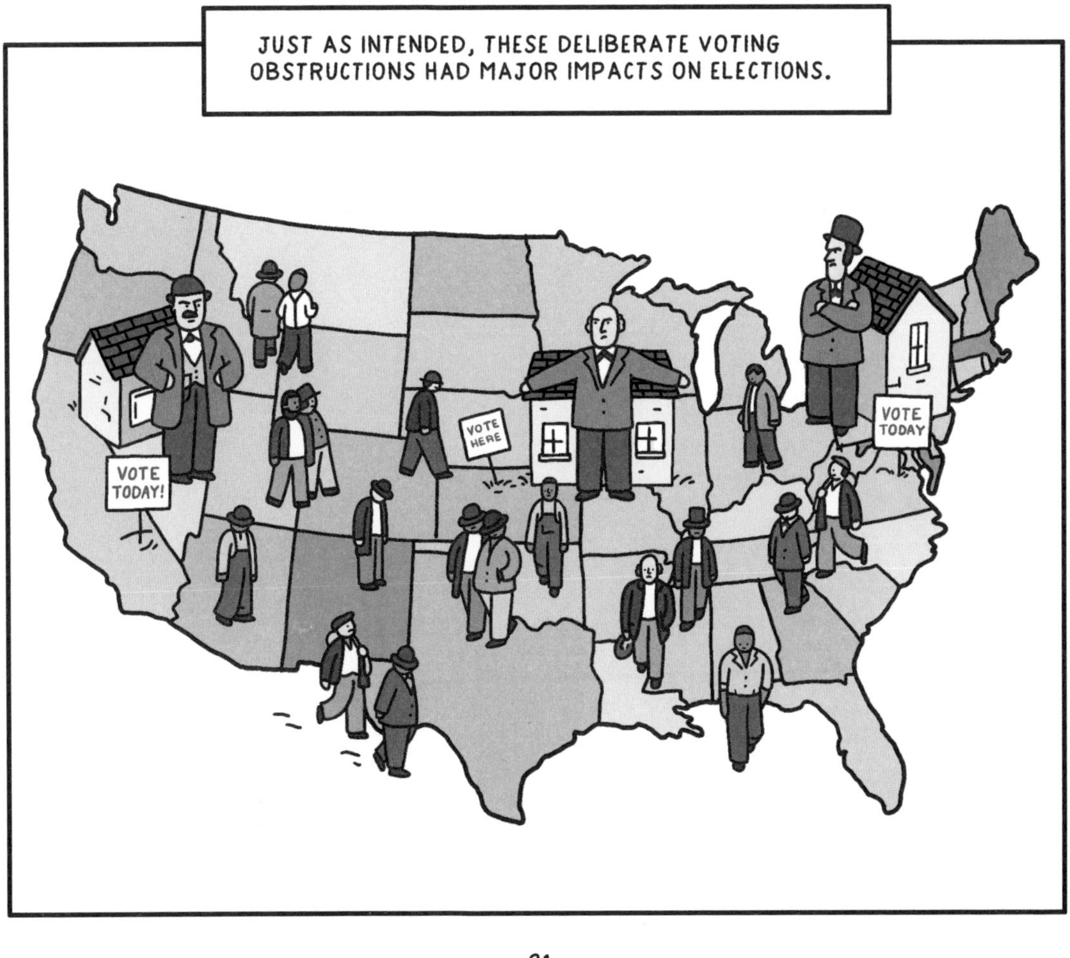
JUST AS INTENDED, THESE DELIBERATE VOTING OBSTRUCTIONS HAD MAJOR IMPACTS ON ELECTIONS.
VOTE TODAY!
VOTE HERE
VOTE TODAY

GEORGE HENRY WHITE OF NORTH CAROLINA'S 2ND DISTRICT LEFT CONGRESS IN 1901. HE WAS THE LAST AFRICAN AMERICAN CONGRESSMAN ELECTED FROM THE SOUTHEAST UNTIL 1972.

WHEN **ANDREW YOUNG** WAS ELECTED FROM GEORGIA'S 5TH DISTRICT, IT HAD BEEN 71 YEARS SINCE AN AFRICAN AMERICAN REPRESENTED A FORMER CONFEDERATE STATE IN CONGRESS.

ACCORDING TO THE 1910 CENSUS, NEGROES (THAT'S HOW THE CENSUS REFERRED TO THEM THEN) MADE UP **31.6%** OF NORTH CAROLINA'S POPULATION.

NORTH CAROLINA

YET, THERE WAS NOT **A SINGLE AFRICAN AMERICAN** SERVING IN CONGRESS.

ALABAMA

IN 1910, AFRICAN AMERICANS MADE UP **42.5%** OF ALABAMA'S POPULATION.

STILL **NO** REPRESENTATION IN CONGRESS.

SURELY WE ARE REPRESENTED BY AT LEAST **ONE** BLACK PERSON?

SORRY. **NOPE.**

SOUTH CAROLINA

I'M NOT EVEN GOING TO ASK.

MISSISSIPPI

GOOD.

GET OUT, YANKEES! YOU'RE CORRUPT AND YOU'RE GETTING ELECTED WITH THE HELP OF BLACKS. **IT'S NOT FAIR!**

WHITES DIDN'T WANT BLACKS TO VOTE BECAUSE, WELL, THEY WERE RACIST, BUT ALSO IT WAS ABOUT CONTROL.

AS WE SAW IN CHAPTER 3, ORGANIZATIONS LIKE THE REDEEMERS AND THE RED SHIRTS SPRUNG UP IN THE 1870S. THOSE ORGANIZATIONS SCARED PEOPLE TO KEEP THEM FROM VOTING REPUBLICAN.

WE'RE GONNA **REDEEM** THE SOUTH FROM **REPUBLICAN GOVERNANCE** AND THE **HUMILIATION** OF RECONSTRUCTION!

VOTE HERE

IN 1876, **WADE HAMPTON III**'S ELECTION IN SOUTH CAROLINA SYMBOLICALLY ENDED RECONSTRUCTION. HIS CAMPAIGN USED THE RED SHIRTS TO KEEP BLACKS AND REPUBLICANS AWAY FROM THE POLLS.

WE ARE REDEEMED!

THE KEYNOTE OF MY CAMPAIGN WAS WHITE SUPREMACY, AND I BELIEVE I WAS CHIEFLY RESPONSIBLE FOR THE CHOICE OF THE ISSUE.

FURNIFOLD MCLENDEL SIMMONS WAS A SENATOR FROM MY STATE, NORTH CAROLINA, WHO SERVED FROM 1901 TO 1931.

IN ADDITION TO POLL TAXES AND LITERACY TESTS, THE DEMOCRATIC PARTY ALSO HAD "WHITE PRIMARIES" TO CONTROL WHO HELD OFFICE.

WE HAVE THE CANDIDATES WE WANT!

THE DEMOCRATIC PARTY CONTROLLED WHO COULD VOTE IN A PRIMARY, AND THEY WOULD ONLY ALLOW WHITES TO VOTE.

PRIMARY ELECTION TODAY

YOUR KIND CAN'T VOTE. WE DECIDE WHO VOTES.

WE GOT TEXAS, LOUISIANA, AND MISSISSIPPI, AND ALABAMA, AND...

BY CONTROLLING VOTING AND ELECTIONS, THE DEMOCRATS CONTROLLED THE SOUTH.

FROM 1877 TO 1963, IN THE STATES OF TEXAS, LOUISIANA, MISSISSIPPI, ALABAMA, GEORGIA, TENNESSEE, SOUTH CAROLINA, NORTH CAROLINA, AND VIRGINIA, ONLY FOUR REPUBLICANS SERVED AS GOVERNOR.

WITH NO REPRESENTATION, AFRICAN AMERICANS HAD NO WAY TO CHANGE DISCRIMINATION LAWS.

MANY DID LEAVE.
THE GREAT AFRICAN AMERICAN MIGRATION BEGAN AROUND 1916.

FROM AROUND 1916 TO AROUND 1970, ROUGHLY 6 MILLION AFRICAN AMERICANS LEFT THE SOUTH.

I'M GOING TO GET A JOB IN A FACTORY.

ME, TOO.

WE HAVE A CHANCE TO CHANGE THINGS. LOOK AROUND. THERE ARE SO MANY OF US.

THERE'S STRENGTH IN NUMBERS.

WITH THIS MIGRATION, SOME NEIGHBORHOODS IN THE NORTH, LIKE HARLEM, BECAME PREDOMINANTLY AFRICAN AMERICAN.

THIS HELPED LEAD TO ARTISTIC AND CULTURAL REVOLUTIONS, LIKE **THE HARLEM RENAISSANCE.**

I'VE KNOWN **RIVERS:** I'VE KNOWN RIVERS ANCIENT AS THE **WORLD . . .**

LANGSTON HUGHES

DUKE ELLINGTON

THE POETRY OF LANGSTON HUGHES AND THE MUSIC OF DUKE ELLINGTON THRILLED BOTH WHITE AND BLACK AUDIENCES.

WE CAN GO TO AFRICAN LIFE AND GET A CERTAIN AMOUNT OF FORM AND COLOR . . . IN DEVELOPMENT OF AN EXPRESSION THAT INTERPRETS OUR LIFE.

PAINTER **AARON DOUGLAS**

THE **NATIONAL ASSOCIATION FOR THE ADVANCEMENT OF COLORED PEOPLE**, OR NAACP, WAS FOUNDED IN 1909.

PART OF THEIR MISSION WAS TO **"ERADICATE** CASTE OR RACE PREJUDICE AMONG THE CITIZENS OF THE UNITED STATES AND TO ADVANCE THE INTERESTS OF COLORED CITIZENS."

OVINGTON

DU BOIS

STOREY

MOORFIELD STOREY, MARY WHITE OVINGTON, W. E. B. DU BOIS, AND SEVERAL OTHERS FOUNDED THE NAACP IN NEW YORK.

BLACK PEOPLE MOVING UP NORTH HELPED THE NAACP TO RECRUIT.

IN THE SOUTH, BLACKS COULDN'T VOTE, AND MANY WERE BEING LYNCHED.

THE NAACP OPPOSED PRESIDENT WILSON WHEN HE BROUGHT SEGREGATION TO GOVERNMENT POLICY AND WORKPLACES.

THIS IS WHAT IS BEST. SEPARATE BUT **EQUAL**, MR. PRESIDENT.

AND THEY TOOK LEGAL ACTION TO TRY TO CHANGE RESTRICTIVE VOTING LAWS.

AND THE NAACP FOR YEARS TRIED TO GET LAWS PASSED AGAINST LYNCHING.

WALTER FRANCIS WHITE SPENT HIS EARLY YEARS IN THE NAACP INVESTIGATING LYNCHINGS.

I HEARD ABOUT THAT BLACK BOY GETTING STRUNG UP.

SOME FOLK DON'T KNOW THEIR PLACE.

ALTHOUGH WALTER WHITE WAS BLACK, HE LOOKED WHITE.
THAT ALLOWED HIM TO DO UNDERCOVER WORK.

THESE DARKIES ARE GETTING UPPITY. WE MIGHT NEED TO FASHION A COUPLE MORE NECKTIES FOR THEM.

WHITE AND THE NAACP LET PEOPLE KNOW ABOUT THE THREAT OF LYNCHING AND THEN TRIED TO GET THE FEDERAL GOVERNMENT TO PASS ANTI-LYNCHING LEGISLATION.

WE ALL VOTE "NO." YOUR LAW DOESN'T PASS.

THE SOUTHERN POLITICIANS ALWAYS VOTED AGAINST THE NAACP OR FILIBUSTERED TO KEEP THE BILL FROM GETTING TO A VOTE.

IN 1930, THE NAACP, ALONG WITH THE AMERICAN FEDERATION OF LABOR, HELPED KEEP **JOHN J. PARKER** OF NORTH CAROLINA FROM BEING CONFIRMED AS A SUPREME COURT JUSTICE.

BECAUSE, WHEN HE WAS RUNNING FOR GOVERNOR IN 1920, PARKER SAID . . .

THE NEGRO AS A CLASS DOES NOT DESIRE TO ENTER POLITICS. THE REPUBLICAN PARTY OF NORTH CAROLINA DOES NOT DESIRE HIM TO DO SO.

REMEMBER HOW BLACK PEOPLE COULDN'T VOTE?

WELL, BECAUSE OF THAT, THEY COULDN'T GET ENOUGH LEGISLATORS ELECTED TO CHANGE THE LAWS.

THE NAACP STARTED A LEGAL DEFENSE FUND TO DEFEND BLACK PEOPLE FALSELY ACCUSED AND TO FIGHT FOR THE RIGHTS OF BLACK PEOPLE IN COURT.

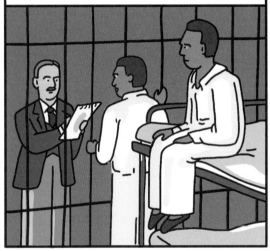

THAT BECAME THE NAACP'S STRATEGY: THEY KNEW THEY COULDN'T GET ENOUGH SUPPORTERS **ELECTED,** BUT THEY COULD STILL FIGHT FOR THEIR RIGHTS IN THE COURTS.

IN 1940, DR. **LONNIE SMITH** TRIED TO VOTE IN A DEMOCRATIC PRIMARY IN TEXAS. HE WASN'T ALLOWED TO, SO HE SUED. HIS LAWYER WAS **THURGOOD MARSHALL.**

SMITH WON IN *SMITH V. ALLWRIGHT.* SUPREME COURT CHIEF JUSTICE **HARLAN F. STONE** MADE THE FOLLOWING STATEMENT:

THE RESTRICTED PRIMARY DENIES DR. SMITH HIS EQUAL PROTECTION UNDER THE LAW ACCORDING TO THE 14TH AMENDMENT.

THIS OPENED UP TEXAS POLITICS AND BEGAN THE PROCESS OF DISMANTLING "WHITE" PRIMARIES. IT SEEMED LIKE A SMALL STEP, HOWEVER . . .

IT WAS A SIGNIFICANT VICTORY.

NOW WE CAN VOTE IN THE PRIMARY.

VOTE TODAY

OF COURSE, THERE WERE MANY MORE FIGHTS TO COME.

THURGOOD MARSHALL GREW UP IN BALTIMORE. HE WENT TO ELEMENTARY SCHOOL AT HENRY HIGHLAND GARNET SCHOOL.

MARSHALL WAS DESCENDED FROM SLAVES ON BOTH SIDES OF HIS FAMILY. AS HE GREW UP, HE REALIZED THAT THE LAW WAS A POWERFUL TOOL.

MARSHALL DECIDED TO HEAD UP THE NAACP LEGAL DEFENSE FUND. HE WAS GOING TO SPEARHEAD CHANGE THROUGH THE COURTS.

THEY STARTED WINNING CASES. YOU KNOW ABOUT *SMITH V. ALLWRIGHT.* BUT THERE WERE OTHERS . . .

THERE WAS *SHELLEY V. KRAEMER,* WITH CHIEF JUSTICE **FRED M. VINSON** PRESIDING. KRAEMER'S NEIGHBORHOOD HAD A COVENANT THAT PROHIBITED AFRICAN AMERICANS FROM LIVING THERE.

LOUIS KRAEMER'S DEFENSE ARGUED THAT THE NEIGHBORHOOD WAS A PRIVATE ORGANIZATION AND THUS COULD SET ITS OWN RULES.

YOU CAN'T LIVE HERE.

FOR DECADES, WHITE NEIGHBORHOODS KEPT BLACKS OUT. BUT THAT CHANGED IN 1948.

AND THEN THERE WAS A CASE INVOLVING SCHOOLS IN TOPEKA, KANSAS: *BROWN V. BOARD OF EDUCATION.*

STATE ENFORCEMENT OF RESTRICTIVE COVENANTS VIOLATE THE EQUAL PROTECTION CLAUSE OF THE 14TH AMENDMENT.

SUMMER SCHOOL

SEPARATE BUT EQUAL, THEY SAID.

SEGREGATION. BLACK CHILDREN COULDN'T ATTEND WHITE SCHOOLS, EVEN IF THE WHITE SCHOOL WAS CLOSER TO WHERE THEY LIVED.

MARSHALL WON THE CASE. CHIEF JUSTICE **EARL WARREN** SAID . . .

SEPARATE EDUCATIONAL FACILITIES ARE INHERENTLY UNEQUAL.

CONGRATULATIONS! YOU WIN THE RIGHT TO GO TO SCHOOL.

WINNER

OF COURSE, NOT ALL STATES COMPLIED RIGHT AWAY. **ORVAL FAUBUS,** THE GOVERNOR OF ARKANSAS, CALLED IN THE NATIONAL GUARD TO KEEP BLACK STUDENTS SEGREGATED.

THAT'S RIGHT, ORVAL. WE'VE GOT TO **HOLD** OUR GROUND.

SLOWLY, THINGS BEGAN TO CHANGE. AND NOT JUST IN THE SOUTH.

SCHOOLS IN BLACK NEIGHBORHOODS IN THE NORTH WERE IN POOR SHAPE AND OVERCROWDED.

BROWN SPURRED ON BLACK PEOPLE IN THE NORTH TO ACTION, TOO.

AND THERE WERE OTHER, DEVASTATING, EVENTS THAT INSPIRED PEOPLE TO ACTION. LIKE THE VICIOUS MURDER OF FOURTEEN-YEAR-OLD **EMMETT TILL.**

ROSA PARKS WAS ARRESTED FOR NOT GIVING UP HER SEAT ON A BUS.

RALPH ABERNATHY AND MARTIN LUTHER KING JR. HELPED ORGANIZE A MONTGOMERY BUS BOYCOTT BY BLACK PEOPLE.

FOR 381 DAYS, THEY BOYCOTTED BUS SERVICE IN MONTGOMERY.

AND THEN THE CITY OVERTURNED ITS BUS SEGREGATION LAW.

THEY MARCHED AND PROTESTED IN BIRMINGHAM, ALABAMA.

RALPH ABERNATHY, FRED SHUTTLESWORTH, JOSEPH LOWERY, AND MARTIN LUTHER KING JR., ALONG WITH OTHERS, FOUNDED THE **SOUTHERN CHRISTIAN LEADERSHIP CONFERENCE.**

I DON'T KNOW WHAT THE FUTURE MAY HOLD, BUT I KNOW WHO HOLDS THE FUTURE.

THEY WENT TO THE BLACK COMMUNITY, ESPECIALLY CHURCHES, TO ORGANIZE PEOPLE.

DESPITE THE ATTACKS, THEY **PERSISTED.**

WHILE IT WAS A TIME OF CHANGE, THE SOUTH WAS STILL TRYING TO HOLD ON TO THE PAST.

VOTE TODAY

ON JANUARY 14, 1963, **GEORGE WALLACE** GAVE HIS INAUGURAL ADDRESS AS GOVERNOR OF ALABAMA.

I SAY SEGREGATION NOW, SEGREGATION TOMORROW, SEGREGATION **FOREVER**.

ALABAMA

PRESIDENT **JOHN F. KENNEDY** WAS MOVED BY EVENTS IN THE SOUTH TO SPEAK TO THE NATION ON JUNE 11, 1963. IN HIS SPEECH HE MADE THE CASE FOR CIVIL RIGHTS LEGISLATION.

ONE HUNDRED YEARS OF DELAY HAVE PASSED SINCE PRESIDENT LINCOLN FREED THE SLAVES, YET THEIR HEIRS, THEIR GRANDSONS, ARE NOT FULLY FREE.

AUGUST 28, 1963, SAW THE MARCH ON WASHINGTON.

I HAVE A DREAM THAT ONE DAY THIS NATION WILL RISE UP AND LIVE OUT THE TRUE MEANING OF ITS CREED: "WE HOLD THESE TRUTHS TO BE SELF-EVIDENT, THAT ALL MEN ARE CREATED EQUAL."

ON NOVEMBER 22 OF THAT YEAR, PRESIDENT KENNEDY WAS ASSASSINATED.

PRESIDENT **LYNDON B. JOHNSON** FULFILLED KENNEDY'S PROMISE AND SIGNED THE **CIVIL RIGHTS ACT** OF 1964. IT OUTLAWED DISCRIMINATION BASED ON RACE, COLOR, SEX, OR NATIONAL ORIGIN.

WHITES ONLY

IT ALSO OUTLAWED UNEQUAL VOTER REGISTRATION APPLICATION, THINGS LIKE POLL TAXES, AS WELL AS SEGREGATION IN SCHOOLS, EMPLOYMENT, AND PUBLIC ACCOMMODATIONS.

THE CIVIL RIGHTS ACT DIDN'T IMMEDIATELY END OPPRESSION. FOR DECADES, BASICALLY ONLY WHITE PEOPLE VOTED IN THE SOUTH.

VOTE TODAY

IT TOOK THE COURAGE OF PEOPLE FACING CRUELTY AND VIOLENCE TO BRING ABOUT THE VOTING RIGHTS ACT.

IT IS MY DUTY AS A CITIZEN TO VOTE.

TAKE THE **MARCH ON SELMA.** IN 1964, ONLY 2% OF SELMA'S ELIGIBLE BLACK VOTERS WERE REGISTERED TO VOTE BECAUSE THE GOVERNMENT KEPT THEM FROM REGISTERING VIA POLL TAXES AND LITERACY TESTS AND INTIMIDATION.

I AM A CITIZEN, TOO. SO ISN'T IT **MY DUTY** TO VOTE AS WELL?

LET'S NOT GET CARRIED AWAY.

THE INTIMIDATION OF POTENTIAL VOTERS WAS VERY DIRECT.

THE **SOUTHERN CHRISTIAN LEADERSHIP COUNCIL** DECIDED TO MAKE SELMA THE FOCAL POINT OF A BLACK VOTER REGISTRATION CAMPAIGN.

SHAKING HANDS WITH DR. KING IS **HOSEA WILLIAMS**. WILLIAMS WAS A KEY FIGURE IN THE FIGHT FOR VOTING RIGHTS.

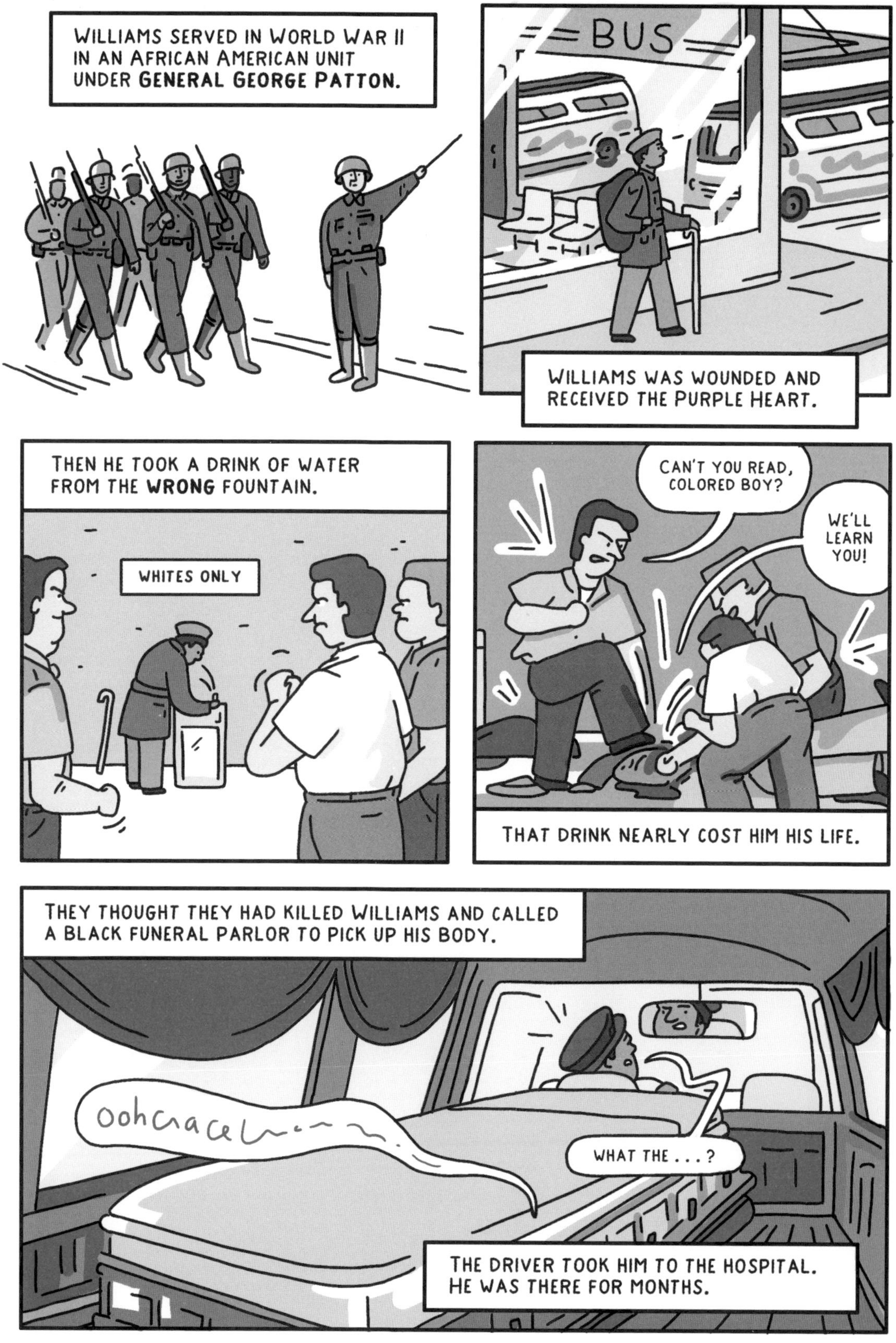
WILLIAMS SERVED IN WORLD WAR II IN AN AFRICAN AMERICAN UNIT UNDER GENERAL GEORGE PATTON.
BUS
WILLIAMS WAS WOUNDED AND RECEIVED THE PURPLE HEART.
THEN HE TOOK A DRINK OF WATER FROM THE WRONG FOUNTAIN.
WHITES ONLY
CAN'T YOU READ, COLORED BOY?
WE'LL LEARN YOU!
THAT DRINK NEARLY COST HIM HIS LIFE.
THEY THOUGHT THEY HAD KILLED WILLIAMS AND CALLED A BLACK FUNERAL PARLOR TO PICK UP HIS BODY.
WHAT THE . . . ?
THE DRIVER TOOK HIM TO THE HOSPITAL. HE WAS THERE FOR MONTHS.

AFTER THAT INCIDENT, WILLIAMS JOINED THE NAACP AND A SHORT TIME LATER JOINED THE SCLC WITH DR. MARTIN LUTHER KING AND RALPH ABERNATHY.

HE LED SIT-INS TO PROTEST SEGREGATED RESTAURANTS. THE ONE IN ST. AUGUSTINE, FLORIDA, RECEIVED NATIONAL ATTENTION.

ON JULY 6, 1964, **JOHN LEWIS**, THE CIVIL RIGHTS LEADER AND LATER CONGRESSMAN, AND A GROUP OF BLACK CITIZENS TRIED TO REGISTER IN SELMA.

YOU ARE ALL UNDER ARREST.

AND IN 1965, TO RAISE AWARENESS OF BLACKS NOT BEING ABLE TO VOTE, HOSEA WILLIAMS HELPED ORGANIZE THE FIRST **SELMA MARCH.**

IF WE GOTTA FIGHT AND DIE FOR AMERICA, WHY SHOULD WE BE TREATED LIKE SLAVES IN AMERICA?

MARCH 7, 1965

THE NEWS SHOWED IMAGES OF MARCHERS BEING BEATEN. PEOPLE AROUND THE COUNTRY SAW WHAT HAPPENED.

THE EVENT GOT ENOUGH ATTENTION THAT PRESIDENT JOHNSON ISSUED A STATEMENT.

I AM CERTAIN AMERICANS EVERYWHERE JOIN IN DEPLORING THE BRUTALITY WITH WHICH A NUMBER OF NEGRO CITIZENS OF ALABAMA WERE TREATED WHEN THEY SOUGHT . . . THE PRECIOUS RIGHT TO VOTE.

THE BEST LEGAL TALENT IN THE FEDERAL GOVERNMENT IS ENGAGED IN PREPARING LEGISLATION WHICH WILL SECURE THAT RIGHT FOR EVERY AMERICAN.

THIS WAS COLD COMFORT, THOUGH. LEGISLATION COULD TAKE **YEARS** TO BE PUT INTO ACTION. IN THE MEANTIME, ANOTHER MARCH WAS ORGANIZED FROM SELMA TO MONTGOMERY.

FIRST, THE ORGANIZERS TRIED TO GET A COURT ORDER TO PREVENT THE POLICE FROM INTERFERING WITH THE MARCH.

YOUR HONOR, TO PROTECT THE RIGHTS OF THE MARCHERS, THIS IS NECESSARY.

FEDERAL JUDGE **FRANK JOHNSON'S** RESPONSE WAS . . .

I AM ISSUING A RESTRAINING ORDER. THE MARCH CANNOT BE HELD NOW AS WE NEED ADDITIONAL HEARINGS ON ITS LEGALITY.

A COMPROMISE WAS REACHED. ON MARCH 9, PROTESTERS MARCHED TO THE EDMUND PETTUS BRIDGE.

DR. KING LED A PRAYER, AND THEN THE MARCHERS TURNED AROUND AND WENT BACK.

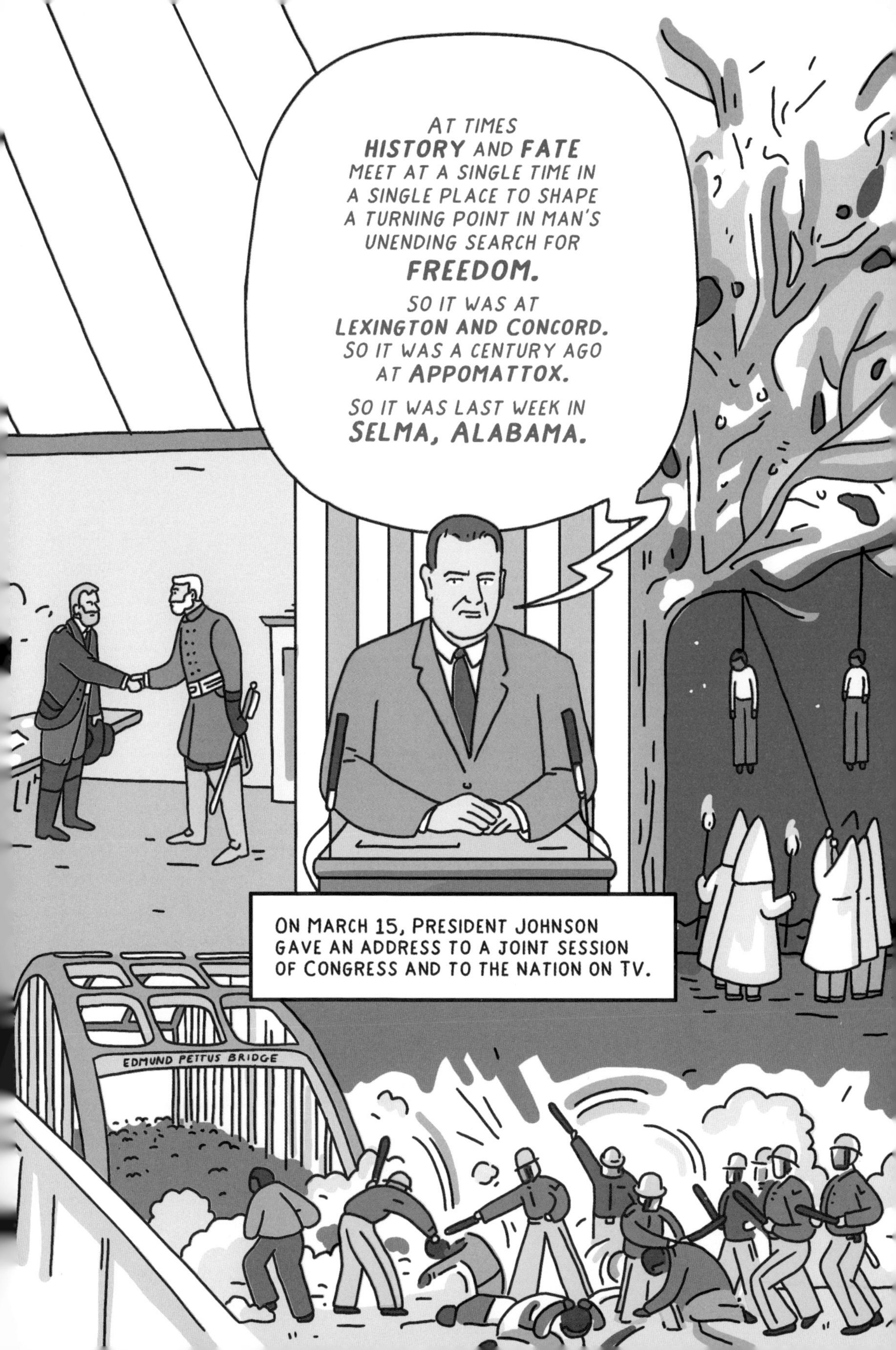
AT TIMES HISTORY AND FATE MEET AT A SINGLE TIME IN A SINGLE PLACE TO SHAPE A TURNING POINT IN MAN'S UNENDING SEARCH FOR FREEDOM.
SO IT WAS AT LEXINGTON AND CONCORD. SO IT WAS A CENTURY AGO AT APPOMATTOX.
SO IT WAS LAST WEEK IN SELMA, ALABAMA.
ON MARCH 15, PRESIDENT JOHNSON GAVE AN ADDRESS TO A JOINT SESSION OF CONGRESS AND TO THE NATION ON TV.
EDMUND PETTUS BRIDGE

THEIR CAUSE MUST BE OUR CAUSE, TOO. BECAUSE IT IS NOT JUST NEGROES, BUT REALLY IT IS ALL OF US, WHO MUST OVERCOME THE CRIPPLING LEGACY OF BIGOTRY AND INJUSTICE. AND WE SHALL OVERCOME.

TWO DAYS LATER, JUDGE JOHNSON LIFTED THE RESTRAINING ORDER.

THE LAW IS CLEAR THAT THE RIGHT TO PETITION ONE'S GOVERNMENT FOR THE REDRESS OF GRIEVANCES MAY BE EXERCISED IN LARGE GROUPS . . .

ON MARCH 21, THE MARCHERS BEGAN THE **THIRD** ATTEMPT OF THEIR MARCH FROM SELMA TO MONTGOMERY.

GOVERNOR **GEORGE WALLACE** WOULDN'T DO ANYTHING TO PROTECT THE MARCHERS, SO PRESIDENT JOHNSON FEDERALIZED THE ALABAMA NATIONAL GUARD.

IT WAS NOT JUST THE MARCH ON SELMA THAT FORCED PRESIDENT JOHNSON'S HAND. OTHER ACTIVISTS ALSO MADE IT CLEAR HE HAD TO PASS LAWS TO PROTECT VOTING.

FANNIE LOU HAMER WAS A SHARECROPPER IN MISSISSIPPI. SHE STARTED PICKING COTTON WHEN SHE WAS SIX YEARS OLD.

IN 1961, SHE HAD TO HAVE SOME MINOR SURGERY. WHILE SHE WAS THERE, THE DOCTORS GAVE HER A MISSISSIPPI APPENDECTOMY, ALSO KNOWN AS A HYSTERECTOMY. SHE NEVER GAVE HER CONSENT FOR THAT PROCEDURE.

LIKE MANY AFRICAN AMERICANS AT THE TIME, HAMER WAS INSPIRED BY BLACK MINISTERS WHO PREACHED ABOUT HAVING THE COURAGE TO VOTE.

A GROUP GOT ON A BUS AND RODE DOWN TO INDIANOLA, MISSISSIPPI, TO REGISTER TO VOTE.

I GUESS IF I'D HAD ANY SENSE, I'D HAVE BEEN **SCARED**—BUT WHAT WAS THE POINT OF BEING SCARED?

THE ONLY THING THEY COULD DO WAS **KILL** ME, AND IT KIND OF SEEMED LIKE THEY'D BEEN TRYING TO DO THAT A LITTLE BIT AT A TIME SINCE I COULD REMEMBER.

YOU'RE UNDER ARREST FOR DRIVING A BUS THAT IS **TOO** YELLOW.

LAW ENFORCEMENT ARBITRARILY MADE RULES TO PREVENT PROTESTING AND VOTING.

THE ACTIVISTS SCRAPED UP ENOUGH MONEY TO GET THE DRIVER OUT OF JAIL.

YOU BETTER WITHDRAW YOUR REGISTRATION. WE'RE NOT READY FOR THAT IN MISSISSIPPI.

I DIDN'T GO DOWN THERE TO REGISTER FOR **YOU.** I WENT DOWN TO REGISTER FOR MYSELF.

AND FOR THAT, HAMER WAS FIRED.

BUT SHE DIDN'T STOP. COMING BACK FROM TRYING TO REGISTER FOLKS ONE NIGHT, SHE WAS ARRESTED.

THE POLICE GOT TWO PRISONERS TO BEAT HER UP.

SHE DIDN'T STOP THEN, EITHER.

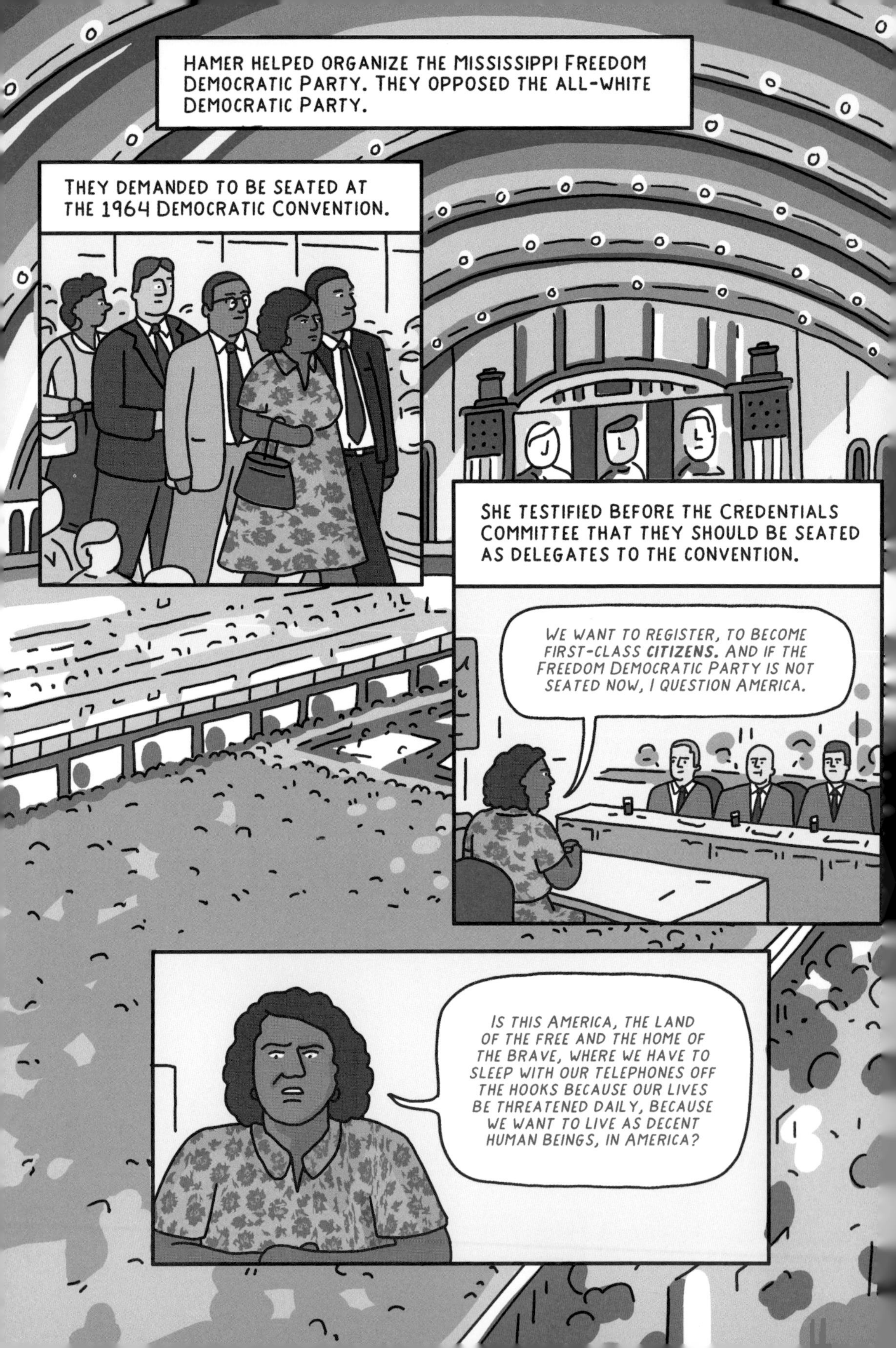
HAMER HELPED ORGANIZE THE MISSISSIPPI FREEDOM DEMOCRATIC PARTY. THEY OPPOSED THE ALL-WHITE DEMOCRATIC PARTY.
THEY DEMANDED TO BE SEATED AT THE 1964 DEMOCRATIC CONVENTION.
SHE TESTIFIED BEFORE THE CREDENTIALS COMMITTEE THAT THEY SHOULD BE SEATED AS DELEGATES TO THE CONVENTION.
WE WANT TO REGISTER, TO BECOME FIRST-CLASS CITIZENS. AND IF THE FREEDOM DEMOCRATIC PARTY IS NOT SEATED NOW, I QUESTION AMERICA.
IS THIS AMERICA, THE LAND OF THE FREE AND THE HOME OF THE BRAVE, WHERE WE HAVE TO SLEEP WITH OUR TELEPHONES OFF THE HOOKS BECAUSE OUR LIVES BE THREATENED DAILY, BECAUSE WE WANT TO LIVE AS DECENT HUMAN BEINGS, IN AMERICA?

HUBERT HUMPHREY APPROACHED THEM WITH A COMPROMISE. THE SITTING DEMOCRATS WOULD SEAT TWO OF THEIR MEMBERS, BUT ONE OF THEM COULDN'T BE HAMER.

WE DIDN'T COME ALL THIS WAY FOR NO **TWO** SEATS.

THE PRESIDENT HAS SAID HE WILL NOT LET THAT ILLITERATE WOMAN SPEAK ON THE FLOOR OF THE DEMOCRATIC CONVENTION.

WE'RE GOING HOME.

HAMER WENT BACK TO MISSISSIPPI AND RAN FOR CONGRESS.

BUT SHE LOST.

HAMER CONTINUED TO FIGHT.

THE PERSEVERANCE AND COURAGE OF HAMER, HOSEA WILLIAMS, AND SO MANY OTHERS HELPED GET PRESIDENT JOHNSON TO SIGN THE VOTING RIGHTS ACT.

THE REAL HERO OF THIS STRUGGLE IS THE AMERICAN NEGRO. HIS ACTIONS AND PROTESTS, HIS COURAGE TO RISK SAFETY AND EVEN TO RISK HIS LIFE, HAVE AWAKENED THE CONSCIENCE OF THIS NATION.

FROM 1900 TO 1965, TWO-THIRDS OF THE 20TH CENTURY, THE VOTING RIGHTS OF AFRICAN AMERICANS WERE NOT PROTECTED BY THE FEDERAL GOVERNMENT.

UNTIL LBJ SIGNED THE VOTING RIGHTS ACT ON AUGUST 16, 1965.

YOU LET US DOWN ON THIS ONE, LBJ.

YOU HAVE TO PASS THE LITERACY TEST TO VOTE.

NOT ANY-MORE.

REMEMBER THE RIDICULOUS HOOPS THAT BLACK VOTERS WERE FORCED TO JUMP THROUGH IN ORDER TO VOTE? THE VOTING RIGHTS ACT DID AWAY WITH THOSE.

VOTE

VOTE

THE ACT OUTLAWED A "VOTING QUALIFICATION OR PREREQUISITE TO VOTING." THAT MEANS ALL OF THESE PEOPLE COULD VOTE.

SEE, THIS PART OF THE LAW WAS CALLED THE GENERAL PROVISION. IT MADE PRACTICES SUCH AS LITERACY TESTS UNLAWFUL. BUT THERE WERE ALSO SPECIAL PROVISIONS TO THE LAW.

ANOTHER SPECIAL PROVISION ALLOWED FEDERAL EXAMINERS TO BE APPOINTED TO OVERSEE VOTER REGISTRATIONS IN CERTAIN DISTRICTS.

HOWEVER, A JURISDICTION **COULD** PETITION FOR EXEMPTION FROM SOME PROVISIONS. THIS WAS A PROCESS KNOWN AS **BAILOUT**.

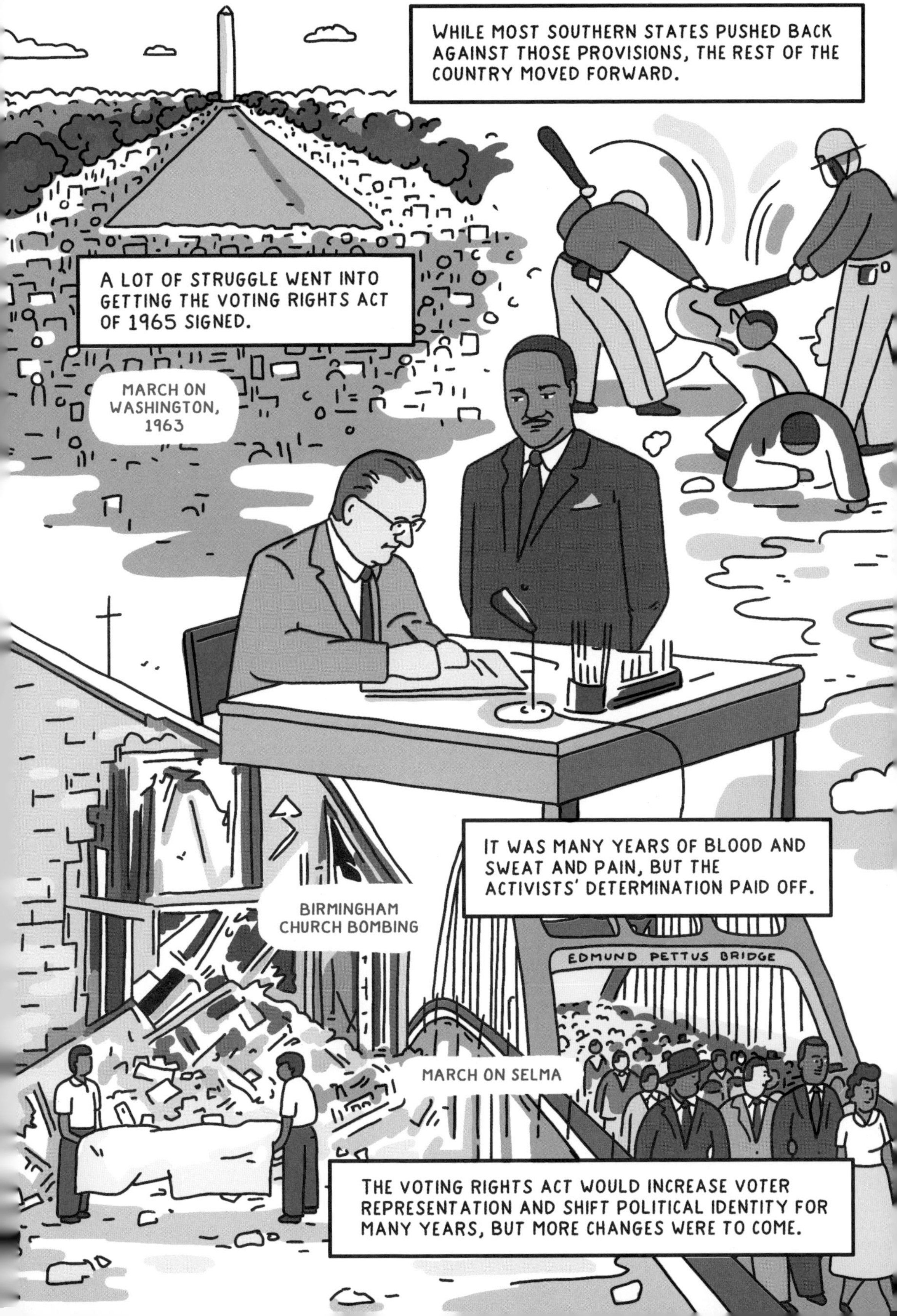
WHILE MOST SOUTHERN STATES PUSHED BACK AGAINST THOSE PROVISIONS, THE REST OF THE COUNTRY MOVED FORWARD.
A LOT OF STRUGGLE WENT INTO GETTING THE VOTING RIGHTS ACT OF 1965 SIGNED.
MARCH ON WASHINGTON, 1963
IT WAS MANY YEARS OF BLOOD AND SWEAT AND PAIN, BUT THE ACTIVISTS' DETERMINATION PAID OFF.
BIRMINGHAM CHURCH BOMBING
EDMUND PETTUS BRIDGE
MARCH ON SELMA
THE VOTING RIGHTS ACT WOULD INCREASE VOTER REPRESENTATION AND SHIFT POLITICAL IDENTITY FOR MANY YEARS, BUT MORE CHANGES WERE TO COME.

CHAPTER 6

A MOVE TO THE LEFT,
A MOVE TO THE RIGHT

1963–2009

THE CIVIL RIGHTS MOVEMENT, THE PUSH FOR THE VOTING RIGHTS ACT, AND ITS PASSAGE HAD A PROFOUND IMPACT ON VOTING DEMOGRAPHICS, ESPECIALLY FOR AFRICAN AMERICANS.

HERE'S 1960 . . .

HOW MANY OF YOU ARE DEMOCRATS?

SEE, IN 1960, 58% OF AFRICAN AMERICANS WERE DEMOCRATS.

IN 1964 . . .

HOW MANY OF YOU ARE DEMOCRATS?

SO NOW, AFTER THE FIRST CIVIL RIGHTS LEGISLATION OF THE EARLY 1960S, 82% OF AFRICAN AMERICANS ARE DEMOCRATS.

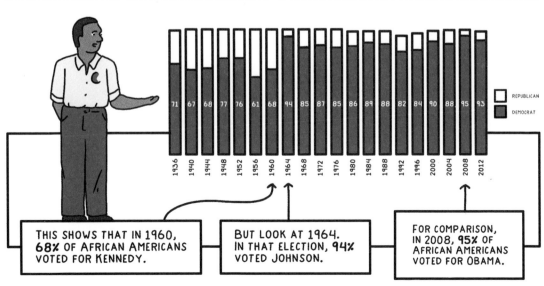

THIS SHOWS THAT IN 1960, 68% OF AFRICAN AMERICANS VOTED FOR KENNEDY.

BUT LOOK AT 1964. IN THAT ELECTION, 94% VOTED JOHNSON.

FOR COMPARISON, IN 2008, 95% OF AFRICAN AMERICANS VOTED FOR OBAMA.

THE VOTING RIGHTS ACT ALSO LED TO MUCH GREATER VOTER PARTICIPATION.

FOR EXAMPLE, IN 1964, IN MISSISSIPPI, BLACK VOTER TURNOUT WAS **6%**. IN 1968, THAT ROSE TO **59%**.

THERE WAS ALSO A BACKLASH AGAINST CIVIL RIGHTS AND THE CHANGING CULTURE OF THE '60S.

SENATOR THURMOND, IT'S TIME.

I AGREE. THE DEMOCRATIC PARTY NO LONGER REPRESENTS THE **TRUE SOUTH**. IT'S TIME WE BECAME REPUBLICANS.

A LOT OF SOUTHERN DEMOCRATS BECAME REPUBLICANS. THEY FELT PRESIDENT JOHNSON HAD ABANDONED THEM.

WHILE MANY SOUTHERNERS LEFT THE DEMOCRATIC PARTY, NORTHEASTERN REPUBLICANS AND NON–SOUTHERN DEMOCRATS SUPPORTED CIVIL RIGHTS LEGISLATION. WHICH . . .

WHICH EVENTUALLY WILL BRING ME, **RICHARD NIXON**, BACK! WE NEED LAW AND ORDER.

IN THE 1964 PRESIDENTIAL ELECTION, JOHNSON WON ALL BUT FIVE STATES. **BARRY GOLDWATER** WON HIS HOME STATE OF ARIZONA AND FOUR DEEP SOUTH STATES—THE FIRST TIME A REPUBLICAN WON STATES IN THE DEEP SOUTH SINCE RECONSTRUCTION.

☐ JOHNSON
■ GOLDWATER

HOW DID GOLDWATER DO IT? WELL . . .

I DID NOT VOTE FOR THE CIVIL RIGHTS LEGISLATION. UNENFORCEABLE GOVERNMENT EDICTS BENEFIT NO ONE.

THERE IS A REASON FOR THE RESERVATION OF "STATES'" RIGHTS.

BARRY **GETS US.** HE UNDERSTANDS WHAT WE NEED TO DO.

SEE? HE UNDERSTANDS STATES' RIGHTS. WE DON'T NEED THE FEDERAL GOVERNMENT TELLING US WHAT TO DO.

IN THE LATE 1960S, THE **VIETNAM WAR** DOMINATED THE HEADLINES.

ON MARCH 31, 1968, LBJ WENT ON TV.

I SHALL NOT SEEK, AND I WILL NOT ACCEPT, THE NOMINATION OF MY PARTY FOR ANOTHER TERM AS YOUR PRESIDENT.

END WAR NOW!

BY 1968, PROTESTS AGAINST THE WAR WERE GAINING POPULARITY.

THEN, ON APRIL 4, 1968, MARTIN LUTHER KING JR. WAS **ASSASSINATED**.

RICHARD NIXON GOT THE ENDORSEMENT OF BARRY GOLDWATER. THAT HELPED HIM WITH THE CONSERVATIVES.

ON JUNE 5, 1968, BOBBY KENNEDY WAS ASSASSINATED.

TIME FOR NIXON!

I BELIEVE IN STATES' RIGHTS AND LAW AND ORDER.

NIXON'S RETURN TO PROMINENCE WAS IMPROBABLE.

IN 1960, HE LOST AN INCREDIBLY CLOSE RACE TO JOHN KENNEDY FOR THE PRESIDENCY. NOTABLY, IT WAS THE FIRST PRESIDENTIAL RACE TO HAVE A DEBATE ON TV, AND THAT DEBATE HELPED THE MORE PHOTOGENIC KENNEDY.

IN THE CALIFORNIA GOVERNOR'S RACE OF 1962, NIXON LOST AGAIN.

I'M SORRY, BUT YOU LOST AND WE WILL HAVE TO SAY GOODBYE TO YOU.

AFTER THAT DEFEAT, NIXON BLAMED THE PRESS, AMONG OTHERS, AND APPEARED TO BE DONE WITH POLITICS. AT HIS PRESS CONFERENCE ON NOVEMBER 7, 1962, NIXON SAID . . .

I LEAVE YOU GENTLEMEN NOW AND YOU WILL WRITE IT. YOU WILL INTERPRET IT. . . . YOU WON'T HAVE NIXON TO KICK AROUND ANYMORE BECAUSE, GENTLEMEN, THIS IS MY LAST PRESS CONFERENCE.

HOWEVER, WITH SO MUCH UNREST, AND THE DEATH OF PROMINENT LEADERS, NIXON SAW THE OPPORTUNITY TO RETURN TO THE SPOTLIGHT. HE WAS ALSO ABLE TO EXPLOIT CHANGES IN VOTING PATTERNS . . .

HARRY DENT SR. OF SOUTH CAROLINA HELPED TO DEVISE A SOUTHERN STRATEGY FOR NIXON'S 1968 CAMPAIGN.

WE EMPHASIZED THAT YOU HAD TO FACE THE FACT THE WHOLE PROBLEM IS REALLY THE BLACKS. THE KEY IS TO DEVISE A SYSTEM THAT RECOGNIZED THIS WHILE NOT APPEARING TO.

NIXON ALSO HAD CHARACTERS LIKE H. R. HALDEMAN ON HIS CAMPAIGN.

WE NEED A NEW RESPECT FOR LAW IN THIS COUNTRY. SOME OF OUR COURTS HAVE GONE TOO FAR IN WEAKENING THE PEACE FORCES IN THIS COUNTRY.

YOU GET IT, DICK. YOU UNDERSTAND THAT THE GOVERNMENT IS **HURTING** SOUTHERNERS.

SEGREGATIONIST GEORGE WALLACE RAN FOR PRESIDENT AS AN INDEPENDENT IN 1968.

WHAT ARE THE REAL ISSUES THAT EXIST TODAY IN THESE UNITED STATES? IT IS THE TREND OF THE PSEUDO-INTELLECTUAL GOVERNMENT . . . LOOKING DOWN THEIR NOSE AT THE AVERAGE MAN ON THE STREET.

MEANWHILE, IN AUGUST, PROTESTERS AT THE DEMOCRATIC NATIONAL CONVENTION IN CHICAGO WERE HARASSED BY POLICE OFFICERS.

CONGRATULATIONS! WE HAVE SOME NICE PARTING GIFTS FOR YOU. YOU WIN **ARKANSAS**, **LOUISIANA**, **MISSISSIPPI**, **ALABAMA**, AND **GEORGIA** IN 1968!

GEORGE WALLACE

YOU DIDN'T WIN THE NORTHEAST, BUT YOU WON **SOUTH CAROLINA**, **NORTH CAROLINA**, AND **TENNESSEE**. AND YOU WIN THE PRESIDENCY!

RICHARD NIXON

ABOUT 95% OF THE BLACK VOTE WENT TO **HUBERT HUMPHREY** AND NOT NIXON.

IN 1968, 84% OF MISSISSIPPI'S **REGISTERED** VOTERS CAST A BALLOT.

BUT HERE'S THE THING: THE PERCENTAGES OF **ELIGIBLE** VOTERS WHO VOTED IN MISSISSIPPI DROPS TO 53%. A GREAT NUMBER OF THE POPULATION WAS NOT EVEN REGISTERED.

IN THE MIDWEST, THE PERCENTAGE OF ELIGIBLE VOTERS WHO VOTED WAS MUCH HIGHER COMPARED TO THE SOUTH, WHERE LARGE NUMBERS OF BLACK PEOPLE WERE NOT REGISTERED.

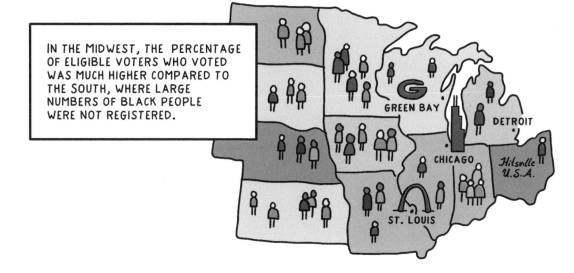

THE **SILENT MAJORITY** CAME THROUGH FOR YOU, DICK. YOU WON 49 OUT OF 50 STATES! THESE NEXT FOUR YEARS WILL BE GREAT. NOTHING CAN DERAIL THIS PRESIDENCY.

HOWEVER, A BREAK-IN AT THE DEMOCRATIC NATIONAL COMMITTEE HEADQUARTERS AT THE **WATERGATE** OFFICE COMPLEX ON JUNE 17, 1972, STARTED AN INVESTIGATION THAT SHOWED THE NIXON ADMINISTRATION HAD COMMITTED CRIMES TO OBTAIN INFORMATION ON POLITICAL OPPONENTS.

WE'LL SHOW THOSE DEMOCRATS BY **STEALING** THESE FILES . . .

AND NO ONE WILL EVER FIND OUT.

NIXON RESIGNED.

GERALD FORD BECAME PRESIDENT, AND THEN **JIMMY CARTER** RAN AGAINST FORD IN 1976.

CARTER WAS A SOUTHERNER, A FORMER GOVERNOR OF GEORGIA. SO, IN 1976, HE WAS ABLE TO ATTRACT VOTES IN THE SOUTH.

AFTER **NIXON** RESIGNED, THE REPUBLICAN PARTY HAD SOME PROBLEMS. ONE PROBLEM WAS THAT **RONALD REAGAN,** FORMER MOVIE STAR, AND FORMER GOVERNOR OF CALIFORNIA, RAN FOR THE NOMINATION AGAINST FORD.

VOTE FOR ME.

VOTE FOR ME.

REAGAN   FORD

FORD ULTIMATELY WON THE NOMINATION, BUT **CARTER** WON THE PRESIDENCY.

BEING A SOUTHERNER HELPED CARTER WIN THE SOUTH.

CARTER'S COALITION DIDN'T LAST. REAGAN LAUNCHED HIS 1980 CAMPAIGN FOR PRESIDENT IN PHILADELPHIA, MISSISSIPPI. REAGAN HAD A CLEAR PLAN.

LEE ATWATER WAS A REPUBLICAN CAMPAIGN CONSULTANT IN SOUTH CAROLINA. HE WORKED ON STROM THURMOND'S CAMPAIGNS AND FOR OTHER REPUBLICANS. IN THE EARLY 1980S, HE WENT TO WORK FOR THE REAGAN ADMINISTRATION AND THEN WAS THE CAMPAIGN DIRECTOR FOR HIS 1984 REELECTION.

THE SOUTHERN STRATEGY WORKED AGAIN. CARTER WON HIS HOME STATE OF GEORGIA, BUT THE REST OF THE SOUTH WENT TO REAGAN.

IN 1984, REAGAN WINS IN A LANDSLIDE, CARRYING ALL OF THE SOUTH.

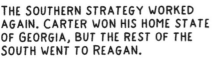

WHITE SUPPORT IN THE SOUTH WAS HIGH FOR REAGAN. THEY WERE ABLE TO WIN OVER MODERATE AND CONSERVATIVE WHITE DEMOCRATS.

REAGAN GETS IT!

REAGAN KNOWS WHAT AMERICA NEEDS.

ATWATER SPOKE IN BLUNT, OFFENSIVE LANGUAGE ABOUT HOW THE '84 CAMPAIGN WORKED.

IT'S THE REAGAN REVOLUTION.

IT'S ALL ABOUT THE SOUTHERN STRATEGY.

YOU START OUT IN 1954 SAYING "N—, N—, N—."

WHOA, WHOA. WHAT ARE YOU SAYING?

AS I WAS SAYING. BY 1968 YOU CAN'T SAY "N—"; THAT HURTS YOU. BACKFIRES. SO YOU SAY STUFF LIKE FORCED BUSING, STATES' RIGHTS, AND ALL THAT STUFF.

ANOTHER REPUBLICAN, **GEORGE H. W. BUSH**, WON THE PRESIDENCY IN 1988. BUT DEMOCRAT **BILL CLINTON** DEFEATED HIM IN 1992.

BEING A SOUTHERNER HELPED CLINTON. HE WON HIS HOME STATE OF ARKANSAS, HIS RUNNING MATE'S HOME STATE OF TENNESSEE, AND GEORGIA.

THE POPULARITY OF THE THIRD-PARTY CANDIDATE **ROSS PEROT**, WHO SPLIT SOME OF THE REPUBLICAN VOTE, DIDN'T HURT, EITHER.

READ MY LIPS: NO NEW TAXES.

IN 2000, HOWEVER, **AL GORE** RAN FOR PRESIDENT. IN A CLOSE RACE, HIS OPPONENT, **GEORGE W. BUSH**, WON ALL OF THE SOUTH.

BARACK OBAMA BECAME THE FIRST AFRICAN AMERICAN PRESIDENT WHEN HE WAS ELECTED IN 2008.

OBVIOUSLY THIS WAS AN HISTORIC EVENT.

IN FACT, OBAMA WON MY OWN STATE OF NORTH CAROLINA. OBAMA'S SUCCESS WAS DUE PARTLY TO THE LARGE TURNOUT OF AFRICAN AMERICAN VOTERS. AFRICAN AMERICAN VOTER TURNOUT IN 2008 WAS 65%. IN 2012, IT REACHED AN ALL-TIME HIGH OF ALMOST 67%.

HOWEVER, THE AFRICAN AMERICAN INCREASE IN VOTING IN 2012 IN NORTH CAROLINA WAS OFFSET BY AN INCREASE IN REPUBLICAN VOTER TURNOUT. MALE REPUBLICAN TURNOUT INCREASED FROM 70.2% TO 72.2%.

LARGER NUMBERS OF PEOPLE VOTING HELPED **BOTH** PARTIES.

CHAPTER 7

PARTY ALL
THE TIME
2009–2016

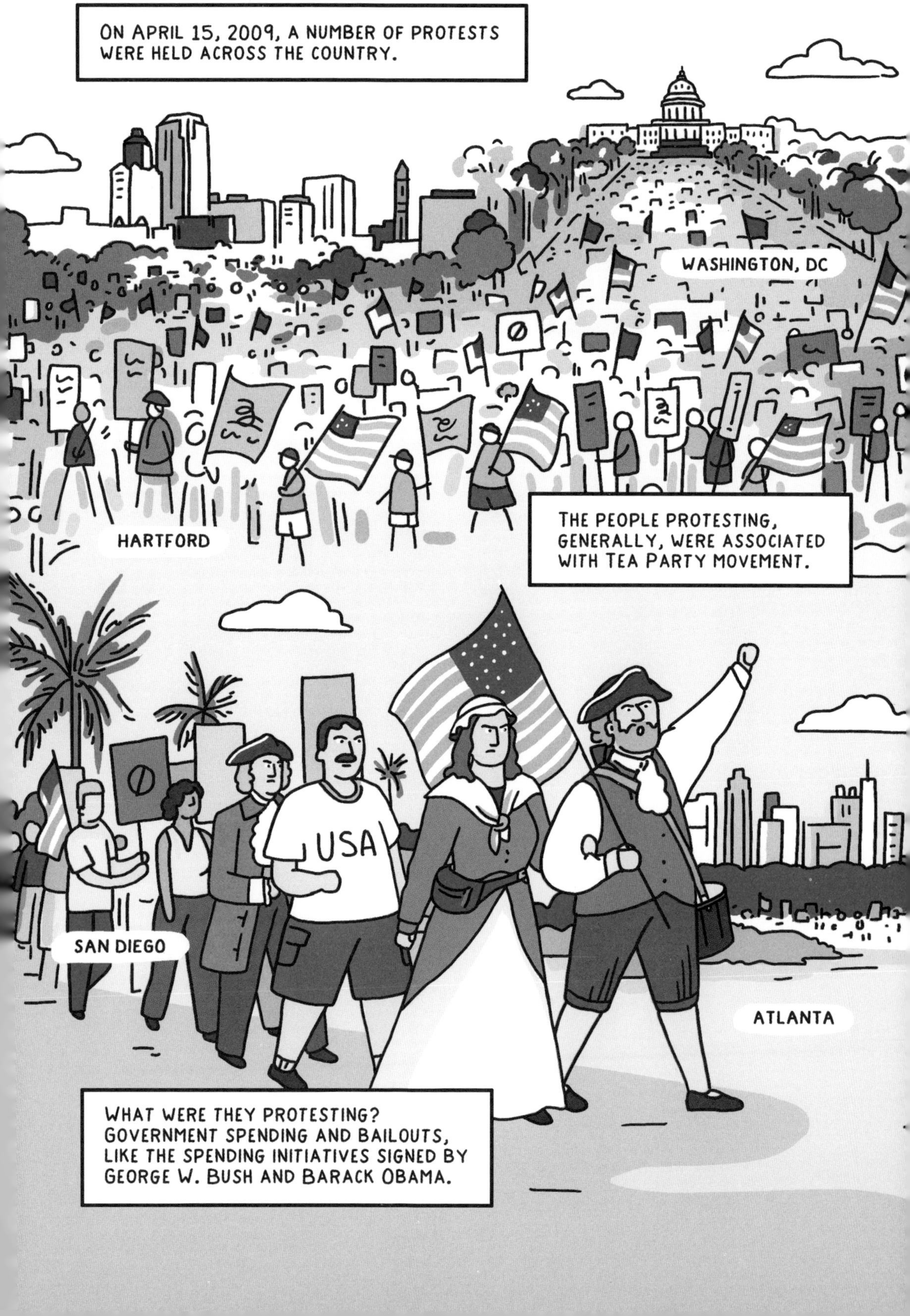
ON APRIL 15, 2009, A NUMBER OF PROTESTS WERE HELD ACROSS THE COUNTRY.
WASHINGTON, DC
HARTFORD
THE PEOPLE PROTESTING, GENERALLY, WERE ASSOCIATED WITH TEA PARTY MOVEMENT.
USA
SAN DIEGO
ATLANTA
WHAT WERE THEY PROTESTING? GOVERNMENT SPENDING AND BAILOUTS, LIKE THE SPENDING INITIATIVES SIGNED BY GEORGE W. BUSH AND BARACK OBAMA.

THE TEA PARTY BECAME NATIONAL WHEN **RICK SANTELLI**, A CNBC FINANCIAL ANALYST, WENT ON A BIT OF A RANT IN FEBRUARY 2009.

THE GOVERNMENT IS PROMOTING BAD BEHAVIOR. THIS IS AMERICA! HOW MANY OF YOU PEOPLE WANT TO PAY FOR YOUR NEIGHBOR'S MORTGAGE THAT HAS AN EXTRA BATHROOM AND THEY CAN'T PAY THEIR BILLS?

WE'RE THINKING OF HAVING A CHICAGO TEA PARTY IN JULY. ALL YOU CAPITALISTS THAT WANT TO SHOW UP TO LAKE MICHIGAN, I'M GONNA START ORGANIZING.

AFTER SANTELLI'S CALL TO ACTION, TEA PARTY RALLIES SPRANG UP ACROSS THE COUNTRY.

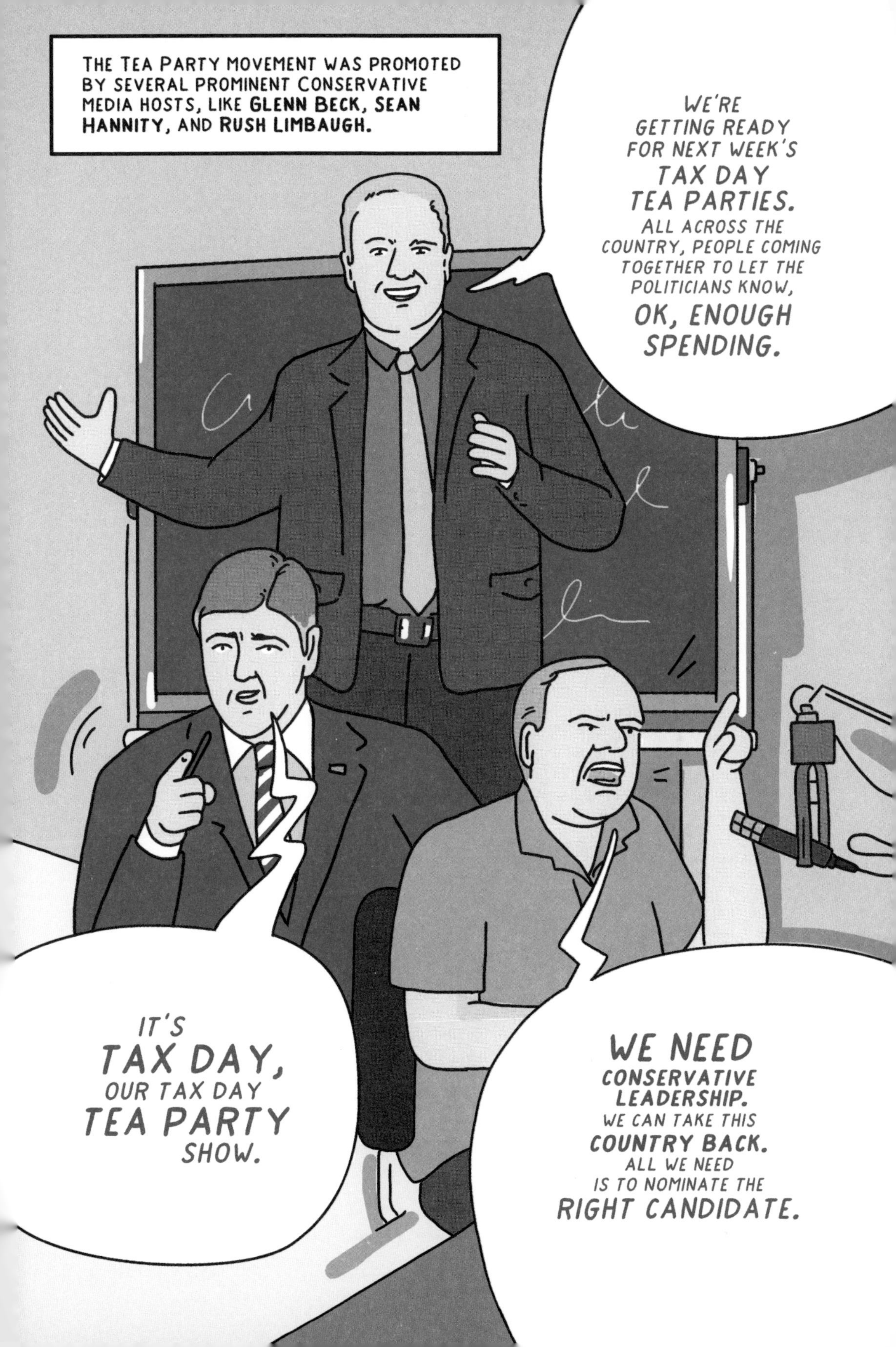
THE TEA PARTY MOVEMENT WAS PROMOTED BY SEVERAL PROMINENT CONSERVATIVE MEDIA HOSTS, LIKE **GLENN BECK, SEAN HANNITY**, AND **RUSH LIMBAUGH.**
WE'RE GETTING READY FOR NEXT WEEK'S TAX DAY TEA PARTIES. ALL ACROSS THE COUNTRY, PEOPLE COMING TOGETHER TO LET THE POLITICIANS KNOW, OK, ENOUGH SPENDING.
IT'S TAX DAY, OUR TAX DAY TEA PARTY SHOW.
WE NEED CONSERVATIVE LEADERSHIP. WE CAN TAKE THIS COUNTRY BACK. ALL WE NEED IS TO NOMINATE THE RIGHT CANDIDATE.

ON JANUARY 21, 2010, THE SUPREME COURT DECIDED THE LANDMARK CASE *CITIZENS UNITED V. FEDERAL ELECTIONS COMMISSION.*

THIS DECISION MEANT CORPORATIONS AND LABOR UNIONS COULD SPEND UNLIMITED FUNDS ADVOCATING FOR INDIVIDUAL CANDIDATES.

SUDDENLY, EVEN MORE MONEY POURED INTO ELECTIONS, AND THE TEA PARTY BENEFITED. POLITICAL ACTION COMMITTEES GREW IN PROMINENCE.

TEA PARTY PATRIOTS

AMERICANS FOR PROSPERITY

FreedomWorks

National Tea Party Federation

Join Tea Party Nation!

WHILE SOME TEA PARTY ORGANIZATIONS SPRUNG OUT OF GRASSROOTS MOVEMENTS, OTHERS WERE GENERATED BY WEALTHY LIBERTARIANS, LIKE **DAVID** AND **CHARLES KOCH.**

TEA PARTY EXPRESS

THE **KOCH BROTHERS** WERE POLITICALLY ACTIVE BILLIONAIRES WHO RAN KOCH INDUSTRIES. THE YOUNGER OF THE TWO, DAVID, PASSED AWAY IN AUGUST 2019.

KOCH INDUSTRIES STARTED AS AN OIL REFINERY.

THE COMPANY NOW HAS ANNUAL REVENUE WELL OVER **$100 BILLION**. IT IS THE SECOND-LARGEST PRIVATELY OWNED COMPANY IN THE UNITED STATES.

IN 1928, THEIR FATHER, **FRED KOCH**, FOUNDER OF KOCH INDUSTRIES, WENT TO THE SOVIET UNION TO BUILD OIL WELLS.

KOCH CAME TO HATE THE AUTHORITARIAN AND EVIL STALIN REGIME.

AND KOCH THOUGHT COMMUNISTS WERE TRYING TO TAKE OVER AMERICA. IN 1939, HE SELF-PUBLISHED A 39-PAGE PAMPHLET TITLED, "A BUSINESS MAN LOOKS AT COMMUNISM."

FRED KOCH THOUGHT THE COMMUNIST PARTY HAD INFILTRATED VARIOUS LEVELS OF AMERICAN SOCIETY.

THE ATMOSPHERE IN MOST OF THE LARGE UNIVERSITIES IS DEFINITELY SOCIALIST IF NOT PRO-COMMUNIST.

THE SUPREME COURT HAS REPEATEDLY THWARTED THE WILL OF CONGRESS AS REGARDS COMMUNISTS.

IN 1958, KOCH WAS ONE OF THE FOUNDERS OF THE **JOHN BIRCH SOCIETY**.

THE UNITED NATIONS, THE WORLD COURT, AND WORLD GOVERNMENT ARE INSTRUMENTS THE KREMLIN INTENDS FOR THE SUBTLE TAKEOVER OF AMERICA.

THE JOHN BIRCH SOCIETY OPPOSED THE CIVIL RIGHTS MOVEMENT AND SAW COMMUNIST ACTIVITY ALMOST EVERYWHERE.

YOU GUYS ARE FAR REMOVED FROM COMMON SENSE.

JOHN BIRCH

EVEN OTHER CONSERVATIVES, LIKE *NATIONAL REVIEW* FOUNDER **WILLIAM BUCKLEY**, THOUGHT THE BIRCH SOCIETY WAS TOO EXTREME.

CHARLES AND DAVID GOT THEIR AFFINITY FOR SMALL GOVERNMENT AND FREE MARKET ADVOCACY FROM THEIR FATHER, NOT TO MENTION A SENSE OF WHAT MONEY CAN BUY IN THE FEDERAL GOVERNMENT . . .

DAVID KOCH RAN AS THE LIBERTARIAN CANDIDATE FOR VICE PRESIDENT IN 1980.

LET'S MAKE THE LIBERTARIAN PARTY A FORCE THAT WILL ROLL BACK THE COERCIVE FORCE OF GOVERNMENT.

BUT THE LIBERTARIANS HARDLY RECEIVED ANY VOTES.

THE BROTHERS DECIDED THAT THEY NEEDED A BETTER STRATEGY TO INFLUENCE ELECTIONS.

THEY SPENT MILLIONS FUNDING GROUPS LIKE **CITIZENS FOR A SOUND ECONOMY.**

CITIZENS FOR A SOUND ECONOMY

HERE'S THE INFORMATION. REMEMBER, VOTE **NO** ON TOBACCO TAXES.

AS SOON AS THAT CHECK CLEARS, YOU'LL HAVE MY SUPPORT FOR THE TOBACCO COMPANIES.

THE KOCH BROTHERS REALIZED THEY COULD INFLUENCE POLITICIANS AND POLICY THROUGH NONPROFIT POLITICAL ADVOCACY GROUPS LIKE CITIZENS FOR A SOUND ECONOMY.

AMERICANS FOR PROSPERITY IS A GRASSROOTS ORGANIZATION COMMITTED TO ENGAGING CITIZENS IN THE NAME OF LIMITED GOVERNMENT AND FREE MARKETS ON THE LOCAL, STATE, AND FEDERAL LEVELS.

EVENTUALLY, AMERICANS FOR PROSPERITY REPLACED CITIZENS FOR A SOUND ECONOMY. THE KOCH BROTHERS ARE ONE OF THE MAJOR FINANCIAL CONTRIBUTORS TO AMERICANS FOR PROSPERITY.

TA-DA! YOU ARE NOW AMERICANS FOR PROSPERITY.

SEE, THESE ARE **NONPROFIT** THINK TANKS AND ORGANIZATIONS, SO THEY DON'T HAVE TO DISCLOSE EXACTLY WHO THEIR DONORS ARE. SO PEOPLE ARE ABLE TO, IN A WAY, HIDE THEIR DONATIONS.

GLOBAL WARMING ALARMISM

IN 2008, AMERICANS FOR PROSPERITY TRAVELED TO 40 CITIES IN HOT-AIR BALLOONS LIKE THIS ONE IN A CAMPAIGN AGAINST TAKING MEASURES TO COMBAT GLOBAL WARMING.

GLOBAL WARMING IS A MYTH. THESE PEOPLE WANT TO **RAISE** YOUR TAXES AND LIMIT YOUR FREEDOM.

IN 2010, AFP MADE A MAJOR PUSH FOR REPUBLICAN CONGRESSIONAL CANDIDATES. THEY HAD A NATIONWIDE BUS TOUR TO ORGANIZE TEA PARTY GROUPS.

THEY HELPED TRAIN TEA PARTY GROUPS ON HOW TO DO VOTER REGISTRATION DRIVES.

YOU NEED TO TARGET AREAS WHERE THERE ARE REPUBLICANS. WE NEED TO GET THE **REPUBLICAN** VOTE OUT!

NOW REMEMBER, WE HAVE TO GET THE VOTE OUT FOR **RAND PAUL.** RAND PAUL IS OUR GUY TO HELP STOP OBAMA.

THEY MADE SURE THAT THEIR CANDIDATES WERE SUPPORTED.

I'VE NEVER BEEN TO A TEA PARTY EVENT. NO ONE REPRESENTING THE TEA PARTY HAS EVER EVEN APPROACHED ME.

FIVE YEARS AGO, MY BROTHER CHARLES AND I PROVIDED THE FUNDS TO START AMERICANS FOR PROSPERITY. IT'S BEYOND MY WILDEST DREAMS HOW AFP HAS GROWN INTO THIS ENORMOUS ORGANIZATION.

IN 2009, DAVID KOCH ADDRESSED THE **DEFENDING THE AMERICAN DREAM SUMMIT,** WHICH WAS SPONSORED BY AMERICANS FOR PROSPERITY.

THE TEA PARTY ENERGIZED VOTERS.

THE 2010 ELECTION SAW A NUMBER OF TEA PARTY CANDIDATES ELECTED, INCLUDING...

RAND PAUL
OF KENTUCKY

MARCO RUBIO
OF FLORIDA

TIM SCOTT
OF SOUTH CAROLINA

IN THE 2010 MIDTERM ELECTIONS, ALL THE TEA PARTY-BACKED CANDIDATES WERE REPUBLICANS.

USA

VOTE TODAY

TEA PARTY CANDIDATES WON 5 OUT OF 10 SENATE RACES AND 40 OUT OF 130 CONGRESSIONAL RACES CONTESTED.

ANOTHER TEA PARTY ISSUE WAS **VOTER FRAUD.**
TEA PARTIERS BELIEVE THERE ARE ILLEGAL VOTES . . .

VOTER FRAUD **IS** A
MAJOR ISSUE. ELECTIONS
ARE NOT FAIR BECAUSE
OF VOTER FRAUD.

DON'T BELIEVE ME?
LISTEN TO **RICK PERRY,**
GOVERNOR OF TEXAS.

FISCAL DISCIPLINE, BALANCED
BUDGETS, AND THE INTEGRITY OF
THE BALLOT BOX ARE CRITICAL
TO THE PEOPLE OF TEXAS.

SEE? THE GOVERNOR OF TEXAS
KNOWS ALL ABOUT ELECTIONS.
AND HE'S NOT THE ONLY ONE.

ILLEGAL VOTING HELPS
DEMOCRATS THE MOST.

PEOPLE DO VOTE WITHOUT BEING A
CITIZEN. IT'S A WINK AND A NOD, WE
ALL KNOW IT IS GOING TO HAPPEN.

MICHELE BACHMANN IS A US
REPRESENTATIVE. SHE RAN FOR
PRESIDENT, SO SHE CLEARLY
KNOWS WHAT SHE IS
TALKING ABOUT.

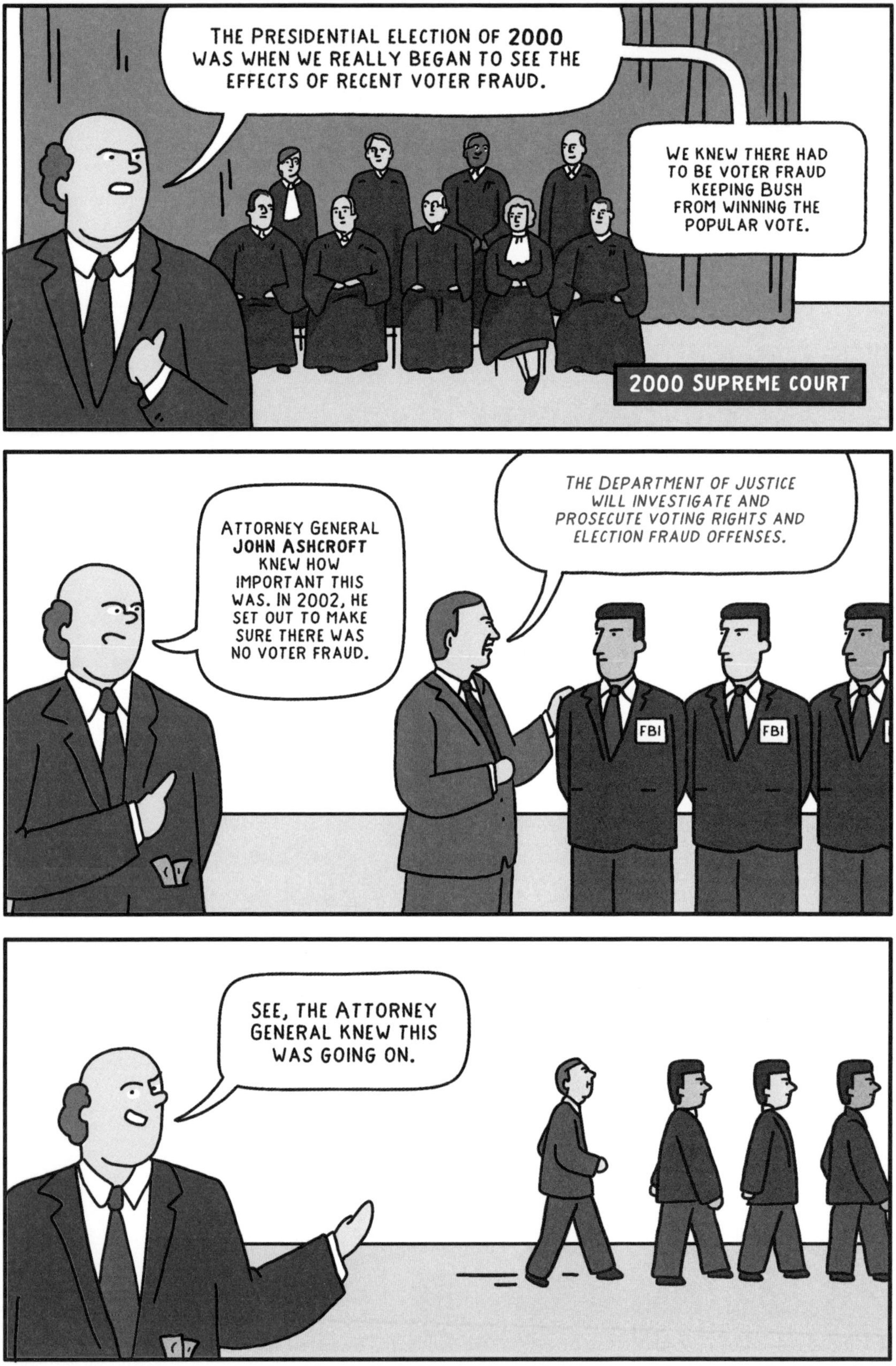
THE PRESIDENTIAL ELECTION OF 2000 WAS WHEN WE REALLY BEGAN TO SEE THE EFFECTS OF RECENT VOTER FRAUD.
WE KNEW THERE HAD TO BE VOTER FRAUD KEEPING BUSH FROM WINNING THE POPULAR VOTE.
2000 SUPREME COURT
ATTORNEY GENERAL JOHN ASHCROFT KNEW HOW IMPORTANT THIS WAS. IN 2002, HE SET OUT TO MAKE SURE THERE WAS NO VOTER FRAUD.
THE DEPARTMENT OF JUSTICE WILL INVESTIGATE AND PROSECUTE VOTING RIGHTS AND ELECTION FRAUD OFFENSES.
FBI
FBI
SEE, THE ATTORNEY GENERAL KNEW THIS WAS GOING ON.

ASHCROFT RESIGNED IN 2004, SO GEORGE W. BUSH SWORE IN A NEW ATTORNEY GENERAL, **ALBERTO GONZALES.**

THANK YOU, MR. PRESIDENT.

LISTEN, ALBERTO. VOTER FRAUD IS A HUGE PROBLEM. LOOK AT PLACES LIKE ALBUQUERQUE, MILWAUKEE, AND PHILADELPHIA.

YOU KNOW THE DEMOCRATS ARE TAKING ADVANTAGE OF VOTER FRAUD.

WE DON'T ACTUALLY HAVE PROOF.

I DON'T HAVE ANY PROOF, EITHER.

NEW MEXICO

MISSOURI

YOU'RE FIRED!

I WOULD NEVER, EVER MAKE A CHANGE IN A US ATTORNEY POSITION FOR POLITICAL REASONS.

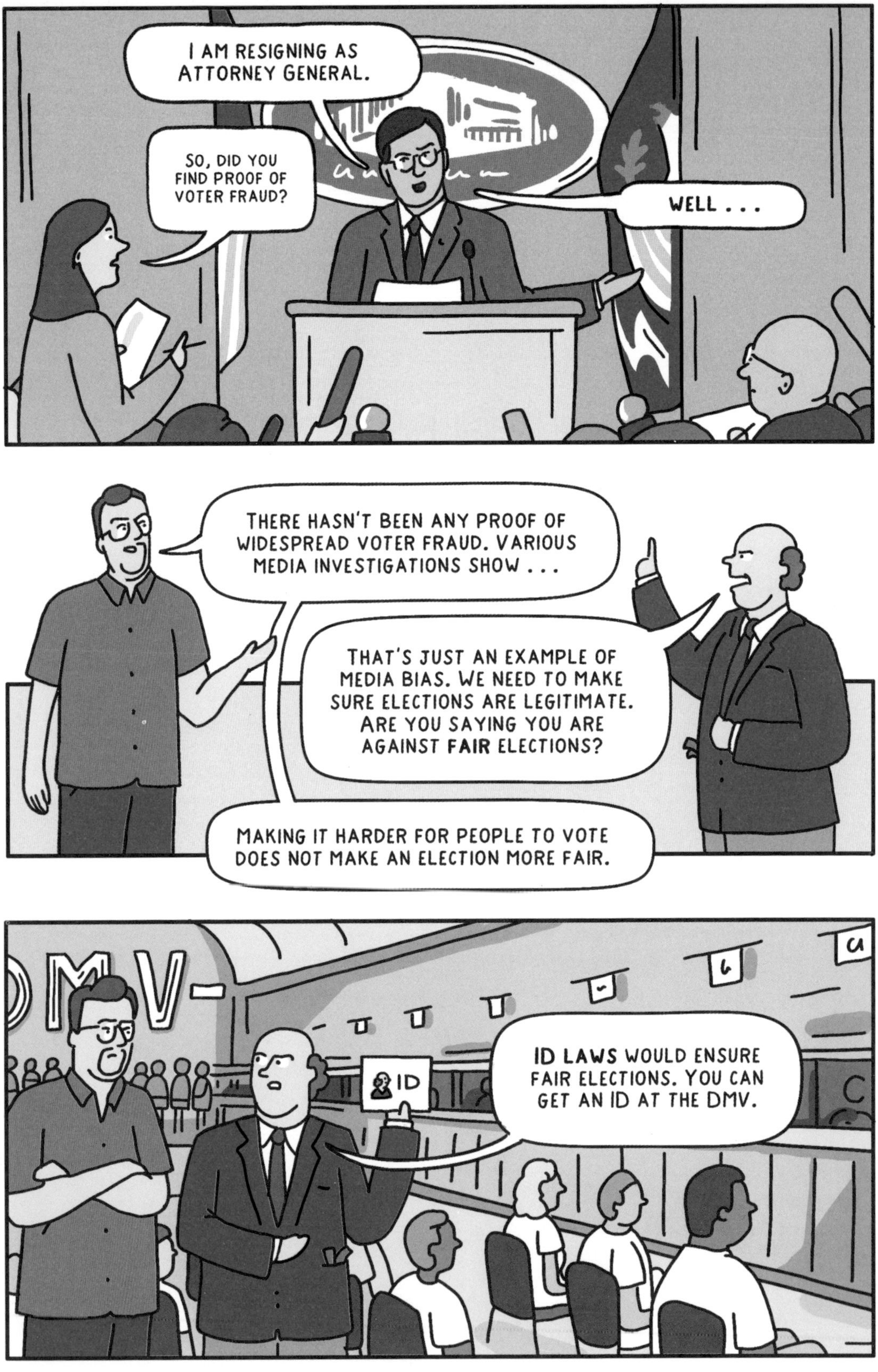
I AM RESIGNING AS ATTORNEY GENERAL.
SO, DID YOU FIND PROOF OF VOTER FRAUD?
WELL . . .
THERE HASN'T BEEN ANY PROOF OF WIDESPREAD VOTER FRAUD. VARIOUS MEDIA INVESTIGATIONS SHOW . . .
THAT'S JUST AN EXAMPLE OF MEDIA BIAS. WE NEED TO MAKE SURE ELECTIONS ARE LEGITIMATE. ARE YOU SAYING YOU ARE AGAINST **FAIR** ELECTIONS?
MAKING IT HARDER FOR PEOPLE TO VOTE DOES NOT MAKE AN ELECTION MORE FAIR.
DMV
ID
ID LAWS WOULD ENSURE FAIR ELECTIONS. YOU CAN GET AN ID AT THE DMV.

YET IN URBAN AREAS, LIKE THE SOUTH SIDE OF CHICAGO, AND EVEN DOWNTOWN RALEIGH, PEOPLE DON'T NEED AN ID AND CANNOT EASILY OBTAIN PHOTO IDS.

THESE URBAN AREAS GENERALLY HAVE A HIGH POPULATION OF MINORITIES WHO TEND TO VOTE DEMOCRAT. REQUIREMENTS LIKE VOTER ID LAWS ARE DIRECTLY TARGETING MINORITIES AND MAKING IT MORE AND MORE DIFFICULT TO VOTE.

PEOPLE ARE POOR HERE, TOO. BUT THEY CAN GET THEIR IDS.

IT'S NOT THE SAME, THOUGH. THESE PEOPLE DON'T RELY ON PUBLIC TRANSPORTATION, FOR INSTANCE. IT'S PROVEN THAT VOTER ID LAWS DISPROPORTIONATELY IMPACT MINORITIES, THE DISABLED, AND THE ELDERLY.

SO VOTER ID LAWS HURT DEMOCRATS, RIGHT? AND THAT'S REALLY WHY THEY OPPOSE THEM.

PHOTO ID LAWS BEGAN POPPING UP IN LOTS OF STATES IN THE MID-2000S.

VOTE HERE

PICTURE ·ID· REQUIRED

AND A BIG HELP FOR A LOT OF STATES WAS THE OVERTURNING OF THE VOTING RIGHTS ACT

IN 2013 THE SUPREME COURT HEARD THE CASE *SHELBY COUNTY V. HOLDER.*

HOLDER WAS ATTORNEY GENERAL DURING BARACK OBAMA'S PRESIDENCY. SHELBY COUNTY IS IN ALABAMA, AND THEY WERE SUING THAT PARTS OF THE VOTING RIGHTS ACT WERE UNCONSTITUTIONAL.

YOU'LL RECALL THAT CERTAIN STATES HAD TO HAVE PRECLEARANCE TO CHANGE THEIR VOTING REGULATIONS. THESE STATES WERE IN THE SOUTH.

PRECLEARANCE IS UNCONSTITUTIONAL BECAUSE IT IS BASED ON 40-YEAR-OLD FACTS HAVING NO LOGICAL RELATIONSHIP TO THE PRESENT DAY.

DOING AWAY WITH PRECLEARANCE EFFECTIVELY NEUTERED THE VOTING RIGHTS ACT BECAUSE NOW THESE STATES COULD CHANGE THEIR VOTING REGULATIONS HOWEVER THEY WANTED.

YEEHAW! NOW WE CAN GET THESE PHOTO ID LAWS PASSED!

AND THAT'S EXACTLY WHAT A NUMBER OF STATES IN THE SOUTH AND OTHER REGIONS DID.

IN 2013, AFTER THE SUPREME COURT DECISION, THE NORTH CAROLINA REPUBLICAN-CONTROLLED LEGISLATURE ENACTED NEW VOTING REQUIREMENTS.

VOTERS MUST SHOW A PHOTO ID. WE WILL NOT ACCEPT STUDENT IDS, GOVERNMENT EMPLOYEE IDS, NOR PUBLIC ASSISTANCE IDS.

NOW WE'RE MAKING PROGRESS!

FURTHER, WE ARE CUTTING DOWN THE NUMBER OF EARLY VOTING DAYS, ELIMINATING SAME-DAY REGISTRATION, AND OUT-OF-PRECINCT VOTING.

WE'RE MAKING AMERICA GREAT AGAIN!

REPUBLICAN GOVERNOR **PAT MCCRORY** SIGNED THE BILL INTO LAW.

BUT THE US ATTORNEY'S OFFICE, LED BY **LORETTA LYNCH**, JOINED THE APPEAL TO FEDERAL APPEALS COURT.

THE THREE-JUDGE PANEL OF THE US 4TH CIRCUIT COURT OF APPEALS HAS STRUCK DOWN OUR BILL THAT CHANGED VOTING REGULATIONS.

DAMN THOSE ACTIVIST JUDGES!

THE COURT FINDS THESE NEW PROVISIONS TARGET AFRICAN AMERICANS WITH ALMOST SURGICAL PRECISION.

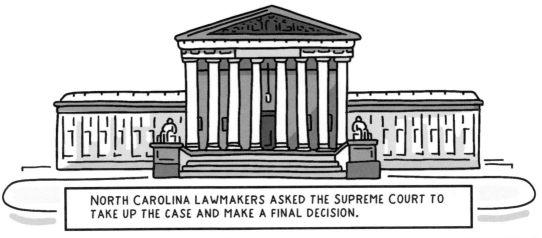

NORTH CAROLINA LAWMAKERS ASKED THE SUPREME COURT TO TAKE UP THE CASE AND MAKE A FINAL DECISION.

NO, WE ARE NOT GOING TO TAKE UP THE NORTH CAROLINA CASE.

JUSTICE JOHN ROBERTS JR.

WHEN THE SUPREME COURT SAID THEY WOULD NOT HEAR THE CASE, IT MEANT THE THREE-JUDGE PANEL'S RULING STOOD.

PRESIDENT PRO-TEMPORE OF THE NORTH CAROLINA SENATE **PHIL BERGER** DID NOT AGREE WITH THE RULING.

ALL NORTH CAROLINIANS CAN REST ASSURED THAT REPUBLICAN LEGISLATORS WILL CONTINUE FIGHTING TO PROTECT THE INTEGRITY OF OUR ELECTIONS BY IMPLEMENTING THE COMMON-SENSE REQUIREMENT TO SHOW A PHOTO ID WHEN WE VOTE.

IT APPEARS THESE VOTER ID LAWS ARE MEANT TO TARGET GROUPS WHO FAVOR DEMOCRATS—AFRICAN AMERICANS, IMMIGRANTS, AND SO ON.

AND REALLY, THIS ISSUE IS AN EXAMPLE OF THE DIVIDE IN THIS COUNTRY.

RURAL AREAS DIVIDED . . .

. . . FROM URBAN AREAS.

WHITES FROM BLACKS.

IT DOESN'T HAVE TO BE THAT WAY. WHY ARE SOME TRYING TO KEEP PEOPLE FROM VOTING? SHOULDN'T WE BE ALLOWING ALL OPINIONS TO BE HEARD AT THE BALLOT? SHOULDN'T WE BE MAKING IT EASIER TO VOTE AND NOT HARDER?

CHAPTER 8

DIVIDE AND
CONQUER
2010–PRESENT

THE WORD **"GERRY-MANDER"** FIRST APPEARED IN 1812 IN THE *BOSTON GAZETTE* NEWSPAPER.

MASSACHUSETTS GOVERNOR **ELBRIDGE GERRY** SIGNED A BILL CREATING A DISTRICT TO ENSURE CERTAIN PARTY REPRESENTATION. THE EDITORIAL CARTOONIST FROM THE *GAZETTE* TURNED IT INTO A CLAWED ANIMAL, AND THUS THE TERM WAS BORN.

LET'S THINK OF GERRYMANDERING AS A GAME OF TWISTER.

IN TWISTER, PEOPLE OFTEN HAVE TO CONTORT THEMSELVES INTO SEEMINGLY IMPOSSIBLE POSITIONS TO WIN.

IN GERRYMANDERING, LEGISLATURES DRAW MAPS OF RIDICULOUS SHAPES TO HELP THEIR PARTIES STAY IN POWER.

WE LIKE TO THINK OF CREATING LEGISLATIVE DISTRICTS AS DOING A JIGSAW PUZZLE. BUT THAT'S NOT HOW IT WORKS.

WE HEAR A LOT ABOUT GERRYMANDERING TODAY. IT IS EASY TO THINK THIS IS A RECENT PHENOMENON, HOWEVER . . .

IN 1788, EVEN BEFORE THE CONSTITUTION WAS RATIFIED, **PATRICK HENRY** AND HIS FOLLOWERS REDREW VIRGINIA'S 5TH CONGRESSIONAL DISTRICT SO HENRY'S POLITICAL OPPONENT, **JAMES MADISON**, WOULD FACE JAMES MONROE, A TOUGHER CANDIDATE.

MR. MONROE

MR. MADISON

MADISON WON ANYWAY.

IN 1842, CONGRESS PASSED AN APPORTIONMENT ACT. THIS SAID THAT CONGRESSIONAL DISTRICTS MUST BE CONTIGUOUS, AND THAT ONE PERSON WAS ELECTED FROM EACH DISTRICT.

PRIOR TO THIS, PEOPLE ALL ACROSS THE STATE COULD VOTE FOR ALL OF THE CANDIDATES, NO MATTER WHAT COUNTY THEY LIVED IN, SO CANDIDATES MIGHT BE FROM ANY COUNTY IN THE STATE.

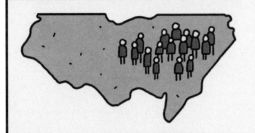

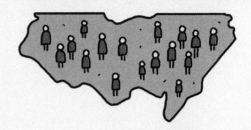

CONTIGUOUS, OF COURSE, MEANS THE DISTRICT HAD TO BE OF ONE PIECE. PREVIOUSLY, A DISTRICT COULD COMPRISE AREAS THAT DIDN'T EVEN TOUCH EACH OTHER.

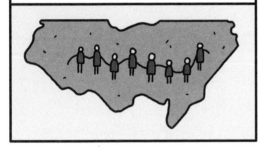

AFTER THE SIGNING OF THE VOTING RIGHTS ACT, SOME STATES CREATED MINORITY/MAJORITY DISTRICTS. THESE DISTRICTS WERE MEANT TO INCREASE MINORITY MEMBERS IN CONGRESS AND TO ENSURE MINORITY VOTES MATTERED.

IN NORTH CAROLINA, IN 1992, THE STATE LEGISLATURE WAS CONTROLLED BY DEMOCRATS. THEIR DRAWN CONGRESSIONAL DISTRICTS INCLUDED ONE MINORITY/MAJORITY DISTRICT.

THE DOJ'S INTERPRETATION OF THE VOTING RIGHTS ACT WAS THAT NORTH CAROLINA NEEDED MORE THAN ONE MINORITY/MAJORITY DISTRICT.

BUT THE DEPARTMENT OF JUSTICE SAID THAT WASN'T GOOD ENOUGH SINCE NORTH CAROLINA HAD A 22% MINORITY POPULATION.

SO, THEY CREATED THE INFAMOUS 12TH. THE 12TH SNAKED ALONG INTERSTATE 85, SOMETIMES BEING ONLY AS WIDE AS THE HIGHWAY.

IN 1993, THE SUPREME COURT RULED IN THE CASE OF *SHAW V. RENO*, THAT THE NEWLY DRAWN 12TH DISTRICT WAS UNCONSTITUTIONAL BECAUSE IT WAS ILLEGAL RACIAL GERRYMANDERING. JUSTICE **SANDRA DAY O'CONNOR** WROTE THE MAJORITY OPINION.

THE DISTRICT BEARS UNCOMFORTABLE RESEMBLANCE TO POLITICAL APARTHEID.

SO, THE DEMOCRATIC LEGISLATURE REDREW THE DISTRICT AGAIN. THE SUPREME COURT DECIDED THE NEW DISTRICT WAS OK BECAUSE IT WAS CREATED TO SECURE THE DEMOCRATS WOULD WIN THE DISTRICT. JUSTICE **STEPHEN BREYER** WROTE THE MAJORITY OPINION.

THEY ATTEMPTED TO PROTECT INCUMBENTS, TO ADHERE TO TRADITIONAL DISTRICTING CRITERIA, AND TO PRESERVE THE EXISTING PARTISAN BALANCE IN THE STATE'S CONGRESSIONAL DELEGATION.

IN 2010, REPUBLICANS IN NORTH CAROLINA RODE THE TEA PARTY WAVE TO VICTORY IN THE LEGISLATURE. IN FACT, THE NORTH CAROLINA SENATE WENT FROM 30–20 DEMOCRAT CONTROL TO 31–19 REPUBLICAN CONTROL.

THIS MEANT THE REPUBLICANS COULD REDRAW THE MAPS.

WHICH THEY DID IN 2011.

AS WE ALREADY SAW, THE COURTS ONCE AGAIN DECLARED THE NORTH CAROLINA LEGISLATURE GUILTY OF ILLEGAL GERRYMANDERING.

WHY ALL THIS FUSS? WELL, WHOEVER CONTROLS THE LEGISLATURE DRAWS THE MAP OF DISTRICTS, WHICH CAN DETERMINE WHO CONTROLS THE STATE LEGISLATURE AND THE STATE'S CONGRESSIONAL REPRESENTATIVES.

IN NORTH CAROLINA, THE VOTING SPLIT IS VERY CLOSE.

MOST OF THE RURAL AREAS IN NORTH CAROLINA VOTE REPUBLICAN, WHILE MOST OF THE URBAN AREAS VOTE DEMOCRATIC. OBAMA WON NORTH CAROLINA NARROWLY IN 2008. ROMNEY WON IT NARROWLY IN 2012. TRUMP'S CUSHION WAS A BIT GREATER IN 2016.

BUT THE STATE LEGISLATIVE SPLIT DOESN'T REFLECT HOW CLOSE VOTING IS OVERALL. AS OF 2019, REPUBLICANS HOLD A 29-21 MAJORITY IN THE STATE SENATE AND A 65-55 MAJORITY IN THE STATE HOUSE OF ASSEMBLY. THAT'S THE POWER OF GERRYMANDERING.

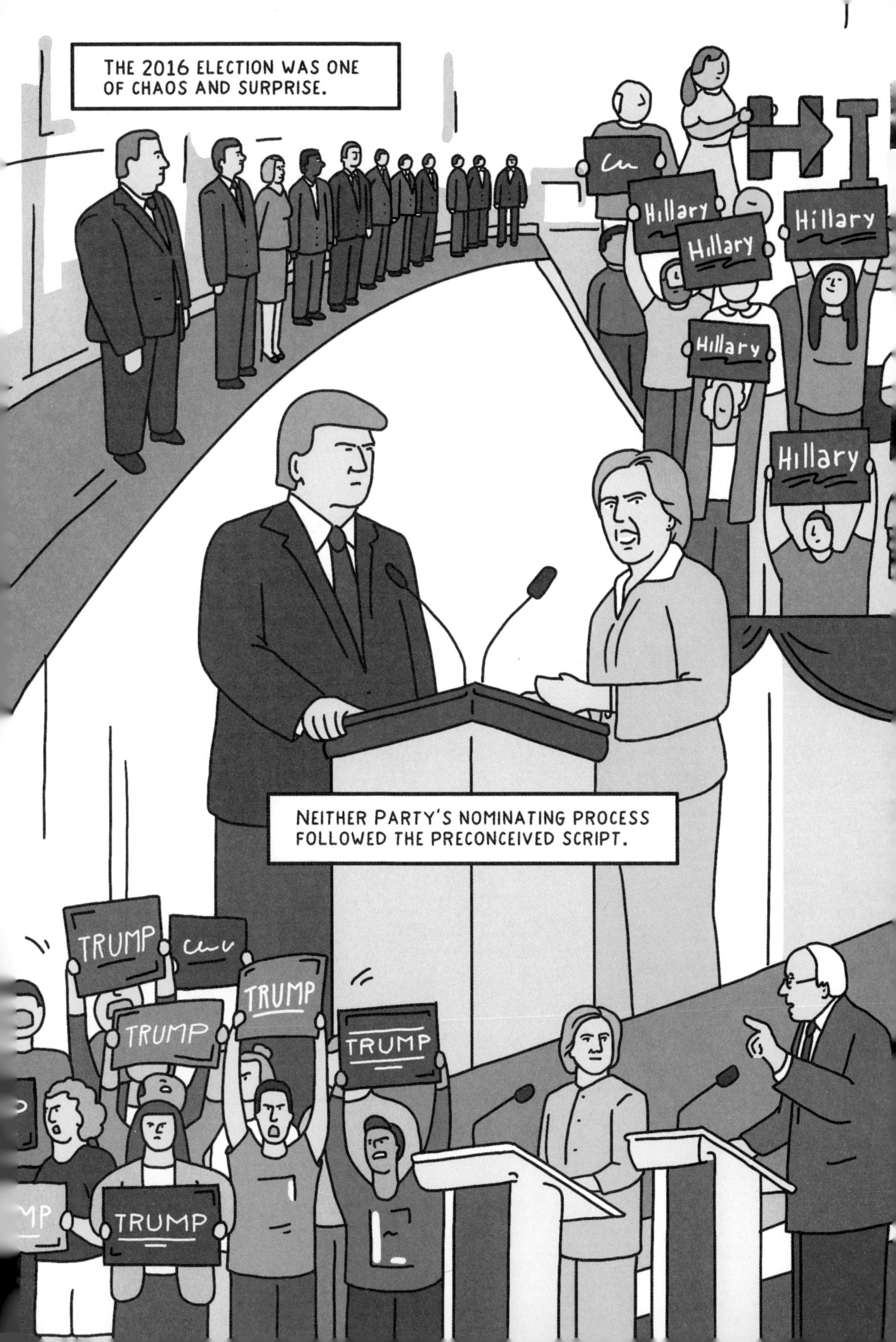

THE 2016 ELECTION WAS ONE OF CHAOS AND SURPRISE.
Hillary
Hillary
Hillary
Hillary
Hillary
NEITHER PARTY'S NOMINATING PROCESS FOLLOWED THE PRECONCEIVED SCRIPT.
TRUMP
TRUMP
TRUMP
TRUMP
TRUMP

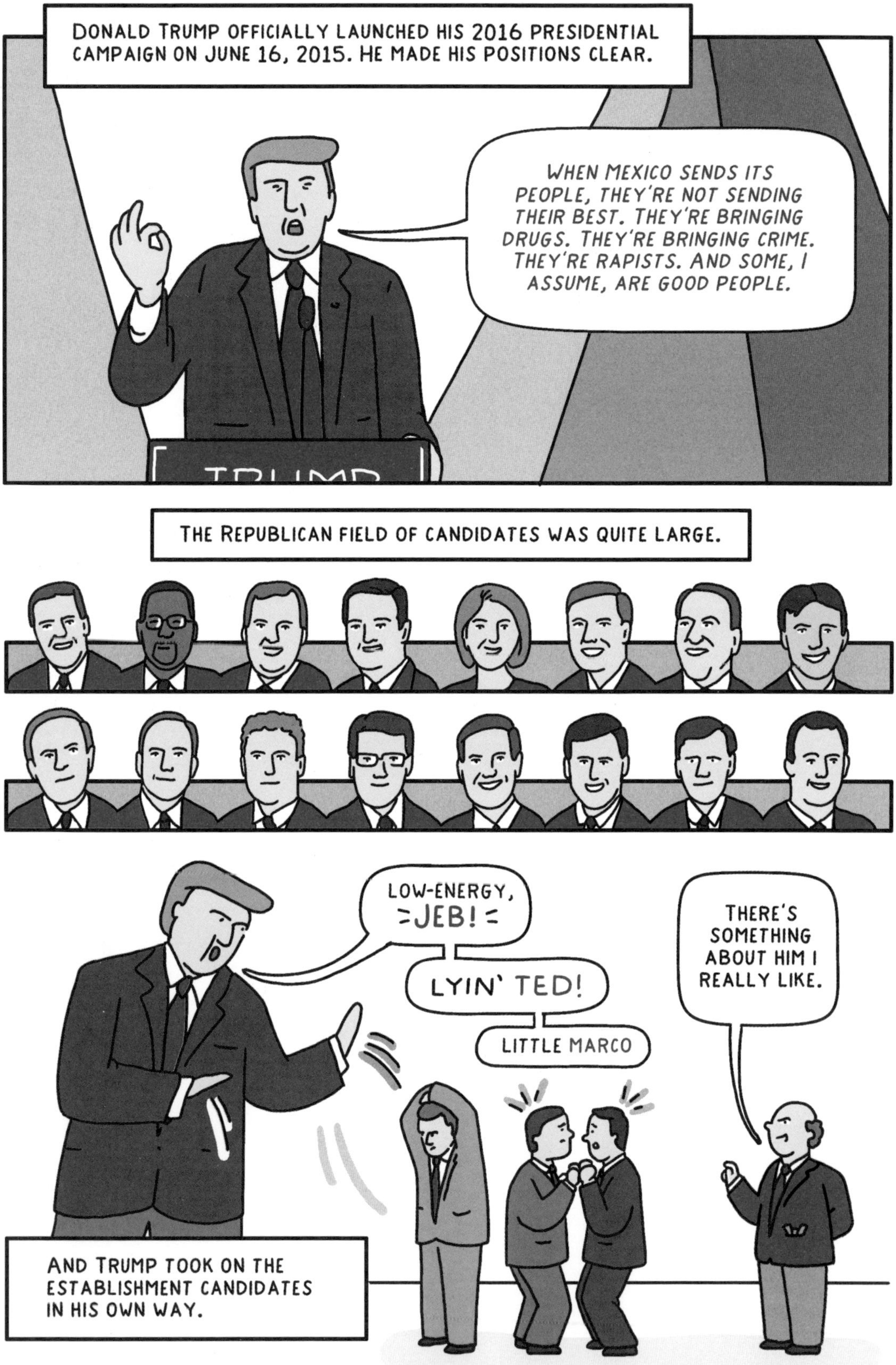
DONALD TRUMP OFFICIALLY LAUNCHED HIS 2016 PRESIDENTIAL CAMPAIGN ON JUNE 16, 2015. HE MADE HIS POSITIONS CLEAR.
WHEN MEXICO SENDS ITS PEOPLE, THEY'RE NOT SENDING THEIR BEST. THEY'RE BRINGING DRUGS. THEY'RE BRINGING CRIME. THEY'RE RAPISTS. AND SOME, I ASSUME, ARE GOOD PEOPLE.
THE REPUBLICAN FIELD OF CANDIDATES WAS QUITE LARGE.
LOW-ENERGY, JEB!
LYIN' TED!
LITTLE MARCO
THERE'S SOMETHING ABOUT HIM I REALLY LIKE.
AND TRUMP TOOK ON THE ESTABLISHMENT CANDIDATES IN HIS OWN WAY.

TED CRUZ DID WIN THE IOWA CAUCUS.
A CAUCUS IS DIFFERENT FROM A PRIMARY.

CAUCUS

CRUZ

IN A CAUCUS, REGISTERED PARTY VOTERS MEET AT A PLACE IN THEIR PRECINCT TO SELECT A CANDIDATE. VOTING IS OFTEN DONE BY JUST A RAISING OF HANDS AND THEN VOTES ARE ADDED UP FROM EACH PRECINCT.

PRIMARY VOTING

VOTE

VOTE

A PRIMARY, HOWEVER, IS MORE LIKE THE GENERAL ELECTION. IT IS DONE BY SECRET BALLOT.

TED CRUZ DIDN'T WIN IOWA: HE **STOLE** IT.

CARSON

RUBIO

CRUZ

TRUMP

IOWA IS NOT A WINNER-TAKE-ALL STATE, SO DELEGATES ARE DIVIDED UP PROPORTIONALLY. CRUZ RECEIVED THE MOST VOTES AND GOT 8 DELEGATES. TRUMP GOT 7, RUBIO 7, AND CARSON 3.

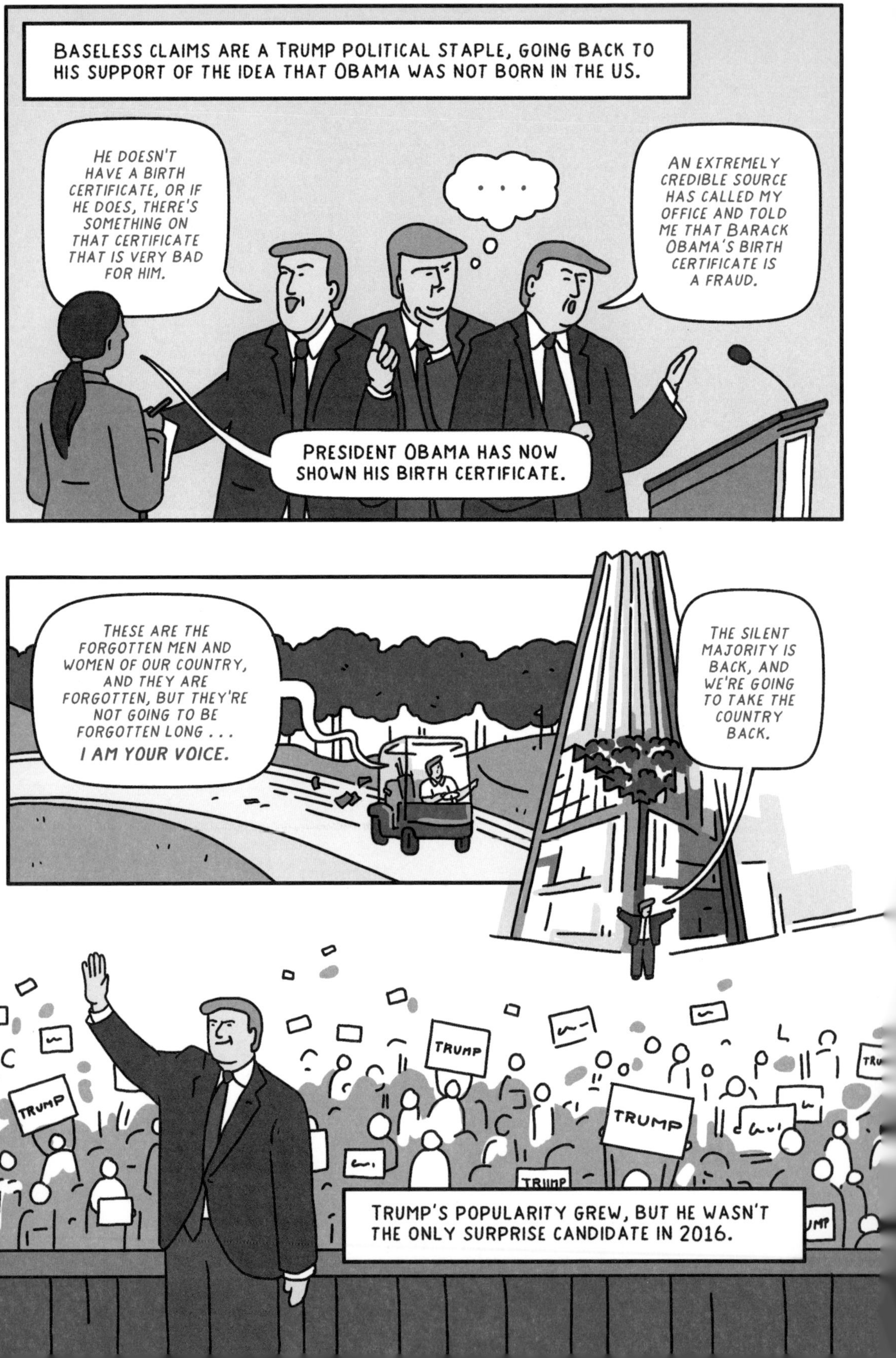
BASELESS CLAIMS ARE A TRUMP POLITICAL STAPLE, GOING BACK TO HIS SUPPORT OF THE IDEA THAT OBAMA WAS NOT BORN IN THE US.
HE DOESN'T HAVE A BIRTH CERTIFICATE, OR IF HE DOES, THERE'S SOMETHING ON THAT CERTIFICATE THAT IS VERY BAD FOR HIM.
. . .
AN EXTREMELY CREDIBLE SOURCE HAS CALLED MY OFFICE AND TOLD ME THAT BARACK OBAMA'S BIRTH CERTIFICATE IS A FRAUD.
PRESIDENT OBAMA HAS NOW SHOWN HIS BIRTH CERTIFICATE.
THESE ARE THE FORGOTTEN MEN AND WOMEN OF OUR COUNTRY, AND THEY ARE FORGOTTEN, BUT THEY'RE NOT GOING TO BE FORGOTTEN LONG . . . I AM YOUR VOICE.
THE SILENT MAJORITY IS BACK, AND WE'RE GOING TO TAKE THE COUNTRY BACK.
TRUMP
TRUMP
TRUMP
TRUMP
TRUMP'S POPULARITY GREW, BUT HE WASN'T THE ONLY SURPRISE CANDIDATE IN 2016.

A PROCLAIMED DEMOCRATIC SOCIALIST, **BERNIE SANDERS** RAN FOR THE DEMOCRATIC PRESIDENTIAL NOMINATION IN 2016.

SANDERS ALSO TAPPED INTO THE DISTRUST OF ESTABLISHMENT POLITICIANS AND MADE A SPIRITED CHALLENGE AT PRESUMPTIVE NOMINEE HILLARY CLINTON.

CLINTON WON THE NOMINATION, ALTHOUGH A NUMBER OF SANDERS'S SUPPORTERS THOUGHT THE SYSTEM WAS UNFAIR AND PREDETERMINED.

IN JULY OF 2016, HACKED DNC EMAILS WERE RELEASED. THESE EMAILS SHOWED HOW THE DNC FAVORED CLINTON OVER SANDERS. THIS REVELATION LED TO THE RESIGNATION OF DNC CHAIR **DEBBIE WASSERMAN SCHULTZ.**

DONNA BRAZILE WAS A LONGTIME CAMPAIGN STRATEGIST AND BECAME THE INTERIM CHAIRPERSON OF THE DEMOCRATIC NATIONAL CONVENTION AFTER DEBBIE WASSERMAN SCHULTZ RESIGNED.

IN HER BOOK ON THE CAMPAIGN, BRAZILE WROTE OF A CONVERSATION SHE HAD WITH GARY GENSLER, THE CFO OF HILLARY CLINTON'S CAMPAIGN.

HE DESCRIBED THE PARTY AS FULLY UNDER THE CONTROL OF HILLARY'S CAMPAIGN.

THESE TYPES OF REVELATIONS DID NOT SIT WELL WITH SANDERS'S SUPPORTERS. MANY SAW THIS AS PROOF THAT THE DEMOCRATIC NOMINATION WAS RIGGED IN FAVOR OF HILLARY CLINTON.

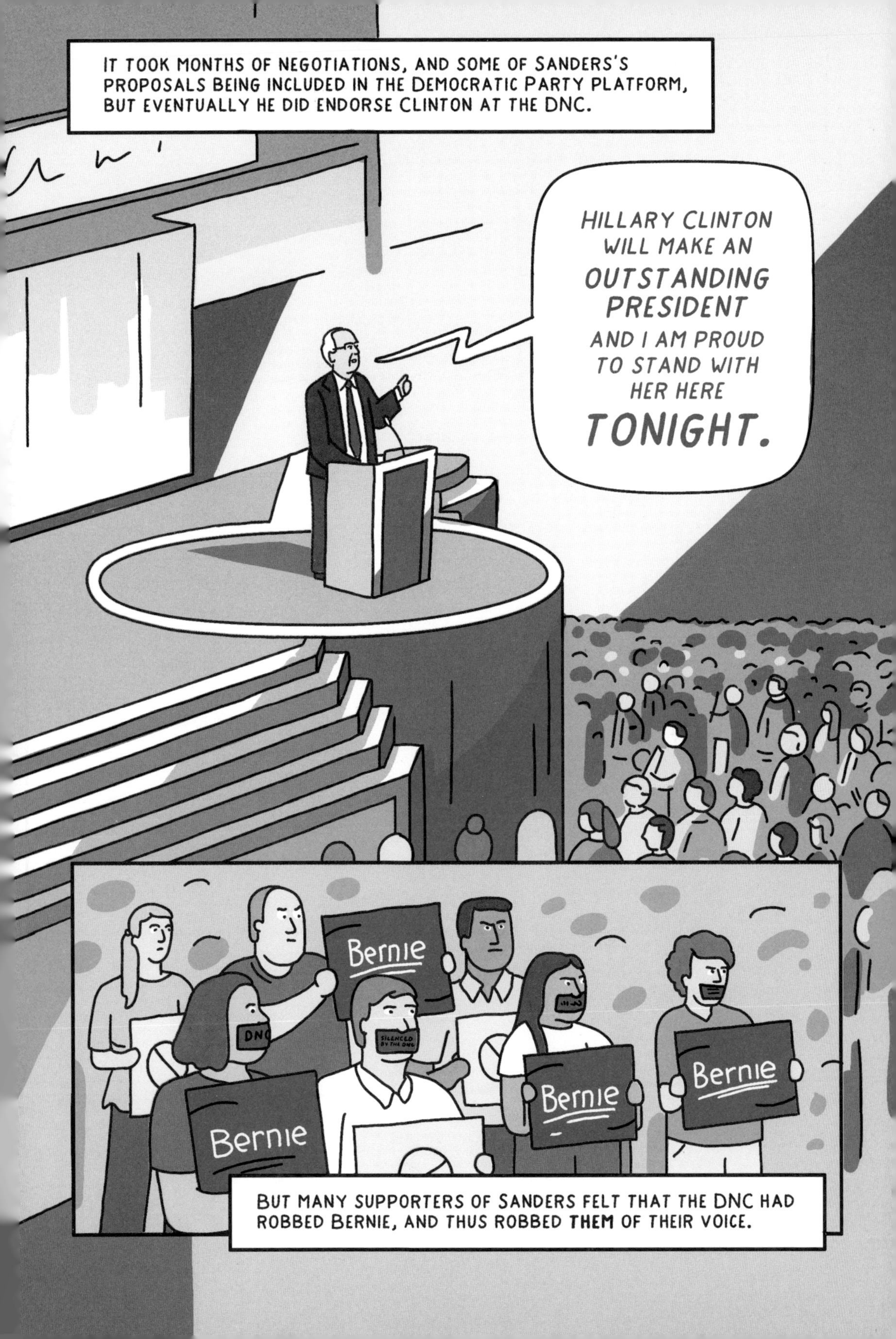

IT TOOK MONTHS OF NEGOTIATIONS, AND SOME OF SANDERS'S PROPOSALS BEING INCLUDED IN THE DEMOCRATIC PARTY PLATFORM, BUT EVENTUALLY HE DID ENDORSE CLINTON AT THE DNC.
HILLARY CLINTON WILL MAKE AN *OUTSTANDING PRESIDENT* AND I AM PROUD TO STAND WITH HER HERE **TONIGHT.**
Bernie
DNC
Bernie
Bernie
Bernie
Bernie
BUT MANY SUPPORTERS OF SANDERS FELT THAT THE DNC HAD ROBBED BERNIE, AND THUS ROBBED **THEM** OF THEIR VOICE.

EVEN IN THE PRIMARIES, VOTERS WERE DIVIDED. IT WAS LIKE THE CANDIDATES HAD CULTS OF PERSONALITY.

DURING THE CAMPAIGN, TRUMP SAID . . .

I COULD STAND IN THE MIDDLE OF FIFTH AVENUE AND SHOOT SOMEBODY, AND I WOULDN'T LOSE ANY VOTERS, OK?

TRUMP SUPPORTERS APPEARED TO LIKE DIVIDING PEOPLE.

BERNIE SANDERS'S SUPPORTERS THOUGHT THEY HAD BEEN OSTRACIZED AND CONQUERED BY THE DEMOCRATIC NATIONAL COMMITTEE.

I MEAN, IT SEEMS LIKE WE REALLY GO OVERBOARD TO MAKE SURE ALL THESE OTHER NATIONALITIES NOWADAYS AND COLORS HAVE THEIR FAIR SHAKE OF IT, BUT NO ONE'S LOOKING OUT FOR THE WHITE GUY ANYMORE.

THE MEDIA AND THE DNC COLLUDED TO BLOCK BERNIE SANDERS SO HE WOULDN'T BE SEEN. WE NEED TO HIT THE RESET BUTTON.

THE 2016 ELECTION WAS ANGRY. DIFFERENT FACTIONS DEMANDED TO BE HEARD.

WHITE WORKING-CLASS VOTERS FELT TRUMP GAVE THEM A VOICE. MANY FELT THEY HAD BEEN IGNORED FOR YEARS. SOME SAID ILLEGAL IMMIGRATION WAS A BIG FACTOR. OTHERS SAID THEY WERE TIRED OF TRADITIONAL POLITICIANS.

EVANGELICAL CHRISTIANS ALSO SUPPORTED TRUMP IN LARGE NUMBERS, MANY SAYING THE COUNTRY WAS MOVING AWAY FROM THEIR VALUES. TRUMP RECEIVED 80% OF THE WHITE EVANGELICAL VOTE, MORE THAN GEORGE W. BUSH RECEIVED IN 2004.

IN MY OPINION, DONALD TRUMP LIVES A LIFE OF LOVING AND HELPING OTHERS AS JESUS TAUGHT IN THE GREAT COMMANDMENT.

AND I BELIEVE THAT AT THIS ELECTION, GOD SHOWED UP.

PROMINENT EVANGELICAL LEADERS, **JERRY FALWELL JR.** AND **FRANKLIN GRAHAM**, BOTH FROM POWERFUL EVANGELICAL FAMILIES, SUPPORTED TRUMP.

SOME SANDERS SUPPORTERS, AGAIN FEELING LIKE THEY WEREN'T BEING HEARD, VOTED FOR TRUMP. ONE REPORT ESTIMATES THAT 12% OF SANDERS SUPPORTERS ENDED UP VOTING FOR TRUMP OVER CLINTON.

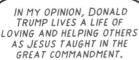

WE'VE GOT SOMEWHERE TO BE . . .

THE COALITION OF EVANGELICALS AND WHITE WORKING-CLASS VOTERS HELPED GIVE TRUMP HIS VICTORY IN THE ELECTORAL COLLEGE.

TRUMP WON THE PRESIDENCY DESPITE CLINTON WINNING THE POPULAR VOTE. LATER, WE LEARNED THERE MAY HAVE BEEN OTHER FACTORS INFLUENCING THE RESULTS OF THIS ELECTION.

 306 trump ✔

clinton 232

207 ELECTORAL VOTES TO WIN

46.4% VOTES
62,984,825

48.5% VOTES
65,853,516

NOT LONG AFTER THE FINAL RESULTS, US INTELLIGENCE AGENCIES CONFIRMED THAT RUSSIANS HAD INTERFERED IN THE ELECTION.

THE FBI, THE CIA, AND THE NATIONAL SECURITY AGENCY ALL CONCLUDED THAT RUSSIANS INTERFERED IN THE PRESIDENTIAL ELECTION.

A LOT OF THE INTERFERENCE WAS DONE BY STORIES THROUGH SOCIAL MEDIA, LIKE FACEBOOK.

AFTER A LONG INVESTIGATION, NATIONAL SECURITY ADVISOR GENERAL **H. R. MCMASTER** SAID IT WAS CLEAR THAT THE RUSSIANS MEDDLED IN THE ELECTION, TRUMP TWEETED THAT IT HAD NO IMPACT.

US REPRESENTATIVE **JOHN LEWIS**, WENT AS FAR AS TO SAY TRUMP WAS AN ILLEGITIMATE PRESIDENT BECAUSE OF THE RUSSIAN INTERFERENCE.

Donald J. Trump ✔
@realDonaldTrump

☞ Follow

General McMaster forgot to say that the results of the 2016 election were not impacted or changed by the Russians.

8:22 PM - 19 Feb 2018

24,748 Retweets 90,984 LIKES

WITH TRUMP DOMINATING THE NEWS CYCLE, THE 2018 MIDTERMS WERE MAINLY ABOUT HIM. FORMER PRESIDENT OBAMA, STILL EXTREMELY POPULAR AMONG DEMOCRATS, CAMPAIGNED TO GET THE VOTE OUT FOR DEMOCRATS.

THE PERCENTAGE OF TOTAL VOTES CAST IN THE 2018 MIDTERM WAS 53.1 FOR DEMOCRATS AND 45.1 FOR REPUBLICANS.

SO HOW COME THE DEMOCRATS DIDN'T WIN EVEN MORE SEATS IN THE HOUSE AND TAKE THE SENATE?

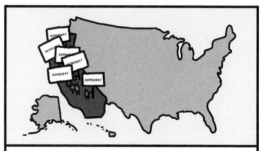

WELL, HEAVY DEMOCRATIC STATES, LIKE CALIFORNIA, HELPED PUSH THOSE NUMBERS.

CERTAINLY, TRUMP BEING PRESIDENT HELPED DRIVE RECORD TURNOUT.

TRUMP CORRECTLY POINTED OUT THAT THE GAINS DEMOCRATS MADE IN 2018 DID NOT EQUAL THE GAINS REPUBLICANS MADE IN THE 2010 MIDTERMS.

DID THE ELECTION JUST PROVE HOW DIVIDED THE COUNTRY WAS?

THE MIDWEST, A KEY AREA IN DECIDING THE 2016 PRESIDENTIAL ELECTION, ONCE AGAIN WAS A MICROCOSM OF VOTING PATTERNS FOR THE COUNTRY.

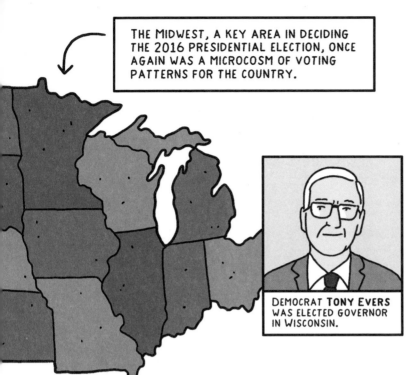

DEMOCRAT **GRETCHEN WHITMER** WAS ELECTED GOVERNOR IN MICHIGAN.

DEMOCRAT **TONY EVERS** WAS ELECTED GOVERNOR IN WISCONSIN.

REPUBLICAN **MIKE DEWINE** WAS ELECTED GOVERNOR IN OHIO.

DEMOCRATS WERE ABLE TO APPEAL TO MORE SUBURBAN VOTERS IN 2018 THAN THEY WERE IN 2016.

AS IN THE SOUTH, HOWEVER, MIDWESTERN RURAL AREAS REMAINED PREDOMINANTLY REPUBLICAN.

THE 2018 ELECTION ALSO HAD VOTING CONTROVERSIES. FOR ONE, FLORIDA, ESPECIALLY BROWARD COUNTY, ONCE AGAIN HAD INSANELY LONG LINES FOR VOTING.

FLORIDA

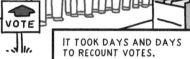

I WILL NOT SIT IDLY BY WHILE UNETHICAL LIBERALS TRY TO STEAL THIS ELECTION.

IT TOOK DAYS AND DAYS TO RECOUNT VOTES.

FLORIDA'S REPUBLICAN GOVERNOR **RICK SCOTT**, AND 2018 SENATE CANDIDATE, SAW DEMOCRATIC SHENANIGANS.

GEORGIA

GEORGIA'S GOVERNOR'S RACE WAS ONE OF THE MOST HOTLY CONTESTED. **STACEY ABRAMS** SOUGHT TO BE THE FIRST AFRICAN AMERICAN GOVERNOR. **BRIAN KEMP**, HER OPPONENT, WAS THE SECRETARY OF STATE.

KEMP'S OFFICE PURGED AROUND 500,000 VOTERS FROM THE ROLLS. ONE REASON WAS BECAUSE PEOPLE HAD NOT VOTED IN SIX YEARS. KEMP APPEARED TO BE TRYING TO BLOCK SUPPORT FOR ABRAMS.

THEN ON ELECTION DAY, THERE WERE PROBLEMS WITH BROKEN VOTING MACHINES AND NOT ENOUGH VOTING MACHINES IN SOME GEORGIA PRECINCTS.

AND YES, THESE PRECINCTS WERE MOSTLY IN MINORITY AREAS.

ARIZONA

REPUBLICAN **MARTHA MCSALLY** AND DEMOCRAT **KYRSTEN SINEMA** WERE IN A TIGHT RACE FOR THE RETIRING SENATOR **JEFF FLAKE'S** SEAT IN ARIZONA.

REPUBLICANS IN ARIZONA FILED A LAWSUIT THE DAY AFTER THE ELECTION CLAIMING THAT THE STATES ELECTION RECORDERS DO NOT USE A UNIFORM SYSTEM TO ALLOW VOTERS TO ADJUST MAIL-IN BALLOTS.

THE ARIZONA SENATE RACE WAS NATIONAL NEWS, COVERED BY ALL FORMS OF MEDIA. POLITICS IS COVERED 24 HOURS A DAY, LONG REMOVED FROM THE DAYS OF A 30 MINUTE NIGHTLY NEWS BROADCAST ON JUST THREE NETWORKS.

THE FAIRNESS DOCTRINE STIPULATED THAT BROADCAST MEDIA, SUCH AS THE NEWS, HAD TO PRESENT ISSUES IN AN HONEST AND EQUITABLE MANNER. HOWEVER, THE DOCTRINE WAS REVOKED IN 1987, AND MEDIA BEGAN TO CHANGE.

WHILE THE DOCTRINE DIDN'T COVER CABLE NEWS, THIS DECISION DID INFLUENCE CABLE NETWORKS. NOW WE HAVE POLITICAL CHEERLEADERS ON CABLE NEWS.

[O]BSTRUCTIONIST DEMOCRATS ARE SHOWING THAT THEY'RE HYPOCRITES, POLITICAL OPPORTUNISTS, AND TOTAL FLIP FLOPPERS.

SEAN HANNITY

"[THE BROADCASTER] MUST AFFIRMATIVELY ENDEAVOR TO MAKE ... FACILITIES AVAILABLE FOR THE EXPRESSION OF CONTRASTING VIEWPOINTS HELD BY RESPONSIBLE ELEMENTS WITH RESPECT TO THE CONTROVERSIAL ISSUES PRESENTED."

REPUBLICANS ARE DESPERATELY TRYING TO HANG ON TO POWER BY STOKING FEAR AND RESENTMENT WITHIN THE REPUBLICAN BASE ...

CHRIS HAYES

TRUMP LAUNCHED A VOCIFEROUS ATTACK ON ANY NEWS SOURCES CRITICAL OF HIM, REINFORCING HIS SUPPORTERS' BELIEF THAT THE MEDIA IS BIASED AGAINST THEM.

A FEW DAYS AGO, I CALLED THE FAKE NEWS THE ENEMY OF THE PEOPLE, AND THEY ARE—THEY ARE THE ENEMY OF THE PEOPLE.

IN FACT, IN DECEMBER 2018 THE SENATE RECEIVED A REPORT FROM OXFORD UNIVERSITY AND GRAPHIKA, A NETWORK ANALYSIS FIRM. THE REPORT STATED, "SOCIAL MEDIA HAVE GONE FROM BEING THE NATURAL INFRASTRUCTURE FOR ... COORDINATING CIVIC ENGAGEMENT TO BEING ... MANIPULATED BY CANNY POLITICAL CONSULTANTS ..."

THE GOVERNMENT NOW HAS IRREFUTABLE PROOF THAT ANY MEDIA CAN BE MANIPULATED, AND THIS DISCLOSURE HAS TAKEN ITS TOLL.

IF AMERICANS CAN'T TRUST THE MEDIA AND NEWS OUTLETS, HOW CAN AMERICANS PREVENT THEMSELVES FROM BEING INFLUENCED BY MISINFORMATION? WHAT ABOUT TRUSTING **POLITICIANS**? WELL . . .

POLITICIANS OFTEN APPEAR TO NOT LISTEN TO THEIR CONSTITUENTS.

PLUS, IT IS REALLY HARD TO DEFEAT AN INCUMBENT. LOBBYISTS POUR SO MUCH MONEY INTO CAMPAIGNS AND POLITICAL ACTION COMMITTEES.

MONEY BUYS ADS SO THAT ALL THE VOTERS KNOW WHO A CANDIDATE IS. AND THIS OFTEN LEADS TO . . .

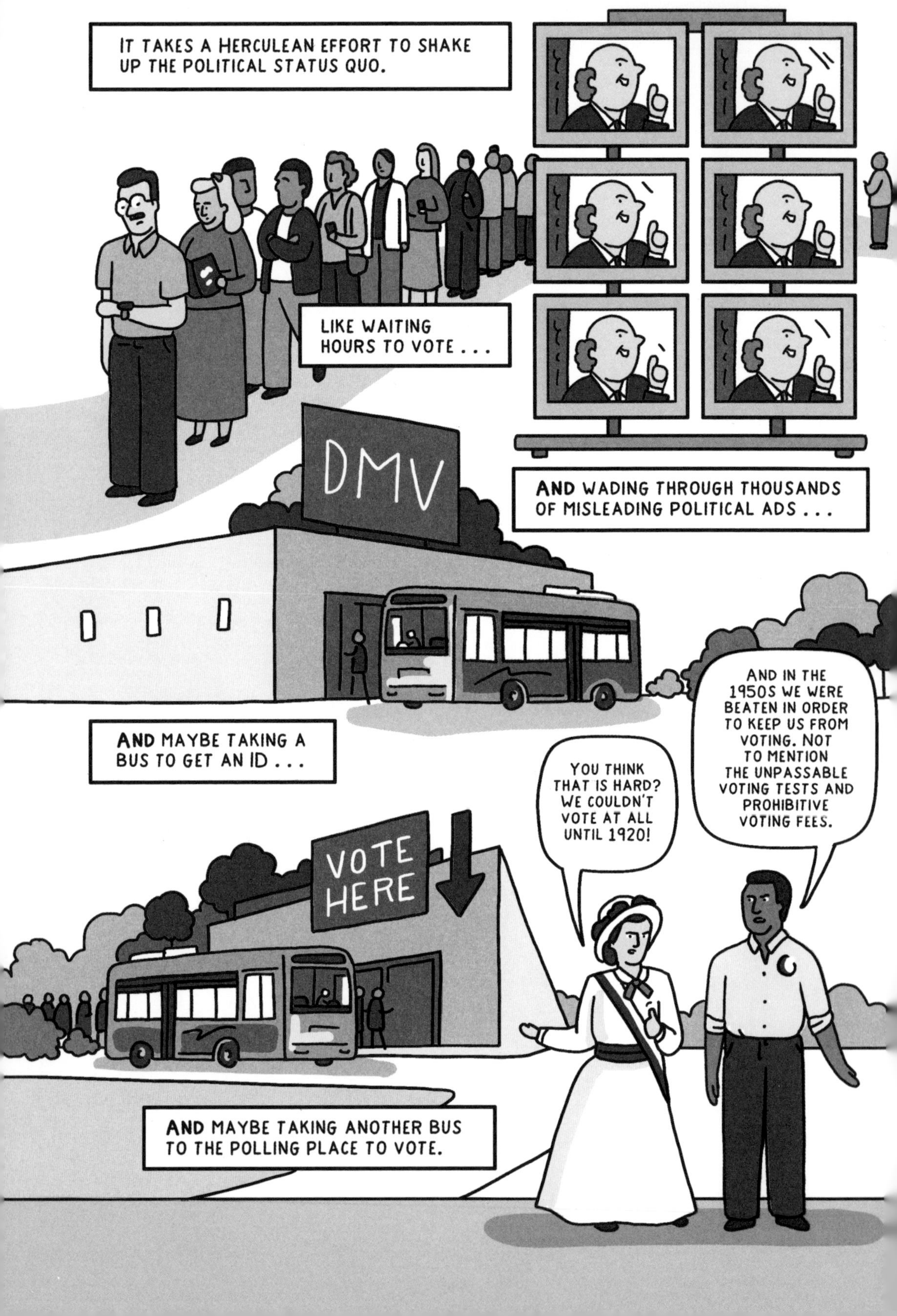
IT TAKES A HERCULEAN EFFORT TO SHAKE UP THE POLITICAL STATUS QUO.
LIKE WAITING HOURS TO VOTE . . .
AND WADING THROUGH THOUSANDS OF MISLEADING POLITICAL ADS . . .
DMV
AND MAYBE TAKING A BUS TO GET AN ID . . .
VOTE HERE
YOU THINK THAT IS HARD? WE COULDN'T VOTE AT ALL UNTIL 1920!
AND IN THE 1950S WE WERE BEATEN IN ORDER TO KEEP US FROM VOTING. NOT TO MENTION THE UNPASSABLE VOTING TESTS AND PROHIBITIVE VOTING FEES.
AND MAYBE TAKING ANOTHER BUS TO THE POLLING PLACE TO VOTE.

PERHAPS **PARTY OVER COUNTRY** IS THE NEW NORMAL.

PERHAPS WE WILL HAVE POLITICIANS WHO WILL CONTINUE TO TRY TO KEEP PEOPLE FROM VOTING.

BUT MAYBE WE CAN HAVE MORE COMPROMISE.

MAYBE WE CAN ACTUALLY MAKE IT EASIER FOR MORE PEOPLE TO VOTE.

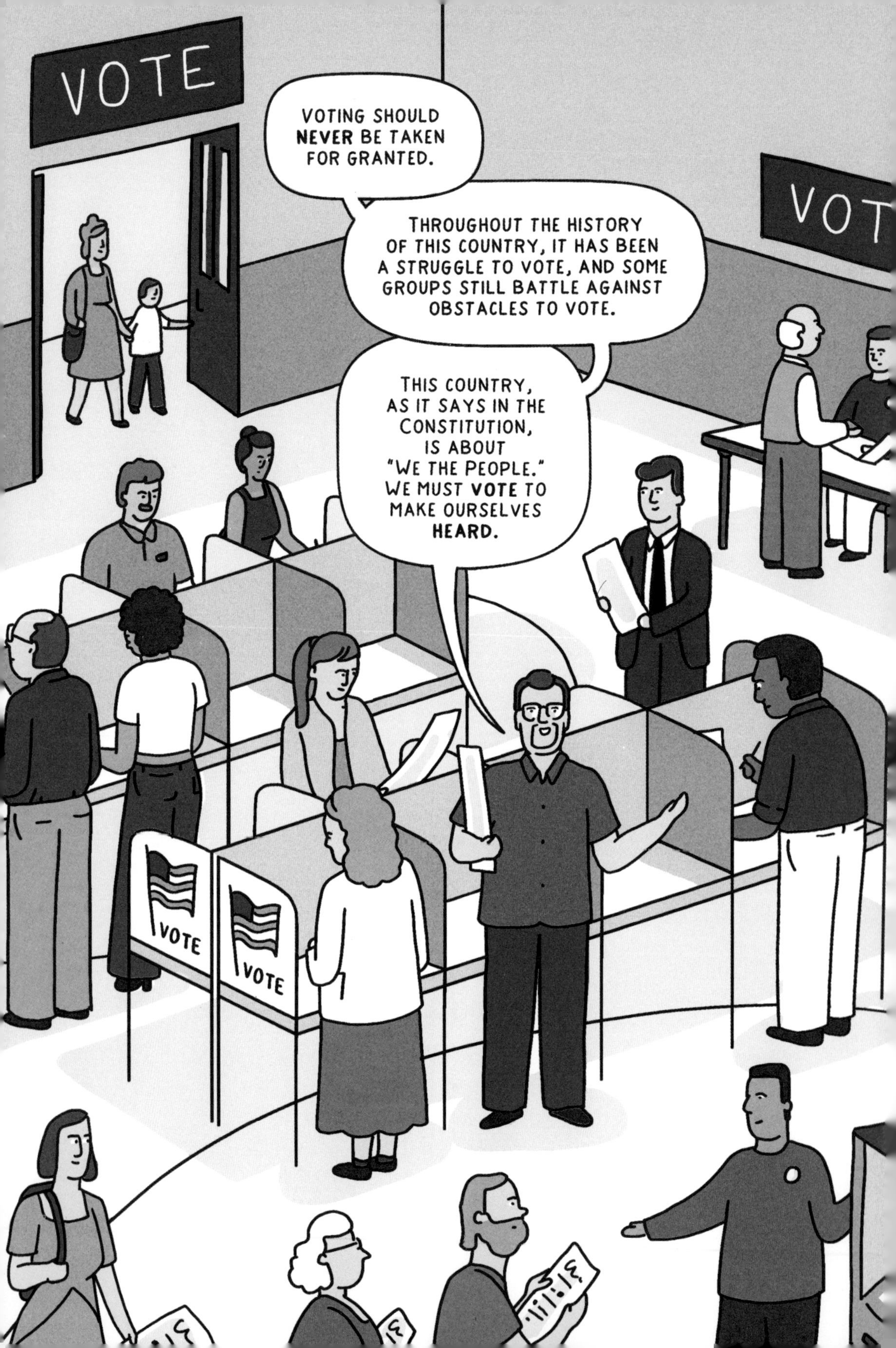
VOTE
VOTING SHOULD NEVER BE TAKEN FOR GRANTED.
VOT
THROUGHOUT THE HISTORY OF THIS COUNTRY, IT HAS BEEN A STRUGGLE TO VOTE, AND SOME GROUPS STILL BATTLE AGAINST OBSTACLES TO VOTE.
THIS COUNTRY, AS IT SAYS IN THE CONSTITUTION, IS ABOUT "WE THE PEOPLE." WE MUST VOTE TO MAKE OURSELVES HEARD.
VOTE
VOTE

EPILOGUE

EVERY VOTE COUNTS

ELECTIONS HAVE CONSEQUENCES. PRESIDENT TRUMP APPOINTED TWO SUPREME COURT JUSTICES IN HIS FIRST TWO YEARS. CONSERVATIVES SAW AN OPPORTUNITY TO HELP THEIR AGENDA.

PERHAPS IN RESPONSE TO PRESIDENT TRUMP'S COURT APPOINTEES, WE HAVE SEEN STATE LEGISLATURES TAKE UP A WIDE RANGE OF LAWS, FORCING THE COURTS AND CONGRESS TO DETERMINE THEIR VIABILITY.

ALSO OF IMPORTANCE, THE PRESIDENTIAL ELECTION, CONGRESSIONAL ELECTIONS, AND STATE ELECTIONS WILL SET THE COURSE FOR HOW THE COUNTRY MOVES FORWARD.

THE FUTURE OF ISSUES LIKE *ROE V. WADE*, GUN RIGHTS, LGBTQ+ RIGHTS, CITIZENSHIP, HEALTH CARE, AND EDUCATION WILL BE DETERMINED.

LEGISLATIVE AGENDAS ARE CREATED BY VOTERS. THE ELECTION OF CANDIDATES, VOTED IN BY PEOPLE LIKE YOU AND ME, SETS THE PATH OF LEGISLATION GOING

THIS IS WHY THE OLD CLICHÉ "MY VOTE DOESN'T MATTER" IS SO INFURIATING. EVERY VOTE MATTERS! YOU VOTE FOR THE CANDIDATES YOU BELIEVE BEST REPRESENT YOUR OPINIONS.

THIS IS ALSO WHY GETTING INVOLVED IN VOTING REGISTRATION IS SO IMPORTANT. YOU SHOULD KNOW YOUR STATE'S GUIDELINES REGARDING REGISTRATION. EACH STATE CONTROLS ITS OWN VOTING REGULATIONS.

REGISTER

VOTE

IT COUNTS!

SOME STATES HAVE EARLY VOTING; OTHERS DO NOT. SOME STATES HAVE SAME-DAY REGISTRATION; OTHERS DO NOT. SOME STATES REQUIRE A PHOTO ID; OTHERS DO NOT. ON THE FOLLOWING PAGES ARE THE VOTING WEBSITES FOR EACH STATE. VISIT YOUR LOCAL WEBSITE SO YOU CAN BE PREPARED TO VOTE.

YOUR VOTE COUNTS.

ALABAMA: sos.alabama.gov/Alabama-votes

ALASKA: elections.alaska.gov

AMERICAN SAMOA: americansamoaelectionoffice.org

ARIZONA: azsos.gov/elections

ARKANSAS: sos.arkansas.gov/elections

CALIFORNIA: sos.ca.gov/elections

COLORADO: sos.state.co.us/pubs/elections/main.html

CONNECTICUT: portal.ct.gov/en/SOTS/Common-Elements/V5-Template---Redesign/Elections--Voting--Home-Page

DELAWARE: elections.delaware.gov/index.shtml

DISTRICT OF COLUMBIA: dcboe.org

FLORIDA: dos.myflorida.com/elections

GEORGIA: georgia.gov/popular-topic/voting

GUAM: gec.guam.gov

HAWAII: elections.hawaii.gov

IDAHO: sos.idaho.gov/elect/index.html

ILLINOIS: elections.il.gov

INDIANA: in.gov/sos/elections

IOWA: sos.iowa.gov

KANSAS: sos.ks.gov/elections/elections_registration_ceo.asp?

KENTUCKY: elect.ky.gov/Pages/default.aspx

LOUISIANA: sos.la.gov/ElectionsAndVoting/Pages/default.aspx

MAINE: maine.gov/sos/cec/elec/index.html

MARYLAND: elections.maryland.gov

MASSACHUSETTS: sec.state.ma.us/ele

MICHIGAN: michigan.gov/sos/0,1607,7-127-1633---,00.html

MINNESOTA: sos.state.mn.us

MISSISSIPPI: sos.ms.gov/Elections-Voting/Pages/default.aspx

MISSOURI: sos.mo.gov/elections

MONTANA: sosmt.gov/elections

NEBRASKA: sos.ne.gov/elec

NEVADA: nvsos.gov/sos/elections

NEW HAMPSHIRE: sos.nh.gov

NEW JERSEY: njelections.org

NEW MEXICO: sos.state.nm.us

NEW YORK: elections.ny.gov

NORTH CAROLINA: ncsbe.gov/ncsbe

NORTH DAKOTA: vip.sos.nd.gov/PortalList.aspx

NORTHERN MARIANA ISLANDS: votecnmi.gov.mp

OHIO: sos.state.oh.us/elections/#gref

OKLAHOMA: ok.gov/elections

OREGON: sos.oregon.gov/voting-elections/Pages/default.aspx

PENNSYLVANIA: dos.pa.gov/VotingElections/Pages/default.aspx#.VSPix-PnF-aU

PUERTO RICO: eac.gov/voters/puerto-rico-elections-office

RHODE ISLAND: elections.ri.gov

SOUTH CAROLINA: scvotes.org

SOUTH DAKOTA: sdsos.gov/about-the-office/board-of-elections/default.aspx

TENNESSEE: sos.tn.gov/elections

TEXAS: sos.state.tx.us/elections/index.shtml

US VIRGIN ISLANDS: vivote.gov

UTAH: elections.utah.gov

VERMONT: sec.state.vt.us/elections.aspx

VIRGINIA: elections.virginia.gov

WASHINGTON: sos.wa.gov/elections

WEST VIRGINIA: sos.wv.gov/elections/pages/default.aspx

WISCONSIN: elections.wi.gov

WYOMING: soswy.state.wy.us/elections

You can volunteer for a political party
to register people to vote in your state.
However, there are nonpartisan organizations
that register people as well.
Nonpartisan voter registration organizations include:

LEAGUE OF WOMEN VOTERS: lwv.org

ROCK THE VOTE: rockthevote.org

NONPROFIT VOTE: nonprofitvote.org

VOTO LATINO: votolatino.org

NOTES

General Reference

Keyssar, Alexander. *The Right to Vote: The Contested History of Voting in the United States.* New York: Basic Books, 2000, revised edition 2009.

Chapter 1. By the People, For the People

7 "Down with Hillary!": Andrew Wyrich, "Here are the Facebook ads Russia used in its 2016 election influence scheme," *Daily Dot*, November 1, 2017, www.dailydot.com/layer8/russia-facebook-ads-2016-election/.

7 "Like and Share": Ibid.

7 "All Those in Favor": Rob Tornoe, "Here's what fake Russian Facebook posts during the election looked like," *Philadelphia Inquirer*, October 6, 2017, www.inquirer.com/philly/news/politics/presidential/facebook-russia-fake-posts-trump-election-clinton-20171006.html.

7 "Press 'Like' to Help": Cecilia Kang, Nicholas Fandos, Mike Isaac, "Russia-Financed Ad Linked Clinton and Satan," *New York Times*, November 1, 2017, www.nytimes.com/2017/11/01/us/politics/facebook-google-twitter-russian-interference-hearings.html.

10 "Jews will not replace us!" [Emphasis added is mine.]: Yair Rosenberg, "'Jews will not replace us': Why white supremacists go after Jews," *Washington Post*, August 14, 2017, www.washingtonpost.com/news/acts-of-faith/wp/2017/08/14/jews-will-not-replace-us-why-white-supremacists-go-after-jews/?utm_term=.f94cc7102dd5.

10 "You also had some very fine people": Meghan Keneally, "Trump lashes out at 'alt-left' in Charlottesville, says 'fine people on both sides,'" CNN, August 15, 2017, abcnews.go.com/Politics/trump-lashes-alt-left-charlottesville-fine-people-sides/story?id=49235032.

11 "Why do we want all these people": Eli Watkins, Abby Phillip, "Trump decries immigrants coming from 'shithole countries' coming to US," CNN, last modified January 12, 2018, www.cnn.com/2018/01/11/politics/immigrants-shithole-countries-trump/index.html.

11 "Wouldn't you love to see": Eugene Scott, "President Trump says NFL players who protest shouldn't be in the game—and maybe not even in the country," *Washington Post*, May 24, 2018, www.washingtonpost.com/news/the-fix/wp/2018/05/23/president-trump-wanted-consequences-for-nfl-players-who-protest-racism-before-games-today-he-got-them/?utm_term=.b83c33e6b898.

15 "Are civil rights only for Negroes?": Steven Greenhouse, "Word for Word/Jesse Helms; The North Carolinian has Enemies, But No One Calls Him Vague," *New York Times*, November 27, 1994, www.nytimes.com/1994/11/27/weekinreview/word-for-word-jesse-helms-north-carolinian-has-enemies-but-no-one-calls-him.html?mtrref=www.google.com&gwh=E488AA81372BCCC5281648AD33FB1DAC&gwt=pay.

15 "You needed that job": "Jesse Helms 'Hands' Ad," shown during the 1990 US Senate campaign in North Carolina, www.youtube.com/watch?v=KIyewCdXMzk.

16 "An 'extremely credible' source": Donald J. Trump, August 6, 2012, 1:23 p.m., twitter.com/realdonaldtrump/status/232572505238433794?lang=en.

16 "Our inner cities": Matthew Nussbaum, "Trump at debate: Minorities in cities are 'living in hell,'" *Politico*, September 26, 2016, www.politico.com/story/2016/09/trump-minorities-living-in-hell-228726.

19 "You could see there was blood": Philip Rucker, "Trump says Fox's Megyn Kelly had blood 'coming out of her whatever,'" *Washington Post*, August 8, 2015, www.washingtonpost.com/news/post-politics/wp/2015/08/07/trump-says-foxs-megyn-kelly-had-blood-coming-out-of-her-wherever/?utm_term=.e358715d101c.

19 "This whole two-week effort": Olivia Paschal, "Read Brett Kavanaugh's Defiant Statement to the Senate Judiciary Committee," *Atlantic*, September 27, 2018, www.theatlantic.com/politics/archive/2018/09/brett-kavanaugh-delivers-fiery-opening-statement/571570/.

19 "I tried to yell for help.": Frank Thorp V, Adam Edelman, Rebecca Shabad, "Kavanaugh accuser Ford testifies she 'believed he was going to rape' her," NBC News, September 27, 2018, www.nbcnews.com/politics/supreme-court/kavanaugh-accuser-ford-provides-four-sworn-declarations-supporting-her-allegation-n913216.

22 "[W]e are going to have": Philip Bump, "Wisconsin Republicans shield their voters from the horrors of democratic elections," *Washington Post*, December 5, 2018, www.washingtonpost.com/politics/2018/12/05/wisconsin-republicans-shield-their-voters-horrors-democratic-elections/?utm_term=.5f20d06e3b74.

22 "This legislation needlessly divides": Eileen Belden, "Governor-elect Whitmer Statement On Recent Legislative Actions," Michigantransition.org, December 5, 2018, michigantransition.org/governor-elect-whitmer-statement-on-recent-legislative-actions/.

CHAPTER 2. THE BIRTH OF A NATION: 1776–1861

32 "Madison's proposal was for": "Article 1, Section 2, Clause 3: Records of the Federal Convention," May 30–September 17, 1787, *The Founders' Constitution*, press-pubs.uchicago.edu/founders/documents/a1_2_3s2.html.

34 "The substitution of electors": "Madison Debates, July 19, [1787]," *The Avalon Project: Documents in Law, History and Diplomacy*, avalon.law.yale.edu/18th_century/debates_719.asp.

35 "Men most capable of analyzing": "The Federalist Papers: No. 68," March 14, 1788, *The Avalon Project: Documents in Law, History and Diplomacy*, avalon.law.yale.edu/18th_century/fed68.asp.

38 "The Electors shall meet"; "Thus, the 12th Amendment": June 15, 1804, Constitutioncenter.org, constitutioncenter.org/interactive-constitution/amendments/amendment-xii.

39 Election participation: "Historical Presidential Elections," 270towin.com, www.270towin.com/historical-presidential-elections/.

CHAPTER 3. UNITED WE STAND, DIVIDED WE FALL: 1865–1900

44 "At this second appearing to take the oath": Abraham Lincoln, "Second Inaugural Address of Abraham Lincoln," March 4, 1865, *The Avalon Project: Documents in Law, History and Diplomacy*, avalon.law.yale.edu/19th_century/lincoln2.asp.

44 "With malice toward none": Ibid.

47 "We hold it to be the duty": Thaddeus Stevens, "Reconstruction.; Honorable Thaddeus Stevens on the Great Topic of the Hour. An Address Delivered to the Citizens of Lancaster, Sept. 6, 1865," *New York Times*, www.nytimes.com/1865/09/10/archives/reconstruction-hon-thaddeus-stevens-on-the-great-topic-of-the-hour.html?mtrref=www.google.com&gwh=9AEA37617FA947FAE6A0C8621A5D80E5&gwt=pay.

48 "Every man": Thaddeus Stevens, "What is Needed for Reconstruction," January 3, 1867, Columbia.edu, www.columbia.edu/itc/history/foner/civil_war/linked_documents/what_is_needed.html.

48 "The right of the Citizens": "15th Amendment," February 3, 1870, Cornell Law School, www.law.cornell.edu/constitution/amendmentxv.

51 "Unite with us" [Emphasis added is mine.]: "Louisiana White League Platform," 1874, Facing History and Ourselves, www.facinghistory.org/reconstruction-era/louisiana-white-league-platform-1874.

62 "This is no longer a government": "In Defense of Home and Hearth: Mary Lease Raises Hell Among the Farmers," History Matters, February 5, 2018, historymatters.gmu.edu/d/5304/www.thenation.com/article/how-a-working-class-movement-held-wall-street-accountable-over-100-years-ago/.

CHAPTER 4. RECLAIMING HER TIME! 1807–2016

64 "No person shall vote" [Emphasis added is mine.]: "Did You Know: Women and African Americans Could Vote in NJ before the 15th and 19th Amendments," National Park Service, last updated July 3, 2018, www.nps.gov/articles/voting-rights-in-nj-before-the-15th-and-19th.htm.

67 "It follows that the law gives the husband": "Joyner against Joyner," June 1862 decision, UTexas, la.utexas.edu/users/jmciver/357L/59NC322.html.

71 Seneca Falls Declaration (July 19–20, 1848): "Declaration of Sentiments," National Park Service, last updated February 26, 2015, www.nps.gov/wori/learn/historyculture/declaration-of-sentiments.htm.

72 "We hold woman to be": Frederick Douglass, "The Rights of Women," July 28, 1848, *Uncle Tom's Cabin & American Culture*, utc.iath.virginia.edu/abolitn/abwm03dt.html.

73 "The prejudice against color": William H. Chafe, "Sex and Race: The Analogy of Social Control," *Massachusetts Review*, Vol. 18, No. 1, Spring 1977, www.jstor.org/stable/pdf/25088719.pdf?seq=1#page_scan_tab_contents.

74 "My friends, we must take up": "The Anniversaries, Important Session of the AntiSlavery Society…," *New York Times*, May 10, 1865,www.nytimes.com/1865/05/10/archives/the-anniversaries-important-session-of-the-antislavery-society.html?mtrref=gathkinsons.net&gwh=079BA728CD2ABC51655B606A8B98D27B&gwt=pay.

74 "The best women I know": "Are You A Citizen If You Can't Vote?," Thirteen: Media With Impact, airdate January 31, 2003, www.thirteen.org/wnet/historyofus/web09/segment2.html.

75 "Think of Patrick": "How Early Suffragist Sold Out Black Women," Becky Little, History, updated January 18, 2019, www.history.com/news/central-park-to-get-its-first-ever-statues-of-real-life-women.

76 "No man is good enough": "Topics in Chronicling America—Susan B. Anthony," Newspaper and Current Periodical Reading Room—Library of Congress, July 7, 2015, www.loc.gov/rr/news/topics/susanb.html.

77 "Nowhere gives the power" [Emphasis added is mine.]: "Virginia Minor and Women's Right to Vote," National Park Service, last updated April 25, 2019, www.nps.gov/jeff/learn/historyculture/the-virginia-minor-case.htm.

77 "The Constitution of the United States" [Emphasis added is mine.]: *Minor v. Happersett* (March 29, 1875), Cornell Law School: Legal Information Institute, www.law.cornell.edu/supremecourt/text/88/162.

78 "The right of citizens of the United States": "Susan B. Anthony Amendment," amendment 1878, Faculty of Arts, University of British Columbia, aculty.arts.ubc.ca/mchapman/by_students/mckinney/susan_b.htm.

79 "Roll up your sleeves": "Women in History—Carrie Chapman Catt," Women in History Ohio, last updated on January 16, 2013, www.womeninhistoryohio.com/carrie-chapman-catt.html.

80 "There never will be": Hayley Miller, "Women Are Placing Their 'I Voted' Stickers On Susan B. Anthony's Grave," *Huffington Post*, November 6, 2018, www.huffpost.com/entry/women-voters-midterms-susan-b-anthony_n_5be1cb73e4b04367a8811b07.

81 "I regard the concurrence of the Senate": "President Wilson's Address to the Senate, September 30, 1918," National Park Service, www.nps.gov/nr/twhp/wwwlps/lessons/139LafayettePark/139facts3.htm.

82 "Some leaders are born women.": Women's Words to Lead By," AAUW, March 21, 2016, www.aauw.org/2016/03/21/words-to-lead-by/.

82 "We say keep your change": David Briggs, "Can Faith Moderate US Gun Culture? Studies Link Religion to Lower Devotion to Firearms," *Huffington Post*, November 14, 2014, www.huffpost.com/entry/can-faith-moderate-us-gun_b_6155098.

82 "I believe that the rights of women": "The Hillary Doctrine," Gayle Tzemach Lemmon, *Newsweek*, March 6, 2011, www.newsweek.com/hillary-doctrine-66105.

CHAPTER 5. JIM CROW STRIKES BACK! 1890–1965

87 "We consider the underlying fallacy": "Plessy v. Ferguson 1896," US National Archives & Records Administration, www.ourdocuments.gov/print_friendly.php?flash=false&page=&doc=52&title=Plessy+v.+Ferguson+%281896%29.

89 Questions from voting literacy tests: "The Rise and Fall of Jim Crow," Thirteen: Media With Impact, airdate October 1–22, 2002, www.thirteen.org/wnet/jimcrow/voting_literacy.html.

89 Questions from voting literacy tests: Rebecca Onion, "Take the Impossible 'Literacy Test' Test Louisiana Gave Black Voters in the 1960s," *Slate,* June 28, 2013, slate.com/human-interest/2013/06/voting-rights-and-the-supreme-court-the-impossible-literacy-test-louisiana-used-to-give-black-voters.html.

93 "The keynote of my campaign": "The 1898 Election in North Carolina—Furnifold Simmons," University of North Carolina Library, exhibits.lib.unc.edu/exhibits/show/1898/bios/simmons.

96 "I've known rivers": Langston Hughes, "The Negro Speaks of Rivers," *The Norton Anthology of American Literature: Volume 2*, eds. Wayne Franklin, Philip F. Gura, Jerome Klinkowitz, Arnold Krupat, and Mary Loeffelholz (New York: Norton, 2012), 1038–39.

96 "We can go to African life": Alexandra Duncan, "Aaron Douglas: African American Painter and Graphic Artist," The Art Story, January 14, 2109, www.theartstory.org/artist-douglas-aaron-life-and-legacy.htm.

99 "The Negro as a class": John Johnston Parker, NCPedia, www.ncpedia.org/biography/parker-john-johnston.

102 *Smith v. Allwright* ruling: *Smith v. Allwright* (1944), Cornell Law School: Legal Information Institute, www.law.cornell.edu/supremecourt/text/321/649/.

103 "State enforcement of restrictive covenants": *Shelley v. Kraemer* (1948), Justia, supreme.justia.com/cases/federal/us/334/1/.

103 "Separate educational facilities are": "Separate Is Not Equal: Brown v. Board of Education," Smithsonian National Museum of American History, americanhistory.si.edu/brown/history/5-decision/courts-decision.html.

106 "I don't know what the future may hold": "Ralph Abernathy," Law Library—American Law and Legal Information, law.jrank.org/pages/3894/Abernathy-Ralph-David.html.

107 "I say segregation now" [Emphasis added is mine.]: "'Segregation Forever': A Fiery Pledge Forgiven But Not Forgotten," NPR, January 10, 2013, www.npr.org/2013/01/14/169080969/segregation-forever-a-fiery-pledge-forgiven-but-not-forgotten.

107 "One hundred years": "President Kennedy Addresses the Nation on Civil Rights" NBC News, New York, NY: NBC Universal, 06/11/1963. Accessed November 3, 2018 from NBC Learn: archives.nbclearn.com/portal/site/k-12/browse/?cuecard=1679.

108 "I have a dream": Martin Luther King Jr., "I Have a Dream," speech delivered at the March on Washington, August 28, 1963.

112 "If we gotta fight and die": Richard Wormser, *The Rise and Fall of Jim Crow: The Companion to the PBS Television Series* (New York: St. Martin's Press, 2014), 162.

113 "I am certain Americans everywhere": "Johnson condemns violence against Negro demonstrators," UPI, March 9, 1965, www.upi.com/Archives/1965/03/09/Johnson-condemns-violence-against-Negro-demonstrators/4542138151843/.

113 "The best legal talent": "On This Day in History," LBJ Presidential Library, March 9, 1965, www.lbjlibrary.net /collections/on-this-day-in-history/march.html.

113 "I am issuing a restraining order.": Jack Bass, "The Selma March and the Judge Who Made it Happen," *Alabama Law Review*, 2016, www.law.ua.edu/lawreview/files/2011/07/The-Selma-March-and-the-Judge-Who-Made-It-Happen.pdf.

115 "At times history and fate meet": "'And We Shall Overcome': President Lyndon B. Johnson's Special Message to Congress," History Matters, March 15, 1965, historymatters.gmu.edu/d/6336/.

116 "Their cause must be our cause, too.": Ibid.

116 "The law is clear": "Alabama: The Selma-to-Montgomery March," National Park Service, last updated July 28, 2017, www.nps.gov/places/alabama-the-selmatomontgomery-march.htm.

118 "I guess if I'd had any sense" [Emphasis added is mine.]: DeNeen L. Brown, "Civil rights crusader Fannie Lou Hamer defied men—and presidents—who tried to silence her," *Washington Post*, October 6, 2017, www .washingtonpost.com/news/retropolis/wp/2017/10/06/civil-rights-crusader-fannie-lou-hamer-defied-men-and-presidents-who-tried-to-silence-her/?utm_term=.afe3eed6b2cb.

118 "The only thing they could do" [Emphasis added is mine.]: Ibid.

119 "I didn't go down there to register for you." [Emphasis added is mine.]: "'I Didn't Know Anything About Voting:' Fannie Lou Hamer on the Missippppi Voter Registration Campaign," History Matters, interview dates April 14, 1972 and January 25, 1973, historymatters.gmu.edu/d/6918/.

120 "We want to register" [Emphasis added is mine.]: "Fannie Lou Hamer: Testimony Before the Credentials Committee, Democratic National Convention," *American Public Media*, testimony date August 22, 1964, americanradioworks.publicradio.org/features/sayitplain/flhamer.html.

120 "Is this America": Ibid.

121 "We didn't come all this way " [Emphasis added is mine.]: Nicholas Targ, "Human Rights Hero: Fannie Lou Hamer," American Bar Association, June 30, 2017, www.americanbar.org/groups/crsj/publications/human_ rights_magazine_home/human_rights_vol32_2005/spring2005/hr_spring05_hero/.

121 "The President has said": DeNeen L. Brown, "Civil rights crusader Fannie Lou Hamer defied men—and presidents—who tried to silence her," *Washington Post*, October 6, 2017, www.washingtonpost.com/news /retropolis/wp/2017/10/06/civil-rights-crusader-fannie-lou-hamer-defied-men-and-presidents-who-tried-to-silence-her/?utm_term=.afe3eed6b2cb.

122 "The real hero of this struggle": "Transcript of the Johnson Address on Voting Rights to Joint Session of Congress," *New York Times*, March 16, 1965, movies2.nytimes.com/books/98/04/12/specials/johnson-rightsadd .html.

CHAPTER 6. A MOVE TO THE LEFT, A MOVE TO THE RIGHT: 1963–2009

129 "I did not vote for": "Barry Goldwater for President 1964 Campaign Brochure," 4President, www.4president .org/brochures/goldwater1964brochure.htm.

129 "There is a reason for the reservation: "Barry Goldwater for President 1964 Campaign Brochure," 4President, www.4president.org/brochures/goldwater1964brochure.htm.

130 "I shall not seek": Ron Elving, "Remembering 1968: LBJ Surprises Nation with Announcement He Won't Seek Reelection," NPR, March 25, 2018, www.npr.org/2018/03/25/596805375/president-johnson-made-a-bombshell-announcement-50-years-ago.

132 "I leave you gentlemen": Julian Zelizer, "You won't have Trump to kick around anymore?" CNN, October 21, 2016, www.cnn.com/2016/10/21/opinions/would-trump-follow-nixon-example-on-concession-speech-zelizer/index.html.

133 "We emphasized that you had to": Associated Press, "Haldeman Diary Shows Nixon Was Wary of Blacks and Jews," *New York Times*, May 18, 1994, www.nytimes.com/1994/05/18/us/haldeman-diary-shows-nixon-was-wary-of-blacks-and-jews.html.

133 "We need a new respect for law": Richard Nixon for President 1968 Campaign Brochure, 4President, www.4president.org/brochures/1968/nixon1968brochure.htm.

133 "What are the real issues": J. David Hoeveler Jr., *The Postmodernist Turn: American Thought and Culture in the 1970s*, (Ithaca, NY: Rowman and Littlefield, 2004), 138.

139 "As I was saying. By 1968": Rick Perlstein, "Exclusive: Lee Atwater's Infamous 1981 Interview on the Southern Strategy," *Nation*, November 13, 2012, www.thenation.com/article/exclusive-lee-atwaters-infamous-1981-interview-southern-strategy/.

140 "Read my lips": "1988 flashback: George H. W. Bush says 'Read my lips: No new taxes," NBC News, December 4, 2018, www.nbcnews.com/video/1988-flashback-george-h-w-bush-says-read-my-lips-no-new-taxes-1388261955924.

CHAPTER 7. PARTY ALL THE TIME: 2009–2016

144 "The government is promoting": Jeff Cox, "5 years later, Rick Santelli 'tea party' rant revisited," CNBC, February 24, 2014, www.cnbc.com/2014/02/24/5-years-later-rick-santelli-tea-party-rant-revisited.html.

144 "We're thinking of having": Ibid.

145 "We're getting ready for": Theda Skocpol and Vanessa Williamson, "The Fox in the Tea Party, Reuters, December 21, 2011, blogs.reuters.com/great-debate/2011/12/21/the-fox-in-the-tea-party/.

145 "It's Tax Day, our Tax Day Tea Party show.": Ibid.

145 "We need conservative leadership." [Emphasis added is mine.]: Rush Limbaugh, "Keynote Address to the Conservative Political Action Committee," American Rhetoric, delivered February 28, 2009, www .americanrhetoric.com/speeches/rushlimbaughcpac2009.htm.

148 "The atmosphere in most": Fred Koch, "A Business Man Looks at Communism," 1939, The University of Southern Mississippi Library, digitalcollections.usm.edu/uncategorized/digitalFile_d98568b6-791e-47cf-b1dd-fb51b5c10a74/.

148 "The Supreme Court has repeatedly": Ibid.

148 "The United Nations, the World Court": Ibid.

148 "You guys are far removed": Alvin Felzenberg, "The Inside Story of William F. Buckley Jr.'s Crusade against the John Birch Society," *National Review*, June 20, 2017, www.nationalreview.com/2017/06/william-f-buckley-john-birch-society-history-conflict-robert-welch/.

149 "Let's make the Libertarian Party": Nicholas Confessore, "Quixotic Campaign Gave Birth to Koch's Powerful Network," *New York Times*, May 17, 2014, www.nytimes.com/2014/05/18/us/politics/quixotic-80-campaign-gave-birth-to-kochs-powerful-network.html.

151 "I've never been to a Tea Party event.": Andrew Goldman, "The Billionaire's Party," *New York* magazine, July 23, 2010, nymag.com/nymag/features/67285/index2.html.

151 "Five years ago, my brother": "Tea Party movement: Billionaire Koch brothers who helped it grow," *Guardian*, October 13, 2010, www.theguardian.com/world/2010/oct/13/tea-party-billionaire-koch-brothers.

153 "Fiscal discipline, balanced budgets": Terrence Stutz, "Perry Declares voter ID, balanced budget amendment priorities for Texas Legislature, *Dallas Morning News*, January 2011, www.dallasnews.com/news /news/2011/01/20/perry-declares-voter-id-balanced-budget-amendment-priorities-for-texas-legislature.

153 "People do vote without being a citizen.": Robert Costa, "Bachmann: Obama turning 'illiterate' immigrants into Democratic voters," *Washington Post*, November 19, 2014, www.washingtonpost.com/news/post-politics /wp/2014/11/19/bachmann-obama-turning-illiterate-immigrants-into-democratic-voters/?utm_term=.344adfb7b52a.

154 "The Department of Justice will investigate": "Prepared Remarks of Attorney General John Ashcroft Voting Integrity Symposium," Justice.gov, delivered October 8, 2002, www.justice.gov/archive/ag/speeches/2002/100 802ballotintegrity.htm.

155 "I would never, ever make a change": "Senate Panel Postpones Gonzales Appearance," NPR, April 16, 2007, www.npr.org/templates/transcript/transcript.php?storyId=9605720?storyId=9605720.

159 "Preclearance is unconstitutional": John Schwartz, "Between the Lines of the Voting Rights Act Opinion," *New York Times*, June 25, 2013, archive.nytimes.com/www.nytimes.com/interactive/2013/06/25/us/annotated-supreme-court-decision-on-voting-rights-act.html.

160 "The court finds these new provisions": Christopher Ingraham, "The 'smoking gun' proving North Carolina Republicans tried to disenfranchise black voters," *Washington Post*, July 29, 2016, www.washingtonpost.com /news/wonk/wp/2016/07/29/the-smoking-gun-proving-north-carolina-republicans-tried-to-disenfranchise-black-voters/?utm_term=.07d5be913e51.

161 "All North Carolinians can rest assured": Robert Barnes, "Supreme Court won't review decision that found NC voting law discriminates against African Americans," *Washington Post*, May 15, 2017, www.washingtonpost.com /politics/courts_law/supreme-court-wont-review-decision-that-found-nc-voting-law-discriminates-against-african-americans/2017/05/15/59425b1c-2368-11e7-a1b3-faff0034e2de_story.html?utm_term=.e91501eefdd2.

CHAPTER 8. DIVIDE AND CONQUER: 2010–PRESENT

167 "The district bears": *Shaw v. Reno* (June 28, 1993), Cornell University Law School, www.law.cornell.edu/supct /html/92-357.ZO.html.

167 "They attempted to protect incumbents": *Hunt, Governor of North Carolina, et al., v. Cromartie, et al.* (October 1998), Justia, supreme.justia.com/cases/federal/us/526/541/case.pdf.

170 "When Mexico sends its people": Washington Post Staff, "Full text: Donald Trump announces a presidential bid," *Washington Post*, June 16, 2015, www.washingtonpost.com/news/post-politics/wp/2015/06/16/full-text-donald-trump-announces-a-presidential-bid/?utm_term=.bf0799c2d017.

171 "Ted Cruz didn't win Iowa; he stole it." [Emphasis added is mine.]: Robynn Tysver, "'Ted Cruz didn't win Iowa, he stole it,' Donald Trump says 2 days after caucuses," *Omaha World-Herald*, February 4, 2016, www.omaha.com/news /politics/ted-cruz-didn-t-win-iowa-he-stole-it-donald/article_60785558-66e5-5d5b-98d9-dfb121c603a8.html.

172 "He doesn't have a birth certificate": Ben Parker, Stephanie Steinbrecher, and Kelsey Ronan, "Lest We Forget the Horrors: A Catalog of Trump's Worst Cruelties, Collusions, Corruptions, and Crimes," *McSweeney's*, November 5, 2018, www.mcsweeneys.net/articles/the-complete-listing-so-far-atrocities-1-546.

172 "An 'extremely credible' source": Donald J. Trump, August 6, 2012, 1:23 p.m., twitter.com/realdonaldtrump /status/232572505238433794?lang=en.

172 "These are the forgotten men and women" [Emphasis added is mine.]: Philip Rucker and David A. Fahrenthold, "Donald Trump positions himself as the voice of 'the forgotten men and women,'" *Washington Post*, July 22, 2016, www.washingtonpost.com/politics/in-speech-at-republican-national-convention-trump-to-paint-dire-picture-of-america/2016/07/21/418f9ae6-4fad-11e6-aa14-e0c1087f7583_story.html?utm_term=.ab827b60d3c9.

172 "The silent majority is back": Ibid.

174 "He described the party as": Aaron Blake, "Elizabeth Warren and Donna both now agree the 2016 Democratic primary was rigged," *Washington Post*, November 2, 2017, www.washingtonpost.com/news/the-fix/wp/2017/11/02/ex-dnc-chair-goes-at-the-clintons-alleging-hillarys-campaign-hijacked-dnc-during-primary-with-bernie-sanders/?utm_term=.dc1428e1f9f7.

175 "Hillary Clinton will make": Steve Benen, "Bernie endorses, is 'proud to stand with' Hillary Clinton, MSNBC, July 12, 2016, www.msnbc.com/rachel-maddow-show/bernie-sanders-endorses-proud-stand-hillary-clinton.

176 "I could stand in the middle of Fifth Avenue": Jeremy Diamond, "Trump: I could 'shoot somebody and I wouldn't lose voters," CNN, January 24, 2016, www.cnn.com/2016/01/23/politics/donald-trump-shoot-somebody-support/index.html.

176 "I mean, it seems like we really": Greg Sargent, "Donald Trump is giving us all a big middle finger. And his supporters love it," *Washington Post*, January 27, 2016, www.washingtonpost.com/blogs/plum-line/wp/2016/01/27 /donald-trump-is-giving-us-all-a-big-middle-finger-and-his-supporters-love-it/?utm_term=.92572b1609df.

176 "The media and the DNC": Matt Flegenheimer and Colin Moynihan, "Angry Bernie Sanders Supporters Protest Hillary Clinton's Nomination," *New York Times*, July 27, 2016, www.nytimes.com/2016/07/27/us/politics /bernie-sanders-protests.html.

177 "In my opinion": Sarah Pulliam Bailey, "White evangelicals voted overwhelmingly for Trump, exit polls show," *Washington Post*, November 8, 2016, www.washingtonpost.com/news/acts-of-faith/wp/2016/11/09/exit-polls-show-white-evangelicals-voted-overwhelmingly-for-donald-trump/?utm_term=.47af4bbdeacc.

177 "And I believe that"; Lindsey Bever, "Franklin Graham: The media didn't understand the 'God-factor' in Trump's win," *Washington Post*, November 10, 2016, www.washingtonpost.com/news/acts-of-faith /wp/2016/11/10/franklin-graham-the-media-didnt-understand-the-god-factor/?utm_term=.7d798773eff1.

178 "General McMaster forgot . . .": Donald J. Trump, February 17, 2018, 8:22 p.m., twitter.com/realdonaldtrump /status/965079126829871104?lang=en.

181 "I will not sit idly by": Ana Ceballos, "GOP's Rick Scott files lawsuit in Florida elections, accuses officials of 'rampant fraud,'" *USA Today*, November 8, 2018, www.usatoday.com/story/news/politics/elections/2018/11/08 /rick-scott-accuses-florida-election-officials-rampant-fraud/1938131002/.

182 "Obstructionist Democrats are showing": "Kellyanne Conway talks immigration battle, DACA debate," Fox News, January 10, 2018, www.foxnews.com/transcript/kellyanne-conway-talks-immigration-battle-daca-debate.

182 "Republicans are desperately trying": "Republicans stoke fear and resentment," MSNBC, transcript, October 18, 2018, www.msnbc.com/transcripts/all-in/2018-10-18.

182 "A few days ago, I called the fake news": David Jackson, "Trump again calls media 'enemy of the people,'" *USA Today*, February 24, 2017, www.usatoday.com/story/news/politics/2017/02/24/donald-trump-cpac-media-enemy-of-the-people/98347970/.

182 "'Social media have gone from being'": Craig Timberg and Tony Romm, "New report on Russian disinformation, prepared for the Senate, shows the operation's scale and sweep, *Washington Post*, December 17, 2018, www.washingtonpost.com/technology/2018/12/16/new-report-russian-disinformation-prepared-senate-shows-operations-scale-sweep/?utm_term=.6e6e13d9eb45.

Acknowledgments

Many people helped in the creation of *Drawing the Vote*. My heartfelt thanks goes out to all who believed in this book.

Su Wu helped develop and guide this book from the very first inkling of an idea. I thank her for her diligence, hard work, perseverance, and friendship. She is brilliant.

I am also lucky to have worked with Charlotte Greenbaum. She is an inventive, meticulous editor whose goal is to make a book the best it can be. Thank you, Charlotte. And many thanks to the entire Abrams team.

Kati Lacker is an amazing artist, and it is a joy to work with her. Charlotte matched Kati's talent with my script and it was a godsend.

My deepest thanks to Martha S. Jones for sharing some of her history and inspiring thoughts on voting. Also, much appreciation to Kellie Carter Jackson for her kind and insightful review of the manuscript.

Thanks also to Charlie Kochman and Judith Hansen who believed in and advocated for this book from the very beginning.

My wife, Peaches, is a saint. She has encouraged me and supported me and without her patience and inspiration, this book would have remained just an idea. To you, Peaches, all my love.

Lastly, my parents taught me the importance of voting. They also taught me the importance of reading. In all of my endeavors, they have stood by me with unconditional love. Thank you both for all you have given me and continue to give.